NATURAL LANGUAGE UNDERSTANDING
AND LOGIC PROGRAMMING

NATURAL LANGUAGE UNDERSTANDING AND LOGIC PROGRAMMING

Proceedings of the First International Workshop on
Natural Language Understanding and Logic Programming
Rennes, France, 18-20 September, 1984

edited by

Veronica DAHL
Associate Professor
Simon Fraser University
Burnaby, B.C.
Canada

and

Patrick SAINT-DIZIER
I.R.I.S.A.
University of Rennes 1
Campus de Beaulieu
Rennes, France

1985

NORTH-HOLLAND
AMSTERDAM • NEW YORK • OXFORD

© ELSEVIER SCIENCE PUBLISHERS B.V., 1985

All rights reserved. No part of this publication may be reproduced, stored in a retrieval system or transmitted, in any form or by any means, electronic, mechanical, photocopying, recording or otherwise, without the prior permission of the copyright owner.

ISBN: 0 444 87714 2

Published by:
ELSEVIER SCIENCE PUBLISHERS B.V.
P.O. Box 1991
1000 BZ Amsterdam
The Netherlands

Sole distributors for the U.S.A. and Canada:
ELSEVIER SCIENCE PUBLISHING COMPANY, INC.
52 Vanderbilt Avenue
New York, N.Y. 10017
U.S.A.

Library of Congress Cataloging in Publication Data

International Workshop on Natural Language Understanding
    and Logic Programming (1st : 1984 : Rennes, France)
    Natural language understanding and logic programming.

    Includes index.
    1. Programming languages (Electronic computers)--
Congresses. 2. Electronic digital computers--Programming
--Congresses. 3. Logic, Symbolic and mathematical--Con-
gresses. 4. Linguistics--Congresses. I. Dahl,
Veronica, 1950-   . II. Saint-Dizier, Patrick,
1954-   . III. Title.
QA76.7.I578 1984   001.64'24   84-29984
ISBN 0-444-87714-2 (U.S.)

PRINTED IN THE NETHERLANDS

QA
76.7
I578
1984

PREFACE

It is a great pleasure for me to present the proceedings of this
workshop, held in France, where the Prolog language originated in
1971, and where logic based metagrammars were developed in 1975.

Since then, logic programming has been used in many natural
language understanding applications, mainly in the areas of
analysis, metagrammatical formalisms, logical treatment of
linguistic problems, and meaning representations for natural
language.

The particular methods and formal systems developed in this
context usually exhibit several of the attractive features of
logic while remaining in the more pragmatic area of programming:
conciseness, modularity, a declarative meaning that is independent
from machine behaviour, and, most importantly, logical inference.
All of these features, common to logic programming and to logic
metagrammars, have been made possible through a chaining of
various fundamental ideas. Outstanding among these are the
resolution principle, by Alan Robinson, in 1965; Prolog itself, by
Alain Colmerauer, in 1971; and Robert Kowalski's interpretation of
logic as a programming language, in 1974.

In 1975, Alain Colmerauer developed a syntactic variant of Prolog
--metamorphosis grammars--, which serves to describe grammars in
terms of type-zero like rewriting rules. The description turns
into an invisible parser when given to Prolog. We have chosen to
call this and related formalisms logic metagrammars, because they
serve to describe any grammar in terms of logic.

From Colmerauer's original metagrammar formalism, various
formalisms were later developed by Harvey Abramson, Lynette
Hirschman, Michael McCord, Fernando Pereira, Karl Puder, Paul
Sabatier, David Warren and myself.

The machines of a relatively near future are likely to incorporate
many of these and other related capabilities while increasing
their speed manyfold. The Japanese Fifth Generation Computer
project has triggered worldwide efforts towards future generations
of computer systems based on these concepts. The potential in
understanding natural language through logic programming is
growing rapidly, and we might be wise to integrate the various
theoretical and practical aspects involved as we go along, rather
than yielding to the temptation of using all the extra power for
programming ad-hoc systems.

This workshop is the first effort toward such an integration, and
we are proud of counting many linguists as well as computer
scientists and logicians among us. We hope it will be the
beginning of a fruitful interaction.

528788

I would like to thank all the people and institutions that have
made this effort possible: the authors; the referees, the program
committee; the sponsoring organizations: Universite de Rennes I,
Groupe Bull, the American Association for Artificial Intelligence,
and Simon Fraser University; and Patrick Saint Dizier, for a fine
and exhausting job of local organizing.

Veronica Dahl
General Chairman

TABLE OF CONTENTS

1st INTERNATIONAL WORKSHOP ON

NATURAL LANGUAGE

AND

LOGIC UNDERSTANDING

GENERAL CHAIRMAN :

    VERONICA DAHL (*Simon Fraser University, Canada*)

PROGRAMME COMMITTEE :

H. ABRAMSON	(*The British Columbia Univ., Canada*)
A. COLMERAUER	(*GIA, France*)
V. DAHL	(*Simon Fraser Univ., Canada*)
P. DERANSART	(*INRIA, France*)
M. GROSS	(*LADL, France*)
M. McCORD	(*IBM, USA*)
F. PEREIRA	(*SRI, USA*)
L. PEREIRA	(*Univ. Nova de Lisboa, Portugal*)
P. SABATIER	(*CNRS Paris VII, France*)
P. SAINT-DIZIER	(*IRISA, France*)
C. SEDOGBO	(*Bull, France*)

LOCAL ORGANISING COMMITTE :

    PATRICK SAINT-DIZIER (*Univ. of Rennes, France*)

    LOCAL SECRETARIAT : BÉATRICE MARET
                            ELISABETH LEBRET

INVITED SPEAKERS :

DEFINITE CLAUSE TRANSLATION GRAMMARS AND NATURAL LANGUAGE APPLICATIONS
    H. ABRAMSON   (*U.B.C., Canada*)

NOTHING MORE THAN PROLOG
    A. COLMERAUER (*GIA, France*)

LEXICON GRAMMARS AND AUTOMATIC SYNTACTIC ANALYSIS
    M. GROSS   (*LADL, France*)

UNIFICATION IN GRAMMAR
    M. KAY   (*Xerox, USA*)

PARSING AND DEDUCTION
    F. PEREIRA   (*SRI, USA*)

PANELS :

(1) ATTRIBUTE GRAMMARS AND NATURAL LANGUAGE ANALYSIS

    M. COURANT   (*IRISA, France*)
    P. DERANSART   (*INRIA, France*)
    F. PEREIRA   (*SRI, USA*)
    L. TRILLING   (*IRISA, France*)

(2) PROLOG AND NATURAL LANGUAGE ANALYSIS

    A. COLMERAUER (*GIA, France*)
    M. KAY   (*Xerox, USA*)
    F. PEREIRA   (*SRI, USA*)

LIST OF REFEREES

The contributions of the following people who served as referees for the submitted papers are very gratefully acknowledge.

Harvey	Abramson
Janusz S.	Bień
Veronica	Dahl
Pierre	Deransart
Maurice	Gross
Richard	Kittredge
Witold	Lukaszewicz
Yuji	Matsumoto
Michael	Mc Cord
Martha	Palmer
Fernando	Pereira
Luis Moniz	Pereira
René	Quiniou
Paul	Sabatier
Simon	Sabbagh
Patrick	Saint-Dizier
Célestin	Sedogbo
Stanisław	Szpakowicz
Laurent	Trilling
Kuniaki	Uehara
Jacques	Virbel
David	Warren

Natural Language Understanding and Logic Programming
V. Dahl and P. Saint-Dizier (Editors)
© Elsevier Science Publishers B.V. (North-Holland), 1985

HIDING COMPLEXITY FROM THE CASUAL
WRITER OF PARSERS

Veronica Dahl

Computing Sciences Department
Simon Fraser University
Burnaby, B.C.   V5A   1S6
CANADA

We describe how logic programming can be exploited for automating great portions of the parser-writing process. We start by
describing how to write parsers in Prolog, the most widespread
logic programming language, and then go on to logic-based
metagrammars. We show how they can be used as a means for
hiding from the user not only the deductive steps that automate
most of the procedural concerns in parsing, but also the arguments otherwise needed for string manipulation, for context-
sensitivity and transformations, for gapping phenomena, and for
building syntactic and semantic structure from the sentence
being parsed. The article is self contained, and controversial
areas and unsolved problems in this very new field are also
pointed out.

1. INTRODUCTION

The idea of using logic as a programming language [1,2] was put to
practical use in 1971, in the form of Prolog [3,4]. It has since
proved extremely valuable in many ambitious and diverse artificial
intelligence areas, including deductive data bases, robotics,
symbolic integration, expert systems and natural language understanding.

In the last of these areas, logic had traditionally provided a
firm conceptual basis. Its ability to formally deal with the
notion of logical consequence made it particularly attractive to
represent meaning. Typically, extensions of first-order predicate
calculus were used to formally account for those natural language
features that could not be represented in standard PC [5,6,7,8].
The introduction of Prolog has made it possible not only to represent meaning of sentences in terms of logic, but also to use logic
as the programming tool. This provides a unified framework where
logic is used throughout.

The first substantial systems that put these ideas in practice
concerned natural language front ends to an expert system - a
computer configurator [9,10] - and to a database system [11,12].
Both applications were entirely written in Prolog. The Prolog
tool used for natural language analysis was metamorphosis
grammars, a syntactic variant of Prolog developed by A. Colmerauer
[13]. The linguistic and logical principles used were described
in [14], and have also been adapted to processing Portuguese,
French and English. They provided the basis, together with [9],

for the CHAT-80 system [15,16], and inspired many other natural
language processing systems in Prolog (e.g. [17,18]).

The central idea in logic metagrammars is allowing the user to
describe (type-O like) rewriting rules, and making the parse
transparent to the user. This is achieved by Prolog's deductive
mechanism acting as the parser. The price, as is typical of
high-level programming features, is that control is relinquished
to Prolog and parsing proceeds in a blind, top-down, left-to-right
manner, which is not always the most efficient one. Because of
Prolog's power, however, efficiency remains quite impressive for
most regular-sized applications. Also, as Fernando Pereira
pointed out in his invited lecture at this workshop, even DCGs -
the logic metagrammars most close to Prolog - should not be
confused with Prolog itself. They can be parsed in many different
ways, and the fact that doing it through Prolog has been the most
convenient one so far does not preclude better ways from being
found in the future.

Further research involved creating new metagrammatical formalisms.
Some of these were motivated by ease of implementation (Definite
Clause Grammars [19]); others, by a need for more general rules
with more expressive power (Extraposition Grammars [20], Gapping
Grammars [21,22]); others still, with a view toward a general
treatment of some particular language processing problem, such as
coordination (Modifier Structure Grammars [23]), or of automating
some part of the grammar writing process, such as the construction
of parse trees and internal representations [23,24,25]. General-
ity and expressive power seem to have been the main concerns
underlying all these efforts.

There is a controversy presently going on, regarding whether
specialized metagrammar formalisms are really useful. In his
invited lecture at this workshop, A. Colmerauer put forward the
thesis that no more than Prolog is really needed. Marseille's
latest Prolog version - Prolog II - does not include any grammar
formalism at all. New control facilities - namely, a "freezing"
mechanism for postponing execution of certain predicates under
given conditions - are used, and it was shown how to handle
transformations such as relativization and interrogation in pure
Prolog II.

Within the context of logic programming, other possiblilities than
Prolog are emerging. This volume contains a description of
object-oriented parsing in the ESP programming language, by
Miyoshi and Furukawa. This is one of the ongoing efforts relating
to more flexible parsing strategies. Alternative bottom-up parsings have recently been investigated by Porto and Filgueiras [26],
by Matsumoto, Kiyono, and Tanaka (this volume), and by Uehara et
al. [27]. This again is a controversial area at present. A.
Colmerauer has pointed out the loss of control and the difficulty
in producing messages as two main drawbacks of bottom-up parsers
(invited lecture).

Still another interesting development has been a metagrammar based on tree-assembling rather than on rewrite rules (Sabatier, this volume). Central to this approach is the future addition of facilities for the user to impose alternative parsing strategies - this is currently being investigated.

Such a proliferation of research directions raises the question of whether it is indeed possible to construct a formalism that combines efficiency with high expressive power, and that hides from the user all details that can be automated, thus providing a simple way of describing the purely creative grammar-writing aspects. So far it is difficult to see just how much should be made transparent, just how much expressive flexibility is appropriate without the formalism becoming too powerful and introducing new problems on this account, and just how to ensure efficiency without burdening the user with machine-oriented concerns such as control.

Still another crucial question is how appropriate to linguistic theory all our computational proposals are. This workshop included a panel session where A. Colmerauer, M. Kay and F. Pereira discussed some issues related to this question.

It was generally felt, on the linguistic side, that the problems addressed by logic-computational linguistics still lack substantial common points with the problems preoccupying pure linguists. In M. Kay's words, explanations that we do not try to formalize are often more satisfying intuitively. What this probably means, since language automatic processing necessarily involves formalization, is that the two disciplines still haven't developed a common language in which to manipulate concepts that are, indeed, quite akin.

Still, as F. Pereira pointed out, many logic programming results are valid contributions to linguistics (e.g. logic being a powerful notation for grammatical knowledge, parsing viewed as deduction, etc.). But these results have probably not yet been presented in a manner that's useful to other researchers in computational linguistics.

This volume includes a discussion by M. Kay of the advantages of unification as a basis for functional representation constructing grammars, but which argues that logic programming might not be the ideal setting for these grammars. Our feeling is that a better integration of both linguistic and logic-programming results is likely to yield interesting contributions in both areas. Testing given language approaches through executable logic might give more insight into them, and at the same time, linguistic theories might provide firmer bases on which to perfect our language processing mechanisms.

2. WRITING PARSERS THROUGH LOGIC PROGRAMMING

For self-containment of this volume we shall briefly describe the main concepts underlying writing grammars in logic. Prolog being the most widespread logic programming language, we adopt it as our framework.

2.1 BASIC CONCEPTS

Prolog statements are of three types: assertions, rules and queries. The basic building block for all three is called a predication, and has the form:

$$P(t_1, \ldots, t_n)$$

where P is an n-ary predicate symbol and the t_i are terms.

A _term_ is either a variable, a constant, or has the form:

$$f(t_1, \ldots, t_k)$$

where f is a k-ary function symbol, and the t_i are again terms.

An _assertion_ has the form:

$$P(t_1, \ldots, t_n).$$

where P is an n-ary predicate symbol and the t_i are terms. It is taken as asserting that, in the particular world we're modeling, all instances of $P(t_1, \ldots, t_n)$ are true (an instance of an expression is another expression obtained from the first by replacing one or more variables by terms).

A _rule_ has the form:

$$P: - P_1, P_2, \ldots, P_n.$$

where P and the P_i are predications. It is read: any instance P'of P obtained through a given substitution of terms for variables is true if the instances of $P_1, P_2, \ldots$ and P_n obtained by applying the same substitution to each are all true.

A _query_ has the form:

$$? - Q_1, \ldots, Q_n.$$

where the Q_i are predications. It is read: find a substitution of terms for variables that, when applied to $Q_1, Q_2, \ldots$ and Q_n, will result in true instances of the n predications.

Example

Here is a very simple program with four assertions and three rules:

```
sibling(X,Y):- parent(X,Z), parent(Y,Z).

parent(X,Y):- mother(X,Y).
parent(X,Y):- father(X,Y).
```

```
mother(ann,mary).
mother(daniel,mary).

father(ann,tom).
father(daniel,bill).
```

Possible queries to this program are:

```
1)  ?- sibling(ann,daniel).
2)  ?- parent(ann,X).
3)  ?- parent(ann,X), parent(daniel,X).
4)  ?- mother(daniel,ruth).
```

Queries, of course, are meant to have answers, which are automatically found in Prolog through an invisible, automatic deduction process based on resolution [28]. Multiple answers to the same query are possible. For the four queries above, Prolog would respectively print:

```
1)  yes.
2)  X=mary, X=tom.
3)  X=mary.
4)  no.
```

Function symbols, for our purposes, are useful to describe linguistic structures. For instance, the term

```
        noun_phrase(determiner(the),noun(mother))
```

can be used as a syntactic structure for the surface string "the mother". Such strings, in turn, are noted in a more convenient form than the functional notation, as bracketed lists, e.g.: [the,mother].[1]

2.2- WRITING GRAMMARS IN PROLOG

2.2.1- RECOGNITION

Let us first define a Prolog recognizer of sentences in the subset of English consisting of sentences with just a proper noun and an intransitive verb in simple present tense, third person singular. We can simply write:

```
sentence([N,V]):- proper_noun(N), verb(V).

proper_noun(ann).
proper_noun(daniel).
        .
        .
        .

verb(laughs).
verb(smiles).
        .
        .
        .
```

Now we can query the program for acceptance of English sentences, e.g.:

```
?- sentence([ann,smiles]).
?- sentence([ann,reads,the,paper]).
```

However, we sometimes want to refer to a substring rather than to each individual word in the sentence, as in the grammar rule

               sentence--> noun_phrase, verb.

where "noun_phrase" may concern more than one word. To achieve this, we regard each non-terminal as a consumer of part of the input string, and a producer of what's left, e.g. "noun_phrase" could either consume a proper noun and produce the rest of the input string (in our subset, a verb), or it could consume a determiner and a noun and still produce a verb as the remainder to be analysed.

Each non-terminal N can thus be written as a predication

                      N(S,R)

where the variable S stands for the list of input words, and R for the sublist of S that remains after consuming some of the front words while analysing them as an N.

Here is a slightly more complete grammar than the one just shown:

```
sentence(X,Y):- noun_phrase(X,Z), verb(Z,Y).

noun_phrase(X,Y):- proper_name(X,Y).
noun_phrase(X,Y):- determiner(X,Z), noun(Z,Y).

proper_name([ann/R],R).   (2)
proper_name([daniel/R)],R).
        .
        .
        .

determiner([the/R],R).
determiner([a/R],R).
        .
        .
        .

noun([child/R],R).
noun([dog/R],R).
        .
        .
        .

verb ([laughs/R],R).
verb ([smiles/R],R).
        .
        .
        .
```

The first rule is read: "we can analyse a front sublist of list X as a sentence, with remainder Y, if we can recognize a front sublist Z, and then recognize a verb heading Z, with remainder Y".

Queries now look like:

```
?- sentence([the,child,smiles],[]).
?- sentence([daniel,laughs],[]).
```

The price we paid is having two arguments instead of one. This seems particularly cumbersome when the second one is empty, but it does allow the more general rules we need.

2.2.2 PARSING INTO A GIVEN REPRESENTATION

In addition to the two arguments representing the input string and its remainder after a partial recognition, we might want to add more arguments serving to reconstruct some meaning representation we might be interested in.

For instance, we might want to retrieve formulas such as "laughs(daniel)" from sentences such as "daniel laughs", or maybe an equivalent in some other language, such as "rit(daniel)".

With this idea in mind, our first grammar in the previous section becomes:

```
sentence ([N,V],R) :- proper_noun (N,R1), verb (V,R1,R).

proper_noun(ann,anne).
proper_noun(daniel,daniel).
        .
        .
        .

verb(laughs,K,rit(K)).
verb(smiles,K,sourit(K)).
        .
        .
        .
```

The first rule recognizes a proper noun N with representation R1 in the head of the sentence, and passes R1 on to the verb recognizer, which accepts the second word as a verb and uses R1 to build the sentence's representation, R.

Queries now look like:

```
            ?- sentence([ann,laughs],R).
```

i.e., is the string "ann laughs" a sentence, and, if so, what is its representation?

As an answer, Prolog will print:

```
            R= rit(anne).
```

Although extremely simple, this grammar illustrates the basic mechanism for structure buildup: some of the "non terminals" --recognizers-- (e.g. proper_noun) produce partial structure,

which is then passed on to other recognizers (e.g. verb), to be
used in the construction of more complex representations.

We're introducing a temporal notion here (FIRST producing, THEN
passing on...), corresponding to a left-to-right reading of the
rules. Although this is how both Prolog and us English readers
operate, it is worth pointing out that alternative strategies are
certainly possible, but the overall outcome should not be affected
by the particular one chosen.

It is not necessary for a structure produced to be completely
known at the time of (the present partial) recognition. A
transitive verb, for instance, might construct a formula "v(S,O)",
where v is the verb's translation, S the subject's representation,
generated upon recognition of the subject, and O the object's
representation, to be generated next, while recognizing the
object.

3. WRITING PARSERS THROUGH LOGIC-BASED METAGRAMMARS

3.1- CONTEXT-FREE GRAMMARS

The idea of logic-based metagrammars springs from providing the
non-specialist user (e.g. a linguist) with a parsing mechanism for
GRAMMARS s/he can describe in terms of familiar, rewriting rules,
rather than in terms of a -- however high level-- programming
language.

Most computer or procedural-oriented concepts, therefore, must be
hidden from the user. The first obvious step is to get rid of the
cumbersome manipulation of the input strings into lists (cf.
Section 2.2.1). The user should be allowed to write for instance
the second grammar in 2.2.1 as a traditional context-free
grammar, i.e.:

```
sentence --> noun_phrase, verb.

noun_phrase --> proper_name.
noun_phrase --> determiner, noun.

proper_name --> [ann].(3)
proper_name --> [daniel].
         .
         .
         .
etc.
```

Still, we can keep those arguments relating to representation
buildup. Thus, the grammar in 2.2.2 becomes:

```
sentence(R) --> proper_noun(R1), verb(R1,R).

proper_noun(anne) --> [ann].
proper_noun(daniel) --> [daniel].
```

```
        .
        .
        .
verb(K,rit(K))  --> [laughs].
verb(K,sourit(K))  --> [smiles].
        .
        .
        .
```

What we are really doing is hiding the string manipulation from
the user, by means of having a program that translates grammars
such as the above into their equivalent Prolog programs -- such as
the one shown in 2.2.2--, which include explicit arguments for
string consumption. In present implementations, this program is
written in Prolog itself.

Although the parsing mechanism is, therefore, still Prolog's
deductive mechanism, for linguistic purposes we can now visualize
the parsing process as a rewriting process, where unification
rather than simple replacement is involved. UNIFICATION is the
process of finding a substitution of terms for variables which,
applied to two expressions, converts them into the same.

We now show a derivation graph for the above grammar, where the
substitutions needed for rule application are written as labels.

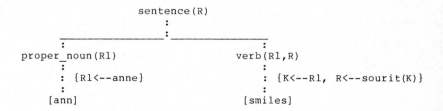

```
                  sentence(R)
                      :
    _____:_____
    :                                  :
proper_noun(R1)                   verb(R1,R)
    :                                  :
    : {R1<--anne}                      : {K<--R1,  R<--sourit(K)}
    :                                  :
  [ann]                            [smiles]
```

Once a variable takes a value in the graph, this value propagates
to all other occurrences of the same variable within the graph.
Thus, binding K to R1 is really giving K the value "anne", so that
the final value for R is "sourit(anne)".

Rules may include procedure calls (noted between braces) in their
right-hand side. These are useful for checking for rule
applicability, for enforcing semantic agreement, etc.

For instance, if we wanted to preclude the verb "to smile" from
being associated with a non-human subject, we could transform the
rule for that verb into:

```
        verb(K, sourit(K))  --> [smiles], {human(K)}.
```

and define the "human" predication through Prolog rules, e.g.:

```
human(daniel).
human(laura).
        .
        .
        .
```

Logic grammars with only "context-free" rules, as the above, have been baptised "Definite Clause Grammars" [19]. The reason is that, as we have seen, they translate straightforwardly into Prolog clauses (by adding two extra arguments for string manipulation), and Prolog clauses are of the type called "definite" or "Horn", which has at most one predication in the left hand side of rules.

Let us also remark that, although definite clause grammars have rules that are morphologically similar to context-free ones, their power is in fact that of type-zero grammars. This is because of grammar symbols being predications rather than simple identifiers. The arguments in grammar symbols can be used to carry contextual information, to achieve transformations, etc.

Because we are thinking of the casual, non-computer oriented user, though, it is perhaps not appropriate to enforce a specific context-free like format where context-sensitivity is less apparent because hidden in argument manipulation. Adding arguments, moreover, might tend to obscure legibility.

The next type of logic metagrammar we examine can accept more than one symbol in a rule's left-hand side.

3.2- CONTEXT-SENSITIVITY. TRANSFORMATIONS.

In metamorphosis grammars (MGs) [13], rules have the form:

$$S\, \alpha \;-\!\!\!-\!\!>\beta$$

where S is a nonterminal (logic) grammar symbol, α is a string of terminals and non-terminals [4], and β is a string of terminals, non-terminals and procedure calls.

As an example, here is an MG that handles relativization by moving an object's trace in front of the verb, so that another rule can then subsume it with a relative marker to produce the pronoun:

```
(1) sentence --> noun_phrase, verb_phrase.

(2) noun_phrase --> determiner, noun, relative.
(3) noun_phrase --> proper_name.

(4) verb_phrase --> verb.
(5) verb_phrase --> trans_ verb, direct_object.
(6) verb_phrase --> moved_dobj, transitive_verb.

(7) relative --> [].
(8) relative --> relative_marker, sentence.
```

(9) direct_object --> noun_phrase.

(10) determiner --> [the].

(11) noun --> [man].

(12) proper_name --> [john].

(13) verb --> [laughed].

(14) trans_verb --> [saw].

(15) relative_marker, noun_phrase, moved_dobj --> rel_pronoun,
                                                   noun_phrase.

(16) relative_pronoun --> [that].

Figure 1 depicts the derivation graph for the noun phrase "the man
that John saw". We abbreviate some of the grammar symbols. Rule
numbers appear as left-hand side labels.

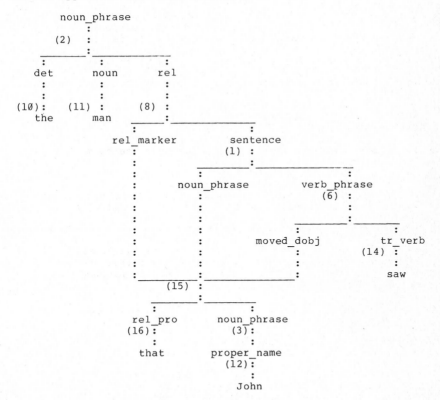

Figure 1. MG derivation graph for "The man that John saw".

3.3- GAP SPECIFICATION

MGs, as we have seen, allow more flexibility than definite clause
grammars (which are a special case of MGs), but make it cumbersome
to relate two constituents that are far apart, and require
explicit specification of all those in between.

Extraposition grammars(XGs) [20] allow us to refer to unspecified
strings of symbols in a rule, thus making it easier to describe
left extraposition of constituents.

XGs allow rules of the form

$$s_1...s_2 \text{ etc.} s_{k-1} \text{ --> } r.$$

where the "..." specify gaps (i.e., arbitrary strings of grammar
symbols), and r and the s_i are strings of terminals and non-
terminals.
The general meaning of such a rule is that any sequence of symbols
of the form

$$s_1 x_1 s_2 x_2 \text{ etc. } s_{k-1} x_{k-1} s_k$$

with arbitrary x_is, can be rewritten into r $x_1 x_2 .... x_{k-1}$.
(i.e., the s_i's are rewritten into r, and the intermediate gaps
(x_i's) are rewritten sequentially to the right of r. For instance,
the XG rule:

        relative_marker...complement --> [that].

allows us to skip any intermediate substring appearing after a
relative marker in the search for an expected complement, and then
to subsume both marker and complement into the relative pronoun
"that", which is placed to the left of the skipped substring.

While, as we have seen, MGs express movement by actually moving
constituents around, DCGs must carry all information relative to
movements within extra arguments. XGs, on the other hand, can
capture left extraposition in an economical fashion: by actually
skipping intermediate substrings rather than shifting the
constituents that follow. Thus, our grammar in 3.2 can be
rewritten in XG terms as:

(1) sentence --> noun_phrase, verb_phrase.

(2) noun_phrase --> determiner, noun, relative.
(3) noun_phrase --> proper_name.

(4) verb_phrase --> verb.
(5) verb_phrase --> trans_verb, direct_object.

(6) relative --> [].
(7) relative --> relative_marker, sentence.

(8) relative_marker ... direct_object --> relative_pronoun.

(9) relative_pronoun --> [that].

(10) direct_object --> noun_phrase.

(11) determiner --> [the].

(12) noun --> [man].

(13) proper_name --> [john].

(14) verb --> [laughed].

(15) trans_verb --> [saw].

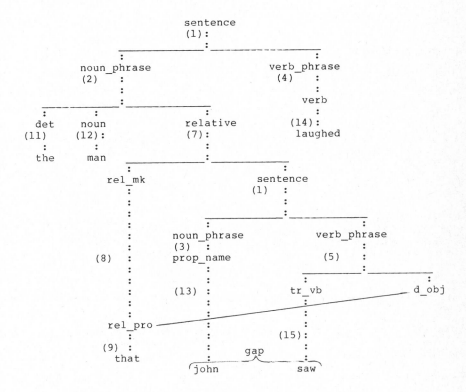

Figure 2.   XG derivation graph for "The man that John saw laughed".

XGs, while useful for economically describing left extraposition, are rather inflexible in that the gaps appearing in the left-hand side MUST be rewritten in consecutive order, and at the end of the right hand side, and also in that gaps must obey the nesting constraint: two gaps must either be totally independent, or one must be completely contained inside the other.

A generalization of XGs, called gapping grammars (GGs), was
devised by the author in 1981, and its uses and potential are
still being investigated [21,22,29].

GGs are the most inclusive logic metagrammar to date. They include
as special cases all other rewriting logic grammar formalisms in
existence. Basically, they are like MGs, except for the addition
of gaps. These gaps are not identified by suspensive dots as in
XGs, but are written "gap(G)", with the variable G denoting the
actual string of constituents conforming the gap. Multiple gaps
are allowed in the same rule, and can be repositiones, duplicated
or deleted in the right-hand side. For instance, the rule:

         A, gap(X), B, gap(Y), C --> gap(Y), C, B, gap(X)

can be applied successfully to either of the following strings:

                        A E F B D C

with gaps X=E F and Y=D, and

                        A B D E F C

with gaps X=[] and Y=D E F. Application of the rule yields

                        D C B E F

and

                        D E F C B

respectively. We can therefore think of the above GG rule as
shorthand for, among others, the two rules:

                   A E F B D C --> D C B E F

and

                   A B D E F C --> D E F C B

GG rules can be considered as meta-rules which represent a
(possibly infinite) set of ordinary grammar rules. They permit one
to indicate where intermediate, unspecified substrings can be
skipped, left unanalysed during one part of the parse and possibly
reordered by the rule's application for later analysis by other
rules.

The explored uses of GGs include:

- left extraposition with more than one gap
- right extraposition
- interaction between different gapping rules
- simpler, higher level grammar formulations
- free word order

Examples of all these uses have been given in [21,22]. Here
let us show one gapping grammar as an example, which
describes the language $\{a^n b^n c^n\}$.

(1) s --> as, bs, cs.

(2) as, gap(G1), bs, gap(G2), cs --> [a], as, gap(G1), [b], bs,
                                    gap(G2), [c],cs.

(3) as, gap(G1), bs, gap(G2), cs --> gap(G1), gap(G2).

Rule (2) simply evens as, bs and cs with a, b, and c, by skipping
any intermediate strings as gaps G1 and G2, which are repositioned
after regenerating as, bs and cs in the right-hand side. Rule (3)
simply makes as, bs and cs vanish by only recopying the gaps found
in between.

4. HIDING STRUCTURE BUILDUP FROM THE USER

We have seen how the introduction of logic-based metagrammars
relieves the user from the routine and cumbersome task of
specifying string-manipulation arguments. Other routine or
semi-routine tasks can be automated, too. Building a parse tree,
for instance, is a boring but not difficult task --at least in the
simplest grammar formalisms, like DCGs. We simply need to add an
argument in each grammar symbol for carrying the piece of
syntactic structure that this symbol contributes to the whole
parse tree. For instance, the rule

                sentence --> noun_phrase, verb_phrase.

becomes

        sentence(s(NP,VP)) --> noun_phrase(NP), verb_phrase(VP).

Of course, the rules for noun_phrase and verb_phrase accordingly
build up their syntactic structures into their argument.

Building a meaning representation, on the other hand, often
involves ingenuity to put together the appropriate pieces with
respect to our particular target language. For instance, the rule:

        sentence(P) --> noun_phrase(X,P1,P), verb_phrase(X,P1).

could be part of a grammar that builds up a first-order logic
representation of the sentence being parsed. X represents the
individual(s) predicated upon (introduced by the subject noun
phrase), and must be carried over to the verb_phrase symbol, to be
used in constructing the (logical) predicate representing the verb
applied to that subject. This predicate, represented by P1, must
in turn be passed along to "noun_phrase", which will use it in
constructing the final representation P of the sentence. For
instance, for "every child laughs", X would remain an unbounded
variable, P1 would be tied to "laugh(X)", and P to "$\forall$ x child(X)

=> laugh(X)".

Of course, we could easily combine the above grammars to obtain
BOTH a parse tree and a meaning representation of the sentence
parsed. It suffices to have extra arguments for each of these,
e.g.:

```
sentence(P,s(NP,VP))  --> noun-phrase(X,Pl,P,NP),
                          verb_phrase(X,Pl,VP).
```

where the last argument in each symbol deals with parse tree
buildup, and the other arguments, with meaning representation.

It is clear that, if we could somehow hide these extra arguments
from the user, our grammar descriptions would become more legible.
Hiding parse-tree arguments is quite straightforward.

Meaning representations in more complex grammars, however, is not
a trivial matter, as these representations usually follow neither
the history of rule application nor the surface ordering of
constituents, and can therefore not be described in sequential
terms.

Arriving at an appropriate meaning representation may involve
complex transformations, change of modifier scopes, etc. It may
not be possible to completely automate this process, but it is
possible to automate some of it, by giving the user a means for
specifing guidelines which the system will consult in order to
construct the final representation. We should allow for these
guidelines to be set in a modular fashion, so that modifications
to the representations obtained can be achieved with just local
changes that are relatively independent from syntax.

Joint research with Michael McCord on coordination [23] yielded as
a by-product a new grammar formalism, modifier structure grammars,
which automates the construction of both parse tree and (in the
modular fashion described above) logical representation.

Simultaneously and independently, restriction grammars were
implemented in Prolog [25]. These also automate parse tree
construction - although not logical representation - within an
augmented context-free framework.

Harvey Abramson later incorporated the idea of automatic buildup
of syntactic and logical form in his Definite Clause Translation
Grammars [24], although less powerfully than in Modifier Structure
Grammars, from the point of view that the former leave scoping and
coordination problems to the user, whereas the latter handle them
automatically.

5.CONCLUSION

We have presented the main ideas and practical aspects underlying
logic based metagrammars for natural language understanding. We
hope to have convincingly argued that these formalisms seem most
suitable for relieving the writer of parsers from machine-dependent

and procedural concerns. We have also compared Prolog-based and logic-grammar based parsers, and conclude that, although their computational power is the same, the expressive power of logic-based metagrammars greatly eases the task by automating some of the grammar-writing process and by hiding from the user some machine-dependent concerns that do not relate directly to the development of a grammar. Even in the case of DCGs, the closest grammar formalism to Prolog, the mere notation in terms of rewriting rules rather than a programming language's rules might make a difference in how comfortable a non-computer-specialist feels with using them.

The process of writing a parser is thus becoming more and more independent from machine and operational concerns, and near to the conceptual level alone. This phenomenon is likely to stimulate more empirical linguistic research, and to allow wider, more economical natural language understanding applications in artificial intelligence. Although much remains to be done, we believe that the combination of these effects already has the potential of producing invaluable results in both fields.

REFERENCES

[1] Kowalski, R., Predicate logic as a programming language, Proc. IFIP 74, North-Holland, Amsterdam (1974), 569-574.

[2] van Emden, M., Programming with resolution logic, in: E. Elcock and D. Michie, eds., Machine Intelligence 8 (Ellis Horwood, Chichester, U.K., 1977).

[3] Colmerauer, A. et al., Un systeme de communication homme-machine en francais, Aix-Marseille Univ. (1973).

[4] Roussell, Ph., Prolog: manuel de reference et d'utilisation, Aix-Marseille Univ. (1975).

[5] Colmerauer, A., An interesting subset of natural language, in: K. Clark and S.A. Tarnlund, eds., Logic Programming (1982), 45-66.

[6] Dahl, V., Quantification in a three-valued logic for natural language question-answering systems, Proc. VI International Joint Conference on Artificial Intelligence, Tokyo (1979).

[7] Pique, J.F., On a semantic representation of natural language sentences, Proc. First International Logic Programming Conference, Marseille (1982), 215-223.

[8] Saint-Dizier, P., Quantifier hierarchy in a semantic representation of natural language sentences (this volume).

[9] Dahl V. and Sambuc R., Un systeme de banque de donnees en logique du premier ordre, en vue de sa consultation en langue naturelle, D.E.A. Report, Aix-Marseille Univ. (1976).

[10] Dahl, V., Logic programming and constructive expert systems, Proc. First International Workshop on Expert Database Systems, South Carolina (1984).

[11] Dahl, V., Un systeme deductif d'interrogation de banques de donnees en espagnol, These de Doctorat de Specialite, Aix-Marseille Univ. (1977).

[12] Dahl V., On database systems development through logic, ACM Transactions on Database Systems, vol. 7, No. 1 (1982) 102-123.

[13] Colmerauer, A., Metamorphosis grammars, in: L. Bolc (ed.), Lecture Notes in Computer Science (Springer-Verlag, vol. 63, 1978) 133-189.

[14] Dahl, V., Translating Spanish into logic through logic, American Journal of Computational Linguistics, vol. 7, No. 3 (1981) 149-164.

[15] Warren, D. H. D., Efficient processing of interactive relational database queries expressed in logic, Dept. A. I., Univ. of Edinburgh (1981).

[16] Warren, D. H. D., An efficient easily adaptable system for interpreting natural language queries, American Journal of Computational Linguistics, vol. 8, No. 3-4 (1982) 110-119.

[17] Coelho, H.M.F., A program conversing in Portuguese providing a library service, Ph.D. Thesis, Univ. of Edinburgh (1979).

[18] McCord, M., Using slots and modifiers in logic grammars for natural language, Artificial Intelligence 18 (1982) 327-367.

[19] Pereira, F.C.N. and Warren, D.H.D., Definite clause grammars for language analysis, Artificial Intelligence, vol.13 (1980) 231-278.

[20] Pereira, F.C.N., Extraposition grammars, American Jounal of Computational Linguistics, vol. 9, No. 4 (1981) 243-255.

[21] Dahl, V. and Abramson, H., On gapping grammars, Proc. Second International Logic Programming Conference, Uppsala (1984) 77-88.

[22] Dahl, V., More on gapping grammars, Proc. Fifth Generation Computer Systems, Tokyo (1984).

[23] Dahl V. and McCord M., Treating coordination in logic grammars, American Journal of Computational Linguistics, vol.9, No. 2 (1983) 69-91.

[24] Abramson, H., Definite clause translation grammars, Proc. IEEE Logic Programming Symposium, Atlantic City (1984) 233-240.

[25] Hirschman, L., and Puder, K., Restriction grammar: a Prolog implementation, in: Warren D.H.D. and van Caneghem, M. (eds.), Logic Programming and its Applications (Ablex, 1984).

[26] Porto, A. and Filgueiras, M., Natural language semantics: a logic programming approach, International Symposium on Logic Programming, Atlantic City (1984) 228-232.

[27] Uehara, K., Ochitani, R., Kakusho, O. and Toyoda, J., A bottom-up parser based on predicate logic: a survey of the formalism and its implementation technique, Proc. 1984

International Symposium on Logic Programming, Atlantic City (1984) 220-227.

[28] Robinson, J.A., A machine-oriented logic based on the resolution principle, Journal of the ACM 12 (1965) 23-44.

[29] Popowich, Fred, The gap stops here, Simon Fraser University (in preparation).

FOOTNOTES

(1) We can think of strings as functional expressions with some symbol standing for "concatenation" as the (binary) function symbol, e.g. ".(the,.(mother,nil))", but we shall stick to the more convenient list notation.

(2) [X/Y] stands for the list with head X and tail Y.

(3) we use square brackets to distinguish terminals from non-terminals.

(4) The actual Prolog implementation of MGs requires in fact that α be a string of terminals alone, but we shall disregard this restriction, since it has been shown [13] to involve no substantial loss with respect to the full MG form.

Natural Language Understanding and Logic Programming
V. Dahl and P. Saint-Dizier (Editors)
© Elsevier Science Publishers B.V. (North-Holland), 1985

NATURAL LANGUAGE INTERFACE
FOR A POLISH RAILWAY EXPERT SYSTEM

Paweł Luboński

Institute of Informatics
University of Warsaw
Warsaw, Poland

The paper describes a natural language understanding
system /for Polish/ which simulates the processing of
enquiries by a railway information office. Some problems connected with computer realization of public
information systems are introduced. A detailed analysis
of the railway information office case is given and basic
rules of interpretation of sentences from a railway
domain-oriented subset of Polish are suggested. The emphasis is on making a dialogue that resembles a natural
one, especially in its dependence of the interpretation
on the context of discourse. Some rather simple data
structures and algorithms are proposed for accomplishing
an interpretation.

INTRODUCTION

In every day life we deal with a variety of public enquiry systems,
e.g. railway or telephone information offices. These systems, irrespective of whether they use electronic equipment or contain
printed information, are operated as a rule by trained personnel.
The reason is, that a typical user of such systems requires some
properties difficult to satisfy in a computer program. The typical
enquirer is a non-expert, who usually doesn´t know an exact structure for the information he wants and cannot express his query
precisely. He prefers colloquial speech and it may be difficult
for him to deal with even a little formalised language. The process of data acquisition may be performed hurriedly or in some
other situation where special stresses are involved.

The outlined conditions of work require a high level of competence
in using a natural language. A human informant, who is an expert,
naturally has that competence, but how to replace him effectively
by a proper computer program is as yet an unsolved problem.

The most important properties desirable for such an automatic
query-answering system are described below and illustrated by a
"natural" dialogue in a railway enquiry-office.

/1/ User: KIEDY MAM POCIAG DO KRAKOWA ?
          When can I set a train to Krakow?
          /literally: "have a train..."/

/2/ System: JEST WIELE POCIAGOW. O JAKIEJ PORZE CHCIAŁBY PAN
            WYJECHAC ?
            There are many trains. What time would you like
            to depart ?

/3/ U: MUSZE BYC NA MIEJSCU PRZED OSMA RANO .
         I must be there before 8 a.m.

/4/ S: JEST POSPIESZNY O 23.15 PRZYJEZDZAJACY DO KRAKOWA O 7.25
         I OSOBOWY O 21.48 PRZYJEZDZAJACY O 6.40.
         There is a fast train at 23.15 arriving in Kraków at
         7.25 and slow   train at 21.48 arriving at 6.40.

/5/ U: CZY OSOBOWY MA WAGON SYPIALNY ?
         Has the slow one got a sleeping-car ?

/6/ S: NIE, ALE MA KUSZETKI .
         No, it hasn't, but it has couchettes.

/7/ U: A TAMTEN ?
         And the other one ?

/8/ S: POSPIESZNY O 23.15 MA WAGON SYPIALNY.
         The fast train at 23.15 has a sleeping-car.

/9/ U: A JAKIES RANO ?
         And any in the morning?

/10/ S: POSPIESZNY O 8.34 I OSOBOWY O 6.15.
         A fast train at 8.34 a.m. and a slow one at 6.15.

/11/ U: A Z REZERWACJA SA JAKIES ?
         With reservable places are there any?

/12/ S: TAK, POSPIESZNY O 8.34.
         Yes, the fast at 8.34.

/13/ U: O KTOREJ GODZINIE ODJEZDZA TEN POPOLUDNIOWY EKSPRES ?
         What time does the afternoon express depart?

In the above dialogue some frequently occuring phenomena of both
syntactic and semantic nature may be observed. A good system should
be able to interpret them correctly.

Idiom. The utterance /1/ is not to be interpreted literally /"when
can I come into possesion of the train"/ but as a question about
departure time.

Indirect answer /3/. Here we deal with two problems. First, we
should infer that if the user must be in Krakow before eight o'clock,
he is interested in trains arriving before this time. Second, in
this way some property of desired trains was stated, but not the
one the system has asked for /i.e. departure time in /2//.

Anaphora /7/.

Another type of reference /5/. The phrase "the slow one" indicates
one of the trains already mentioned and not an arbitrary slow train
to Krakow.

Ellipsis. /7/. A verb phrase is missing in this utterance. Intuitively the phrase contained in the previous user's utterance /5/
is assumed. Similarly there is no verb phrase in /9/ and a destination of travel is not specified; however this utterance is still
quite meaningful.

Unnatural word order /11/. In free-word order languages like
Polish such sentences may be correct syntactically, but not in
respect of style.

Assumption of properties. The context of the utterance /11/ implies
that only morning trains are to be considered.

<u>Unsolvable anaphoric reference</u>. In /13/ the phrase "the afternoon express" points to an object not mentioned earlier in the dialogue, but well-known to both user and system.

System's responses to user's queries in this sample dialogue illustrate some properties desirable for natural language conversational systems. A system not having such properties will probably be less useful and in certain circumstances may cause serious misunderstandings.

<u>Query too general</u> /1/. A full answer could be too extensive. The system asks for a more precise query /2/.

<u>Cooperativeness</u>. The answer /4/ contains not only those data which were asked for /i.e. departure time/, but also others the user could be interested in; in the given context an arrival time is of importance. In /6/ the system not only gives the negative answer, but tries to find any information similar to the desired one.

<u>Automatic disambiguation</u>. Because the meaning of the query /7/ is not self-evident, the system paraphrases its interpretation to formulate the answer. The often used technique to solve such doubts is to ask an user before answering if the given interpretation is valid /as in [1], [2]/. Notice, however, that a system permanently asking for a confirmation of every interpretation could be rather irritating.

<u>Assuming user's intentions</u>. If the query /11/ is interpreted literally, the answer will be simply "yes". However, it should be interpreted as a request to list proper trains.

Let us now consider what information is necessary to interpret a user's utterance correctly in the presence of the problems described above.

a./ Knowledge of user's goals. In the general case identifying user's goals is an extremely complicated task. In the case of given information systems the goal repertory is relatively narrow and it is possible to design a simple algorithm to identify a correct goal [3] .

b./ Knowledge of a history of dialogue. This is useful for example when solving problems of anaphora or ellipsis during a dialogue.

c./ Knowledge of the present "world state". In our example an item of information about time or date could be necessary /e.g. to interpret such queries as: "When will the <u>next</u> train to Krakow arrive?"/. The "world state" notion includes also the present database content. For instance a railway timetable access must be performed to interpret the reference "the afternoon express" in /13/, that means to identify the train.

The last two sets of information /b. and c./ will be called "context" in this paper.

Now two basic notions which determine the meaning of a user's utterance will be defined. The approach presented is similar to those given in [4] .

<u>The topic of an utterance</u> is the main object or notion which the utterance centers around. In our example it is a certain train. Every utterance has its own topic but different utterances can have the same one. A topic need not be explicitly mentioned in a utterance. Consider queries /1/ and /3/. In /1/ the topic containing

"all trains to Kraków" is introduced. The utterance /3/ has the
same topic, but contains no explicit mention of trains. Topics may
change in the course of dialogue; they may also be narrowed as in
/5/ where the topic is a subset of the topic of /4/.

The theme of a utterance is a purpose of this utterance in the
general case. It may be a request to perform some action /e.g. to
supply some information/ or making some assertion. For instance
it can be said that the theme of the utterance /1/ is "a request
to enumerate all trains to Kraków". Notice that the theme in this
meaning usually corresponds with the main verb phrase in a sentence.

RAILWAY CASE STUDY

First, the model of a natural Polish dialogue must be built. It is
a complicated task because an interpretation of a utterance depends
not only on information given directly in the utterance and not
only on the context. The hearer's knowledge, his beliefs about
the speaker's intentions etc. should also be considered [5] .
  However, given a relatively simple situation of dialogue in a
railway information office we can build rather simple model if we
accept some strong assumptions about semantics of utterances and
knowledge and beliefs of both user and system. It seems that the
restrictions are not so large to limit the practical value of presented results of the work.

The following model of the user is introduced:

1. The user's goal is to acquire certain information. Every his
   utterance specifies some range of desired information. So, such
   utterances as "I want to go to Krakow" are to be interpreted
   as requests to list proper trains rather than as just an informative sentence about the user's wishes. Similarly in the
   example at the previous section the utterance /3/ introduces
   additional requirements to the query /1/ and ought to be interpreted as another query.

2. The user is assumed not to have any knowledge about the subject
   of dialogue, i.e. railway timetables in this case. For example
   the system could not assume that he knows that an express train
   has all seats reservable /as it is in Poland/.

3. No user's intentions are known, except those explicitly expressed in his discourse. This means that the system cannot make
   any assumptions about a desired departure time, type of train,
   etc.

For a simplification /because of limited computing resources/ I
make a restriction on the range of accesible information. Namely
queries may concern only trains from Warsaw and only the properties of those trains which are contained in the timetable. Hence
queries like "How late will this train be?" or "Where is the lug-
gage office" are not permitted. In addition I assume that the whole
dialogue consists of pairs /user's query - system's response/
called dialogue_cycles . A single user's utterance may contain
at most one non-complex Polish sentence. Compound sentences /e.g.
"What time does it arrive and what is its route?"/ are not permitted.

Given such assumptions the interpretation of the user's utterance
reduces to :

- determining the topic of the utterance, i.e. the train or group

of trains the utterance refers to;
- determining the theme of the utterance, i.e. establishing
  what information about these trains is desired.

Consider the first of these issues /the second is relatively easily recognizable/. Notice that every query can refer to trains in
two ways. First, it can be a request to enumerate all trains with
specified properties /e.g. "fast, morning, to Krakow"/; second,
some information can be requested about certain /i.e. known
by the user/ train; for example, what time does it arrive at the
station of destination. I call these cases respectively the general query and the specific query.

There are several kinds of reference to trains that may occur in
the sentence /the terminology is mine/:

a./ Reference by specifying attributes. It occurs usually in gene-
    ral queries; e.g. "What are the morning trains to Krakow?"
    A variant of it is relative reference /relative to other
    trains or to present time/; e.g. "earlier", "next".
b. /Anaphora. This usually refers to some train mentioned in dialo-
    gue; e.g. "Has it a sleeping-car?"
c./ Reference by complement. This refers to trains not mentioned
    yet; e.g. "Are there any other trains?"
d./ Indirect reference /see example /3/ in introduction/.

Two or more types of references can be combined in a single query;
e.g. "Have those other fast trains sleeping-cars?"

The fundamental problem of interpreting references is to determine
a basic set of trains. The basic set is the set of trains the topic will be selected from. In the simplest case it contains all
trains of given destination, but this is not a general rule. Consider the example from the introduction again. In the query /5/
there is a reference by attribute "slow". It is intuitively clear,
that such a train ought to be found among those enumerated in the
previous system response /4/ rather than among all trains to Krakow.

The next problem corresponds to assumptive attributes. Consider
another example:

/1/ U: CZY DZIS RANO SA POSPIESZNE POCIAGI DO KRAKOWA ?
       Are there fast trains to Krakow this morning?

/2/ S: TAK, O 8.35.
       Yes, at 8.35 a.m.

/3/ U: A OSOBOWE ?
       And slow ones?

Intuitively , "slow trains this morning" are assumed. As we see,
in some cases attributes may be inherited from previous queries.

In particular there could be no train satisfying a reference. That
situation is interpreted differently, depending on whether the
query is specific or general. For the specific query that implies
an error - the user refers to a nonexisted train or described it
inprecisely. For the general query it means that not all the
user's requirements can be satisfied. In this case the system
ought to attempt to find trains that are as close to these requirements as possible. Suppose that the query is the same as /1/
in the example above, but that there are no such trains. Suppose
then that both a slow train in the morning and a fast train in the

evening exist. Which of them is of interest? To resolve such
ambiguities an order on the set of train attributes is introduced.
In the example intuitively the arrival time is more important
than the type of train. Similarly it could be established that
a date of a journey is more important than time, type of train
than route etc. The order changes if one of the attributes is
assumptive. Suppose that the first system's response /2/ was:
"There is only slow train at 8.35 a.m." The next remark of the
user is:

   /3/ WOLE JECHAC POSPIESZNYM .
       I prefer fast trains.

In the utterance /3/ the "morning" attribute is inherited from /1/,
but the directly-specified type of train dominates over it, so a
suitable answer may be:

   /4/ POSPIESZNY JEST TYLKO O 19.05.
       The only fast train is at 19.05.

ALGORITHMS OF INTERPRETATION

By the interpretation of a user's query I mean the determination
of the /topic-theme/ pair as defoned in the previous section.

The goal of this study is to create a simple method of natural
Polish language interpretation for a specific, well defined domain. It must be emphasized that concepts described below are sub-
stantially influenced by the assumed dialogue restrictions; thus
they could not be widened or transferred to other domains, at least
in a simple way. The value of the concepts is justified by their
practical utility: it appears that the algorithms perform the correct interpretation of an extremely wide set of utterances. Manual
tests on some dozens of original instances of dialogue didn't cause any serious misunderstandings /where by serious misunderstanding
I mean a situation where a user gets information incompatible with
his expectations yet does not realize this/.

The process of interpretation is divided into two phazes. In the
first of them, an input sentence is transformed to the internal
semantic representation. As established by experiments, in most
of the cases a full semantic and syntactic analysis of the sentence is not necessary for valid interpretation; it is sufficient
to extract some well-defined data from the input. Every one of
them is carried by a certain fragment of a sentence, called a seg-
ment_. I assume that a segment is a continous fragment, that
every two segments are separated and that information supplied by
one segment is not influenced by any other segments. With this
assumption the query analysis reduces to detection and analysis of
separated segments. Every word in the sentence has to exactly one
segment, contrary to the approach presented in [6] . Assumed segment classification and motivations for it are introduced below.

a./ Introduction. This supplies information about grammatical number and/or gender of the users, thereby allowing individualization
of system responses.
E.g.: PROSZE NAS POINFORMOWAC
        Please, inform us

b./ Question tag.
E.g.: O KTOREJ GODZINIE   /what time/

c./ Pivot. This contains the main verb phrase of the sentence.
E.g.: PRZYJEZDZA DO KRAKOWA RANO
     arrives in Krakow in the morning

Segments b. and c. together determine the theme of query, i.e. the
type of information desired.

d./ Quantification tag. This category includes anaphoric references and other phrases which influence the basic set selection.
E.g.: ON , TAMTEN , JAKIS , INNY
     it   that   any   other

e./ Attributes. They make a criterion for selection of trains from
the basic set. Any number of attributes may occur under the condition that they are compatible with each other.
E.g.:   Z WAGONEM SYPIALNYM
       with a sleeping-car

f./ Destination. This attribute is distinguished because of its
specific role. Every selected train must be of the proper destination of course, while other specified attributes may not be satisfied.

The internal semantic representation consists of data listed above
represented in a simple formalism. An additional datum, not connected with any segment of a sentence, is the grammatical number of
trains mentioned in the query. It may be useful. For example:

/1/ KIEDY JEST PIERWSZY POCIAG DO KRAKOWA ?
    Whem is the first train to Krakow?

/2/ POSPIESZNY O 10.12.
    The fast at 10.12 a.m.

/3/ A NASTEPNY ?
    And the next ?

/4/ OSOBOWY O 11.56.
    The slow train at 11.56.

/5/ O KTOREJ ONE PRZYJEZDZAJA DO KRAKOWA ?
    What time do they arrive to Krakow?

If in /5/ a pronoun occurs in the singular /"it"/, the query will
refer only to the second train.

For more details about conception and implementation of the first
phase of the interpretation see [7] .

The second phase uses information about the previous course of the
dialogue. This knowledge is recorded in a special data structure
called the context graph. It is a directed graph with every node
representing one of the user's utterances. Every node contains
the following data:
- the topic of the given utterance /i.e. list of trains/;
- the selection criterion /attributes specified in the query/;
- the query type /general or specific, assumptive or specified/.
There is one additional node, not connected with any utterance.
It is called the base and contains the list of all trains of given
destination.

There are two kinds of arcs in the context graph. The chronological arc connects the node of a given discourse with the node of
utterance immediately previous to it in time. The hierarchical one
points to the node which contains a set of trains used as the basic
set during interpretation of a given utterance /i.e. the superset

of the current topic; in the simpliest case it is the base/.
Every node /except the base/ has one arc of each kind leading out
of it. The node of the last utterance is directly accesible and is
called the current node.

I introduce the following definitions:

The explicit query - the query which contains segments determining
the query type /the question tag and/or the pivot/;

The implicit query - in other case;

Incompatible sets of attributes - if they cannot be satisfied by
the same train;

Neutral sets of attributes - if they refer to different properties
of trains; e.g. "fast" and "morning" are neutral with each other;

Specified attributes - attributes mentioned explicitly in the utterance;

Assumptive attributes - those inherited from previous utterances.

Four basic cases may be distinguished, with different methods of
interpretation: the general explicit, the general implicit, the
specific explicit and specific implicit queries. Moreover some
special cases exist. The most important of them are:
- the query with an "other" quantification tag;
- the query specifying a destination /this enforces selection
  the base as a basic set/.

For the sake of brevity I describe here algorithms for only two
of basic cases. The terms "chronologically/hierarchically nearest"
used in the description refer to the first node /of some properties/
reached while searching the graph using arcs of the given type.

1. General explicit queries.

   i. find the chronologically nearest /to current/ node A with
      a general query;

   ii. find the hierarchically nearest /to A/ node B with an att-
       ribute list compatible with specified attributes /in the
       simpliest case A=B may occur/; attributes contained in
       nodes passed on the way, which are neutral with the spe-
       cified ones constitute an assumptive attribute list;

   iii. treat the train set B as a basic set; select trains in
        it according to specified and assumptive attributes;

   iv. if there are no trains satisfying all the attributes,
       pass to the hierarchically next node and repeat iii.;

   v. if the base has been reached, select the trains satisfy-
      ing as many attributes as possible in accordance with
      their priority /notice that specified attributes have an
      upper priority than assumptive/.

2. Specific implicit queries.

   i. find the chronologically nearest node A with an explicit
      query /in fact only at this moment can the query be iden-
      tified as specific/;

   ii. find the chronologically nearest /to A/ node B with att-
       ribute list compatible with specified attributes /A=B
       cannot occur here/; attributes of node A /only!/ neutral
       with specified attributes make up an assumptive attribute

    list;
iii. select trains in B according to the specified attributes;
all must be satisfied; otherwise searching using chronological arcs is continued;

  iv. if the result of selection is imprecise /e.g. reference in
the utterance is in the singular and more than one train
was selected/, assumptive attributes may be used in additional selection; if this also fails, the query is ambiguous.

The general schema of conversation is as follows: when the destination is mentioned the first time /it should occur in the first
user´s utterance for in other case the interpretation will be im-
possible/, the base node is created. Each cycle of dialogue creates a new node describing the given discourse. This node automatically becomes current. There is an exception - when a query is
ambiguous or erroneous and the topic cannot be identified. In such
cases no node is created and after the information for the user
the dialogue proceeds as if the last utterance does not exist.

An example of the usage of desribed algorithms follows.

/1/ U: JAKIE SA RANO POCIAGI DO KRAKOWA PRZEZ KIELCE ?
      What trains are to Krakow through Kielce in the morning?

/2/ S: OSOBOWY 8.46 i POSPIESZNY 10.15.
      The slow at 8.46 and the fast at 10.15.

/3/ U: CZY POSPIESZNY MA MIEJSCA REZERWOWANE ?
      Has the fast one reservable seats?

/4/ S: NIE MA.
      No, it hasn´t.

/5/ U: A TEN OSOBOWY ?
      And the slow one?

/6/ S: MA .
      It has.

/7/ U: CZY SA JAKIES POCIAGI PRZEZ CZESTOCHOWE ?
      Are there any trains via Czestochowa?

/8/ S: RANO NIE MA . JEST TYLKO POSPIESZNY O 21.30.
      There aren´t any in the morning. There is only the fast
      train at 21.30.

After the first two dialogue cycles the following context graph
exists:

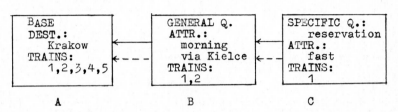

where:

- ←—————————— denotes chronological arcs;
- ←— — — — — — denotes hierarchical arcs;
- numbers stand for train descriptions.

Consider the query /5/. According to rule 2i. we reach the node
C and identify the query as "specific implicit". According to 2ii.
we then reach the node B. Because specified attributes /"slow"/
are compatible with attributes of B, the list of trains B becomes
the basic set. Because there is only one slow train in this basic
set, the topic is identified. The context graph presents itself
now as below:

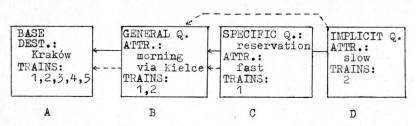

Consider now the query /7/. According to 1i. we reach the node B.
Because attributes "via Kielce" and "via Częstochowa" are incompatible, we pass chronologically to the base. The "morning" attribute becomes an assumptive attribute of the current query /1ii./.
According to 1iii. we select trains in the base A. Because no
train satisfies all requirements, the train which satisfies only
the specified attributes but not assumptive ones is selected. The
final state of the context graph is:

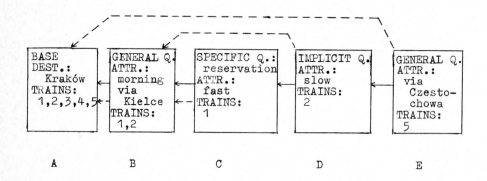

STATE OF WORK

Algorithms described in the paper are implemented in PROLOG as a
part of the railway expert system. In the system the query-interpreter module collaborates with the journey-organizer module.
The journey-organizer is able to find optimal railway connections
between arbitrarily selected two railway stations in Poland, regarding user's requirements. The journey-organizer has access to the
database containing the railway timetable.

It is worth-noticing that the journey-organizer has a greater power
than the query interpreter, i.e. it can answer more complicated
queries than the query-interpreter could accept. Thus the main goal of further work will be to generalize interpretation rules to

a such degree that queries about indirect connections and not only from Warsaw can be accepted.

Two parts of the system run now:
- The journey-organizer. It has been tested on the primitive database describing only few railway routes, because the version of PROLOG interpreter used in this work do not allow for a larger selection of routes.
- A fragment of the query-interpreter which accomplishes the first phase of the interpretation. It is implemented as a relatively big metamorphosis grammar. It is a "railway queries" grammar rather than a grammar of Polish language. A few of the Polish grammar rules are obeyed; that approach allows us to accept many sentences formally invalid but intuitively comprehensible. Ambiguities are eliminated as a rule by accepting only the interpretation that refers to the given domain; e.g. the Polish word "pośpieszny" /fast/ will always be interpreted as a train attribute, although it could also mean "hurried" in a more general context.

The system works on the IBM/370 under the IIUW-PROLOG interpreter [8] , [9] .

CONCLUDING REMARKS

The experimental work described in this paper has permitted an investigation in some depth into the problem of dialogue organization in Polish. There were some attempts to construct a natural language question-answering system for Polish but none of them are operational. It seems that the given system with some extensions has a chance of becoming practically usable. However much work remains to be done, if the extensions mentioned above prove to be succesful, PROLOG will be shown to be an effective instrument for implementing such systems.

REFERENCES

1 Lopes, G.P., Implementing dialogues in a knowledge information system, in: this paper.

2 Szpakowicz,S.,Świdziński,M., A simple dialogue in Polish: Interactive railway guide, in: Bień,J.S. /ed./, Papers in computational linguistics II /IInf UW Reports, Warsaw, 1981/.

3 Allen,J.F.,Perrault,C.R., Participating in dialogues: understanding via plan deduction, AI-MEMO, July 1978.

4 Bullwinkle,C., Levels of complexity in discourse for anaphora disambiguation and speech act interpretation, in: 5th IJCAI, Proceedings of the Conference.

5 Bień,J,S., Multiple environments approach to natural language, Americal Jrnl. of Computational Linguistics, 3 /1976/.

6 Courant,M., Robin,S., Classified advertisement analysis, in: this paper.

7 Luboński,P., Automatyczna informacja kolejowa, implementacja w języku PROLOG, M.Sc.Thesis, IInf Univ. of Warsaw, 1984.

8 Kluźniak,F., Szpakowicz,S., PROLOG /WNT, Warsaw, 1983/.

9 Kluźniak,F., IIUW-PROLOG,in: Logic Programming Newsletter, vol.1, no.1 /Berlin, 1981/.

Natural Language Understanding and Logic Programming
V. Dahl and P. Saint-Dizier (Editors)
© Elsevier Science Publishers B.V. (North-Holland), 1985

CLASSIFIED ADVERTISEMENT ANALYSIS IN THE CONTEXT
OF AN EXPERT SYSTEM IN AD MATCHING

Michèle Courant, Sophie Robin
I.R.I.S.A.
Campus de Beaulieu
35042 RENNES Cédex
France

HAVANE is an expert system in automatic classified adverti-sement matching where the ads are expressed in the usual ad language (as in newspapers). One feature of this natural language corpus is the absence of global syntax. A specification language based on an attribute grammar formalism is defined. This language allows the expert to characterize the acceptable ads. In the framework of a prototype programmed in PROLOG, a parser, which makes use of the ad language proper-ties, is built based on the specifications of an expert. It is a two-level parser and it contains valuation criteria in-tended to select, from among the various meanings of an ad text, the most "pertinent" one. We show that in return, this parsing technique results in specific problems which prove that the ad language, despite its poor syntax, nevertheless requires a fairly elaborate syntactic analysis.

1. INTRODUCTION

HAVANE is a system designed to match automatically classified ads (BOS), (COU). The purpose in building this system is to design an ergonomic system aimed at a large public and built around natural language dialogues.

This application appears original in that it enables a user to select out of a data bank of ads, ads that correspond "best" to his particular advertising needs. Compared to other existing ad services, in current use by newspaper publishing in-dustry, HAVANE therefore offers the advantage of an automated ad selection service.

Moreover, compared to other computer generated ad systems which function via menus (FER), HAVANE, although aimed at performing the same service, doesn't require any modification of normal advertising formats. In particular, the ads are ex-pressed in the usual ad language, found in newspapers.

In addition, HAVANE is conceived of as an expert-system for two reasons :
- constraints of evolutivity of the treated domain and extension to other domains ;
- ergonomic constraints (e.g. necessity of explanation related to the ads selected
  by the system ...).
This choice necessitates the definition of tools intended for experts which will
provide them with the means to express knowledge underlying the applications they
want to carry out.

The implementation of an ad application entails, on the one hand the specification of what is an acceptable ad, and on the other hand the specification of the
notion of complementarity between two ads. This requires the definition of a language for specifying what is an acceptable ad. The language of advertisements in
and of itself constitutes a fairly original corpus, for it is built on the juxtaposition of independent syntactic units, which can be ordered in any sequence. In
view of this, rather than returning to classical techniques of natural languages
parsing (PER), (BIE), we designed both a specification language and a parser which
take account of the ad language properties.

In this paper, we first briefly present the principle underlying the system.
A second section focuses on the nature of the knowledge underlying the implementation of such a system, and describes a specification language based on an attribute grammar formalism. In a third section we describe in detail the parser which
issues from the specifications and we discuss its limitations. In creating HAVANE,
the purpose is obviously not only to design ad systems ; so we show then how the
specification language and the parsing technique can be generalized to other applications. Finally, we consider the expert-system aspect of HAVANE by studying the
problem of automatic reformulation of ad texts. Lastly we discuss certain problems
related to the parsing technique and propose resolutions for them.

2. PRINCIPLE OF THE SYSTEM

The principle of the system can be summed up by the following diagram :

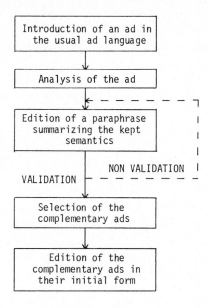

The user expresses his ad in the usual language of newspaper advertisements. Then the system proceeds to analyse it before constructing a paraphrase which summarizes its understanding of the ad. This paraphrase is returned for the user approval. When the user approves it, the system looks for the "complementary" ads. These ads are then returned in their original form.

3. SPECIFICATION

This section first describes the basic knowledge required for the description of acceptable ads and then proposes a language for the specification of this knowledge.

3.1. THE NATURE OF KNOWLEDGE.

Since HAVANE's purpose is advertisement matching, it must first be able to compare ads. This consequently requires the definition of "comparison objects" which will be used in the ad matching. Yet, not all the information which appear in the text of an ad will have relevance to the comparison. For example : the nature of the object (house, apartment, ... in the real estate domain, etc.) is obviously a piece of information which will have to do with the comparison ; on the other hand the advertiser's address is not taken into account in the comparison of two ads.

Consequently, the definition of the comparison objects comes down at the present time to the determining of those elements relevant to the ad comparison. In
so far as these elements are the pivotal point around which analysis and comparison
revolve, their determination constitutes the preliminary step to the specification
of the needed knowledge. Next, the definition of the acceptable ads is accomplished
by establishing the link between the ad language and the comparison objects. However, the ad language is characterized by the absence of a global syntactic structure, due to the elimination of grammatical entities such as articles, pronouns,
prepositions, etc. It is built on the juxtaposition of independent and optional
syntactic units which can be organized in any order (JAY) ; for example *"for sale
house Rennes"* and *"Rennes house for sale"* are two possible ads.

An exhaustive description of this language by means of syntactico-semantic
grammars, often used in natural language processing, turns out to be inadequate
because of the combinatorics involved. The idea is rather to make use of this absence of global syntax and to make a two-level description :
- a lexico-syntactic description of the basic components ;
- a purely semantic global description.

The semantic description is achieved by means of acceptability criteria and
inference rules, which leads to the definition of comparison objects.

At this point, we are in agreement with Pawel Lubonski's assertion *"in most
of the cases a full semantic and syntactic analysis of the sentence is not necessary ... It is sufficient to extract some well defined data from the input.
Every one of them is carried by a certain fragment of sentence, called a segment."*
(LUB).

3.2. THE SPECIFICATION LANGUAGE

Two specification languages have been defined to specify acceptable ads. The-
se languages, which are the Linguistic Analysis Grammars (LAG) for syntax and the
Structure Descriptor for semantics, preserve the distinction established above.
These two tools are built on the same formalism : attributed context-free grammars
(KNU).

From the point of view of specification, the attribute grammars are a simple
and concise formalism. On the one hand it offers an easy implementation in PROLOG.
But in the other hand, it is important to note that this formalism remains free of
implementation problems by leading to some abstraction (MAL). Furthermore, there
exist theoretical results which are useful for verifying the coherence of the specifications (DER). Since the expression of the global semantics of an ad obeys the
compositionnality principle (i.e. is a function of the basic components' seman-

tics), only synthesized attributes are retained. This restriction doesn't alter
the expressive power of the tools and makes the expert's task more simple.

3.2.1. Linguistic analysis grammars

The ad language appears as a syntactically poor language, since it is essentially built on the juxtaposition of independent syntactic units. Among these
units, some are considered "pertinent" in so far as they carry information relevant to ad matching. Consequently, LAGs are aimed at establishing the connection
between the "pertinent" textual elements and the semantic attributes.

A LAG is an attribute grammar, whose terminals are strings encountered in the
ad language.

Example :

    <<direction(offer)>> --> offers / proposal / ...
    <<direction(request)>> --> looks for / ...

These two rules belong to the grammar "direction". This grammar recognizes
strings indicating the transaction direction. The axiom of this LAG has a single
attribute which can take either of two values "offer" and "request". Which one is
chosen depends on wether we find the strings "offers" and "proposal" or "looks
for" in the ad text.

3.2.2. Structure descriptor

The purpose of the Structure Descriptor is the description of acceptable ads
as semantic trees. It is a grammar such that :
- the attributes of its start symbol "ad" are the significant units for the comparison ;
- the terminals of the grammar are the start symbols of the LAGs.

In addition, attribute calculus and coherence checking expressions are tied
to each production of the grammar.

Example :

P1 : <ad(TD.TM.NAT.NB1.NB2...)> --> <transaction(TD1.TM1)>

                                <object(NAT1.NBP1.NBP2)><exchange(...)

    where (1) TD1 = unknown and TM1 = buy-or-sale => TD = offer
              TD1 = unknown and (TM1 = hiring or NBP1 = NBP2) => TD = request
              :
              :

(2) ⎰default(TD) : TD1

(3) ⎰not(NBP1 = NBP2 and TD1 = offer)
    ⎱NAT ≠ unknown

The production P1 specifies that an ad is semantically composed of a "transaction", an "object", and an "exchange". Although the attribute grammar formalism is used here, the juxtaposition of two non-terminals in the right part of a rule does not impose any contiguity and any order on the strings which are recognized by these non-terminals. It is only a semantic structure which is described, and it has no syntactic consequence.

The first three expressions tied to this production convey inference through attribute calculus. The first one (1) means that for lack of any information about the transaction direction and if the transaction mode is "buy-or-sale", one can deduce that the transaction direction is "offer". We are also provided with means to specify easily default values (2).

Finally, the two logical formulas (3) express coherence checking on the attribute values. The first one means that, in case of an offer, it is not possible to mention a number of rooms through an interval. The second one expresses that the "nature-of-object" is mandatory information.

P2 : <transaction(ST1.MT1)> --> <<direction(ST2)>><<mode(MT2)>>
where default(ST1) : ST2
      default(MT1) : MT2
      ⋮

In this production, the "<<...>>" around "direction" and "mode" means that these are terminals of the Structure Descriptor and, therefore, start symbols of the Linguistic Analysis Grammars.

Note :
    Although it doesn't appear in the above examples, the paraphrases may also be built through attribute calculus in the Structure Descriptor as well as in the LAGs.

4. THE PARSER

Within the framework of a prototype programmed in PROLOG, an implementation of the specifications for the real estate domain has already been carried out. The

implementation gave rise to the design of a two-level parser :
- a linguistic level which processes lexical and syntactic problems (ambiguities, ...) ;
- a semantic level which builds the semantic objects (or comprehension) from the
  linguistic results. (The semantic objects represent the different meanings of an
  ad text).

For a given ad, this parser builds all the comprehensions in order to proceed
to a global valuation of the results. For reasons of ergonomy, the idea is, to
provide the user immediately with the paraphrase corresponding to the most "pertinent" comprehension.

This section will proceed by discussing the linguistic and semantic analysis
followed by describing valuation problems and concluding with an illustation.

4.1. LINGUISTIC ANALYSIS

The source string is completely parsed by all the LAGs. One can see in a diagram below that this parsing process may lead to the overlapping of substrings recognized by the different grammars. It is also possible to have multiple success
of a given grammar.

If we call "result" a couple (LAG,substring), we obtain, for example, a set
of results such as :

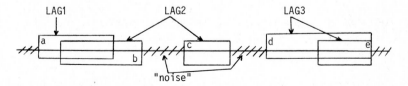

Then, we form sets "without conflict", i.e. such that there exists no overlapping between the substrings of the different couples, and such that a given LAG
appears at most in one couple. At this level valuation criteria are already coming
into play. These criteria are essentially based on the maximum use of the information appearing in the text. Hence, subsets of sets without conflict will never be
retained.

If we refer to the previous figure, two without conflict sets will be built :

{(LAG1,a),(LAG2,c),(LAG3,d)} and {(LAG2,b),(LAG3,d)}.

Neither one of these sets contains the result (LAG3,e) because the grammar LAG3
has recognized an otherwise longer string which doesn't conflict with any other
success. It is here the same choice as in [MAT] which gives priority to the reco-

gnition of the longest string.

4.2. SEMANTIC ANALYSIS

All the sets built during the linguistic phase are submitted to the Structure Descriptor. A set which satisfies acceptability criteria leads to a semantic object.

As soon as one set doesn't satisfy the acceptability constraints (due essentially to contradiction or information insufficiency in the text of the ad), a failure of the ad parsing occurs. The reasons for this failure are explained to the user.

In the opposite case, the system proceeds to a valuation of semantic objects based as well on the maximum information criteria. This valuation gives the order according to which the various comprehensions are submitted to the user through paraphrases.

4.3. VALUATION

During the linguistic analysis phase, several situations may occur :
- overlappings : a substring of the ad is parsed by several grammars ;
- multiple success of a given grammar.

These cases lead to the construction of several comprehensions corresponding to different interpretations of the ad. Then the valuation criteria, acting at the linguistic level as well as at the semantic level, enable the system at times to choose an interpretation which makes sense.

4.3.1. Overlappings

We are considering four cases.

Case 1 :

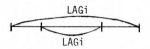

Example : "... great house ..." where the substrings "house" and "great house" are recognized by the same grammar "nature-of-object".

Case 2 :

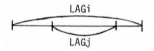

Example : "... brakes 10000 km ..." where the substrings "10000 km" and "brakes 10000 km" are respectively parsed by the grammars "distance" and "state-of-brakes".

These overlapping cases don't cause any ambiguity for a reader. They result from the chosen parsing technique. So it is advisable to grant the success to the larger string.

Case 3 :

Two grammars recognize substrings which can't be distinguished by any context.

Example : "... garage ..." where both the grammar "nature-of-object" and the grammar "garage" recognize the string "garage".

Case 4 :

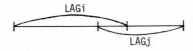

Example : "... garden 250 sqm inhabitable ..." where the strings "garden 250 sqm" and "250 sqm inhabitable" are respectively parsed by the grammar "ground" and the grammar "surface".

These two last cases correspond to real ambiguities. The maximum information criterion of the semantic level will sometimes allow the system to decide between the two hypotheses. The most probable string may be compatible with a greater number of elements appearing in the remainder of the ad. So, it will lead to a more informed semantic object.

4.3.2. Multiple success

Example : "*house for sale, 5 rooms, garden, garage, in Rennes*" where "house" and "garage" are recognized by the grammar "nature-of-object".

This case is processed like overlapping cases 3 and 4 (cf. 4.1). Here too, one of the hypotheses will likely be selected at the semantic level. In the example, the interpretation "*sale of a 5 rooms house in Rennes with garage and garden*" will be retained because it corresponds to a more informed semantic object.

4.4. ILLUSTRATION

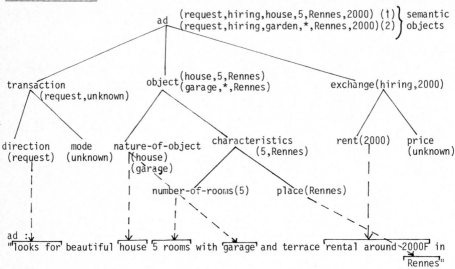

For the ad above, two without conflict sets are built :

$\Big\{$(Direction,"looks for"),(Nature,"house"),(Number-of-rooms,"5 rooms"),
   (Rent,"rental around 2000F"),(Place,"Rennes")$\Big\}$

and

$\Big\{$(Direction,"looks for"),(Nature,"garage"),(Number-of-rooms,"5 rooms"),
   (Rent,"rental around 2000F"),(Place,"Rennes")$\Big\}$

   These sets are submitted to the Structure Descriptor and lead to two seman-
tic trees corresponding to two semantic objects (1) and (2).
   The first one is more informed than the second one.
N.B. : * means "meaningless".

4.5. LIMITATIONS OF THE ANALYSIS TECHNIQUE

   The parser previously described is based on an ad hoc parsing technique which
uses the properties of the ad language. This technique introduces specific problems inherent in the fact that the syntactic analysis is local and the existence
of "noise" in the ad (i.e. substrings not parsed by the LAGs because they are non-
significant for the ad matching).

   Although the chosen valuation criteria attempt to compensate for these limitations, certain aberrations still result. One such aberration is, for example, the
building of two understandings of equal "pertinence" for an ad such as : *"for sale
apartment, 3 rooms, near House of Parliament"*. The two interpretations (*sale of a
3 rooms apartment and sale of a 3 rooms house*) are produced due to the double

success of the LAG "nature-of-object" on the strings "apartment" and "House".

5. EXTENSIONS

The features of the ad language force us to distinguish two levels in its specification. The idea is to make use of the local nature of the syntactic compo- nents ; so the tools placed at the expert's disposal lead him to differentiate the descriptions, of the syntax on the one hand, and of the semantics on the other hand. This choice, particularly suited to the ad language, permits the expert to describe various languages, from relatively poor languages requiring only a key- word analysis, to richer languages such as a subset of French. This ability to describe various languages arises from the freedom which allows the expert to cha- racterize to a greater or lesser extent the syntax and the semantics of the appli- cation language with the LAGs and with the Structure Descriptor. Although the spe- cifications drawn up in the case of HAVANE appear very simple from the linguistic point of view, LAGs are in effect a fairly powerful tool. Since they are built upon an attribute grammar formalism, they enable the expert through the use of non terminals in the right hand parts of rules and attribute calculus expressions, to achieve more complex syntactic descriptions. For example the description can be so complex as to allow a syntactic structure description for French or English sen- tences.

As far as the Structure Descriptor is concerned, it enables the expression of semantic rules related to an object, via coherence constraints and inference rules. In the case of simple applications having few ambiguities, the inference rules may allow the system to interpret a question, on semantic criteria alone, without requiring the user to respect a particular syntax. For instance, a question such as "*hommes yeux bleus bruns*" (blue-eyed brown-haired men) can lead immedia- tely, due to the inference system of the Structure Descriptor, to the interpreta- tion "*looks for men which are blue-eyed and brown-haired*".

In addition to the advertising field, these tools developed in the context of HAVANE, may be applied to other applications involving inquiries. Thus a rail- way information service that deals with questions such as : "*train Paris arrival this evening*" or "*night trains with sleeping cars to Marseille*" falls in this category.

As far as the parser is concerned, since it issues from the implementation of the specifications and is endowed with valuation criteria, it too is generali- sable. This is due to the valuation criteria that have been drawn from common sen- se, and have thus provided satisfying results in the ad case. It is likely to be

applicable to other languages satisfying results in the ad case and may likely be
applicable to other languages.

6. THE EXPERT-SYSTEM FOR THE USER : THE AUTOMATIC REFORMULATION

6.1. WHY REFORMULATION

As seen earlier, the parser produces a set of meanings in order of decreasing
pertinence. These meanings are proposed successively to the user through paraphrases until either the user accepts one or until there are no more possibilities. In
this latter case, the advertiser sees his ad rejected and must formulate another
one. In order to proceed quickly toward the best interpretation and not to reject
completely an ad text, a dialogue must take place after the first paraphrase is
proposed. Then during this dialogue, the system obtains new information, which
allows it, either to find in the comprehensions previously provided the one which
has to be retained, or to build a new meaning by taking into account the further
information. In this latter case, the initial text must be updated in order to
ensure its conformity with the new meaning (It is important to remember that it is
the texts which are returned after a selection of complementary ads and not those
meanings found by the system).

To ensure conformity between text and meaning, the system is given an automatic reformulation capability (COU2).

6.2. THE PROBLEM OF THE AUTOMATIC REFORMULATION

During the reformulation of an ad text, the system has to :
- add new information ;
- modify certain elements ;
- suppress certain information.

Remember that, during the analysis, the system has recognized only the strings
which carry information relevant to ad comparisons. Some elements such as articles,
very subjective adjectives (beautiful, ...), etc. have therefore been ignored.
These elements are, however, very important for the reformulation because they are
tied to substrings which can optionally be delected.

Example : In an ad such as :

"*for sale house wooded ground in Rennes*"

where the strings analysed by the LAGs are underlined. If the context is not taken
into account, the suppression of the information "ground" will lead to the new ad
"*for sale house wooded in Rennes*".

6.3. THE AGREED UPON TECHNIQUE

Two types of solutions are possible :
- a global one, which supposes a complete linguistic analysis of the ads ;
- a local one, accomplished in the same way as the existing parsing technique.

In order to maintain the spirit between the parsing technique and the approach to reformulation, the local solution is chosen, and this leads to tie the contexts to the LAGs.

Therefore a new tool, the "context grammars", which enable the specification of the left and right contexts of each LAG, is defined.

Example : The grammar describing the left context of the LAG "nature of object" could be :

<<nature-of-object-LC>> --> <<article>><<adjective-group>>|<<adjective-group>>

<<adjective-group>> --> <<adjective>><<adjective-sequence>>

<<adjective-sequence>> --> et<<adjective-sequence>>|ou<<adjective-sequence>>|ε

where <<article>> and <<adjective>> are lexical entries.

Addition, suppression and modification rules must be joined to the context specification. The reformulation brings to light additional problems which are examined in detail in (COU2).

7. CONCLUSION

In the context of a prototype, a two-level parser provided with valuation criteria is implemented. This parser has been shown to be quite efficient. Furthermore, for most of ads, the chosen valuation criteria permit the system to lead to the more pertinent meanings. Moreover, the heuristics implemented through the semantic valuation allows the system to arrange the various meanings in a common-sense order.

The parser nevertheless has certain limitations and certain examples reveal that the required robustness cannot be achieved without a more complex syntactic analysis. The expert's description of the ad language accepted by the system cannot be reduced only to the useful linguistic units (i.e. significant for a comparison). Recall the example of section 4.5 "*for sale apartment, 3 rooms, near House of Parliament*" for which the system is led to an aberrant interpretation. Without carrying out a complete, exhaustive syntactic parsing of the ad, one must take into account the syntactic connection of noises to termes around them. Rather than a more precise characterization of the languages generated by the LAGs, we

propose thinking of a characterization of the complementary languages. Perhaps it
suffices to eliminate certain expressions, especially by making use of prepositions. In the example of section 4.5, the non-success of the grammar "nature of
object" on the string "near House" would suppress the aberrant interpretation
"sale of 3 room house" ...

As seen in the previous section, the automatic reformulation of ad texts,
entails furthermore a more elaborate study of the ad language.

We intend to develop the expert-system aspects of the user interface, by the
design of an explanation module and an intelligent dialogue module (BON). An explanation module related to analysis failures is, at the present time, in the develop-
mental stages. The treatment of these failures, owing to the existence of contra-
dictions or insufficient information in the ad, essentially consists of disco-
vering the relevant textual elements by means of applied inference rules. In summary, we note that the work on the parser module and the reformulation module are
both finished. Moreover each work has been carried out independently. The development of the expert-system will proceed in such a way as to achieve an integration
of the two existing modules.

BIBLIOGRAPHY

(BIE) J.S. BIEN, S. SZPAKOWICZ, "Toward a parsing method for free word order lan-
       guages", COLING 82 Abstracts, p. 37-41.

(BON) A. BONNET, "Quelques modes de représentation des connaissances et des méca-
       nismes de raisonnement pour les systèmes experts", AFCET 4ème Congrès,
       Journées de Synthèse 23-24 Janvier 1984.

(BOS) P. BOSC, M. COURANT, S. ROBIN, L. TRILLING, "HAVANE : un système de mise en
       relation automatique de petites annonces", Rapport INRIA n° 223, Juillet
       1983.

(COU1) M. COURANT, S. ROBIN, L. TRILLING, "Un système de traitement de petites an-
       nonces", Journées sur la Programmation en Logique, Plestin-les-Grèves, 25-
       27 Avril 1984.

(COU2) M. COURANT, S. ROBIN, B. VIBET, "La reformulation automatique des petites
       annonces dans le système HAVANE", under publication. Rapport IRISA.

(DER) P. DERANSART, "Logical Attribute Grammars", IFIP 83, R.E.A. Mason (Ed.),
       Elsevier Science Publishers B.V (North-Holland), p. 463-469.

(FER) C. FERRER, "Définition et réalisation d'un système transactionnel réparti", Rapport INRIA, Juin 1981.

(JAY) J.H. JAYEZ, "Une approche de la compréhension par machine du langage naturel", Thèse d'Etat Université de Paris VII, 1979.

(KNU) D. KNUTH, "Semantics of context-free languages", Mathematical System Theory, Vol.2, n°2, 1968 et Vol.5, n°1, 1971.

(LUB) P. LUBONSKI, "Natural language interface for a Polish railway expert system", in this volume.

(MAL) J. MALUSZYNSKI, J.F. NILSSON, "A comparison of the logic programming language PROLOG with two-level grammars", First International Logic Programming Conference, September, 14-17th, 1982.

(MAT) Y. MATSUMOTO, M. KIYONO, H. TANAKA, "Facilities of the BUP parsing system", in this volume.

(PER) F. PEREIRA, D. WARREN, "Definite Clause Grammar for Language Analysis. A survey of the formalism and a comparison with Augmented Transition Networks", Artificial Intelligence, 13, 1980, p. 231-278.

Natural Language Understanding and Logic Programming
V. Dahl and P. Saint-Dizier (Editors)
© Elsevier Science Publishers B.V. (North-Holland), 1985

HANDLING QUANTIFIER SCOPING AMBIGUITIES IN A SEMANTIC
REPRESENTATION OF NATURAL LANGUAGE SENTENCES

Patrick Saint-Dizier
I.R.I.S.A.
Campus de Beaulieu
35042 RENNES Cédex
France

In this paper, we describe a rewrite system whose goal is to
reorder the range of quantifiers introduced by determiners
that appear in natural language sentences so as to produce a
correct formal semantic representation of the meaning of these
sentences. The range of the quantifiers is lowered or raised
by the application of the rewrite system rules. When a sentence
is ambiguous, all the relevant orderings of quantifiers are
produced. Finally, we show how the correct interpretation of an
ambiguous sentence can be selected by using contextual information. Contextual information invalidates or disinvalidates
the application of some rewrite rules.

INTRODUCTION
_____

Our long term goal is to specify a friendly man-machine interface that supports natural language communication. Ultimately, we intend to have software that
will be able to parse and to understand ordinary conversation on a limitied subject
and that will be able to generate answers in natural language and to provide help
to the user.

We have developed a domain independant parser and generator of french. The
subset of french accepted by the parser is quite large and thus, we need a very
comprehensive and robust parser. More precisely, this implies that the parser has
to take into account ambiguities, anaphoras, ellipsis and scoping problems for
quantifiers, adjectives, adverbs, negation, etc ... The result of the parsing process is a semantic representation that can be translated into first order logic.
(See the article by C.B. Schwind in this volume).

The semantic representation is produced from an intermediate syntactic structure in which every syntactic item is linked to its determiner. A separate syntactic level is necessary for handling determiners scoping and, more generally, modifiers scoping. A separate level for the semantic interpretation computation makes
it easier to treat constructions that require syntactic manipulations (cf. sentences with verbs "to be" or "to have" ...). Furthermore, from a methodological point
of view, it is important to have different treatments in separate modules. Modifications can thus be done in better conditions and the program is more readable.
Finally, we think that this decomposition into separate levels has no real conse-
quences on the efficiency of the parser.

In our system, the semantic representation of a sentence is functionnaly
computed in three steps :

    (a) The input sentence is parsed by a Definite Clause Grammar <FPe 80> and a
        syntactico-semantic representation is produced <Sai 83>.

(b) Anaphora resolution is then treated. Semantic and pragmatic information is used to find the appropriate antecedents of pronouns <Sai 85>.

(c) The computation of the range and the scope of quantifiers is carried out.

This article deals with quantifiers scoping and the way to detect and to solve the ambiguities they can introduce. Up to now, this problem has received little attention in linguistics and specially in computational linguistics. Most of the time, those who have studied quantifiers have mentioned that ambiguities may occur in the range and the scope of quantifiers and thus inferencing is required for disambiguation. But, in fact, they have never attempted to provide mechanisms to point out ambiguities and to present a notation that would accomodate inferencing mechanisms. In this article, we first describe a rewrite system whose goal is to build all the different relevant quantifier configurations in the semantic representation of natural language sentences, Then, we show how the correct configuration can be selected by using contextual information.

1 - THE QUANTIFIERS RANGE AND SCOPE PROBLEM

Consider the sentence :

(1)   *"A river runs through every european country."*

In the standard way of representing quantification in logical form, this sentence has two different readings, e.g. quantifier scopings. Moreover, from a truth point of view, for each reading there is a model that satisfies one and not the other. This sentence can be read distributively, with different rivers running through the different european countries or collectively, with a single river running through all the different european countries. In the first case, we say that the determiner "a" is in the scope of the determiner "*every*" or that "*every*" governs "a". The range of "*every*" is higher than the range of "a".

Most of the works done in the field of quantifier scoping does not have a comprehensive set of scoping rules, but rather are satisfied with some rules, defined a priori, that are supposed to produce reasonable readings. This has been the approach taken by W. Woods <Woo 72>, V. Dahl <Dah 77>, <Dah 79>, <Dah 80>, A. Colmerauer <Col 79>, J.F. Pique <Piq 80>, E. Keeman <Kee 80>, J.D. Fodor <Fod 81>, M. Mc Cord <McC 82>, F. Pereira <FPe 83> and R. Cooper <Coo 83>. However, it turns out that in some cases a choice a priori in scoping rules leads to false representations and that the correct representation depends hardly on the context. Consider for instance the sentences :

(2a)   *"All the students work with a micro-computer."*

(2b)   *"All the students work with a VAX."*

The correct interpretation of sentence (2a) occurs when the determiner "*all the*" has "a" in its scope, whereas the correct interpretation of sentence (2b) occurs when the determiner "a" has "*all the*" in its scope because a VAX is often a shared computer.

This example shows that a choice a priori in the range of quantifiers has to be set aside. What is needed, in fact, is a set of rules to produce all the relevant readings of an input sentence and at the same time an adequate use of contextual information to select the correct reading.

Before going on, we will give a brief overview of works related to quantifier scoping.

1.1. V. DAHL'S AND A. COLMERAUER'S APPROACH

The first works on quantifier scoping are the hypotheses formulated by V. Dahl <Dah 77>, <Dah 79>, A. Colmerauer <Col 79> and their revision by J.F. Pique

<Piq 81>. Sentences are here represented by a quantified tree with three branches
where :

- nodes are labeled by quantifiers (with three branches), conjunctions or negations,
- leaves are predicates, variables or constants.

For instance, sentence (1) will be represented by :

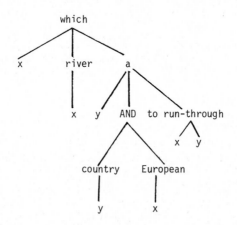

or, if we flatten the tree, by :

    which(x,river(x),a(y,
        AND(country(y),european(y)),to_run_through(x,y)))

For more convenience, we will use this latter formalism for most of our
examples. However, our work can be adapted to other formalisms (See conclusion).
The three hypotheses are :

Hypothesis 1 :
    The quantifier introduced by the article of a verb subject governs quantifiers
introduced by the complements closely linked to this verb if there are any. However, if the subject article is "*un*" (a), that of one of the complements is
"*chaque*" "*chacun des*" (every, each) and there is a constraint of oneness on the
verb argument quantified by the subject, the quantifiers introduced by the verb
complements govern those introduced by the subject.

Hypothesis 2 :
    In a construction including a noun complement, the quantifier introduced by
the complement's article governs that of the common noun except if :

- The article of the complement is indefinite, and the article of the common noun
  is "*tout*", "*chaque*", "*aucun*" (every, each, all, no).
- The article of the complement is in the plural. It is then replaced by "*quelque*"
  (some).
- The article of the common noun is in the plural and the property attached to the
  complement is exclusive on the argument introduced by the common noun.
  In this case it governs the formula attached to the common noun.

Hypothesis 3 :

(a) When a verb has two complements, quantification is in the reverse order to that of appearance.

(b) When a noun has several complements, quantification is made by applying hypothesis 2 in the inverse apparition order.

These hypotheses can represent a large number of natural language sentences. For instance, a distinction is made in the formal representation between the active and the passive voice. However, it turns out that in some cases these hypotheses fail, as in :

(3)   *"One of the pieces that every engine is composed of is made of gold."*

(*Une des pièces dont est composée chaque machine est en or.*)

In this sentence, the quantification *"every"* introduced in the relative clause governs the quantification introduced by *"one of the"*. (See also other examples in section 4).

In the sentence :

(3bis)   *"All the workers have not a lot of free hours."*

(*Tous les travailleurs n'ont pas beaucoup d'heures de libre.*) the quantification introduced by *"all"* governs the other quantifications of the sentence. The negation refers only to the quantification introduced by *"a lot of"*. An equivalent sentence is : *"All the workers have a few free hours."* (*Tous les travailleurs ont peu d'heures de liberté*). We will discuss later the links that can occur between negation and certain determiners.

Furthermore, these hypotheses have the inconvenience (1) of needing semantic information and (2) of introducing a choice a priori in the reordering of quantifiers.

Finally, some expressions such as : *"the complement closely linked to this verb"*, *"a constraint of oneness"* or *"the property attached to the complement is exclusive on the argument"* seems to us a little fuzzy, and the required contextual information is very difficult to specify.

1.2. M. McCORD'S APPROACH : DETERMINERS AS MODIFIERS

M. Mc Cord has developed a quite similar set of rules based on very elegant and appropriate linguistic abstractions <McC 82>. Determiners are considered here as a class of modifiers. M. McCord shows that the semantic hierarchy of modifiers can violate vertical relations in the syntactic tree as well as horizontal (e.g. left-right) relations. For example, in the sentence :

(4)   *"Give me the average level of each student."*

the noun complement *"each student"* is a daughter of the noun phrase *"the average level"* and the noun complement has wider scope than the initial noun phrase.

In his system, M. McCord has divided the semantic interpretation computation process in two stages. The first stage reshapes the syntactic tree so that the modifier reflects the desired semantic hierarchy of determiners. The second stage makes clear the implicit information of modifiers.

1.3. F. PEREIRA'S APPROACH IN CHAT-80

F. Pereira <FPe 83> has adopted and extended the approach taken by Woods in the Lunar system <Woo 72>. His goal is to formulate a very small and, as he says, coarse set of rules that produce reasonable readings.

In the system Chat-80 he has developed with D. Warren, it is interesting to point out that the determiner scope rules assume as default scoping the scoping given by the order of quantification in what he calls the Quant tree. Roughly speaking, for our purpose, in the Quant tree, the determiners appear in their left to right input reading order. Then, he has defined a small set of exceptions to this default rule. An exception rule can be paraphrased by : "If det A appears above det B in the Quant tree, then give B wider scope than A, which would be contrary to the default". Then B governs A. These rules are used for dealing with determiners, negation and interrogative operators.

In Chat-80, determiners are divided into two classes : "strong" determiners (each, any) and "weak" determiners (the others). Any strong determiner governs any weak one. A strong determiner will move up and to left until it finds another strong determiner. When a Quant tree cannot have further up or to the left movements, it is in its final position. It can then be translated into its final semantic representation.

F. Pereira assumes also that no determiner of a modifier (for instance in a relative clause) is allowed to have a larger scope than the modified noun phrase. Although this be true most of the time, there are certain sentences, such as (12) that contradict this assumption.

1.4. DEFINITE PLURAL NOUNS

As shown by V. Dahl <Dah 77>, a correct analysis of definite plural noun phrases is to represent them as introducing sets. The predicate that translates the noun takes sets as arguments and operates on those arguments. This first step in the definite plural nouns representation is important and solves many difficult problems, however some remarks and objections can be made. The main objections to this representation are formulated by F. Pereira, (with whom we agree) :

- the distinction between collective and distributive determiners is removed from the initial representation,

- it remains a major difficulty to represent nested definite plural noun phrases, such as : "*The children of the employees* ..." It is impossible to apply the predicate "*child_of*" to the set of employees and to the set of children to produce a new set.

The approach adopted by F. Pereira <FPe 83> is to use indexed sets. The translation of the above noun phrase is then :

$$\{(x,y) : employee(x) \text{ AND } y = \{z : child\_of(z,x)\}\}$$

This analysis results in a set of pairs (x,y) that seems to us to be more adequate.

On the other hand, another approach has been proposed by J. Hobbs <Hob 83>. He introduces the notion of typical element (or prototype) of a set. Then, the logical formula for a plural noun phrase includes reference to a set and its typical element. Some scope dependencies can also be represented as relations among typical elements.

We will now explain our approach to the quantifier scoping problem. Our starting point is the hypotheses formulated by V. Dahl and A. Colmerauer.

2 - PRODUCTION OF ALL THE RELEVANT REPRESENTATIONS OF A SENTENCE

Our goal is to determine a set of rules that can produce :

(1) a correct logical representation of a sentence from the quantifiers order point of view,

(2) all the relevant interpretations of an ambiguous sentence.

Our work differs slightly from the preceding ones for the following reasons :
- We make no choice a priori when two or more quantifier configurations are possible,
- We have not introduced semantic constraints a priori in the rules because we think that they are sometimes somewhat fuzzy and difficult to specify. We will see in the discussion section how and when semantic and pragmatic considerations can be introduced.
- Our system is a compromise between a local and a global quantifier scoping computation.
- We have taken into account negations because they sometimes interact with quantifiers. For instance, consider the sentence :

(5)   *"All the students have not solved a problem."*

This sentence may have several meanings :

(5a)   *"There is a problem, the same for all the students, that these students have not solved."*

(5b)   *"All the students have not solved a problem, may be a different one for some students."*

But also :

(5c)   *"There is a problem that some students have not solved."*

Note the interaction between *"not"* and *"all the"*. Another example is :

(6)   *"At this time of the year, a lot of fruits does not have much taste."*

This sentence is equivalent to :

(6a)   *"At this time of the year, a lot of fruits have a little taste."*

Our starting point is a left to right reading of an input sentence. A formal representation of the sentence is produced where the quantifiers introduced by the determiners appear in the determiners reading order. From that formal representation, determiners and negations are extracted in order to build what we call a range indicator. The notion of range indicator is purely artificial and it has no linguistic foundation. I will use it for the clarity of my explanations. Finally, a set of rewrite rules are applied on the range indicator in order to modify the order of the quantifiers so as to get a correct formal representation. The determiners range is lowered or raised by these rules.

2.1. CONSTRUCTION OF THE RANGE INDICATOR

In order to build the range indocator, all the determiners and the negations that appear in a surface sentence are indexed according to their order of appearance. If in a sentence there are the determiners : the ... a ... all_the..., then, the determiners are indexed : the1 a2 all_the3.

In order to take into account the specifics of our problem and in order to interface computer applications with a direct and simple natural language, we have classified the determiners in four sets : D, E, Q and U. All the determiners of a given set have the same behaviour towards the other determiners. All the determiners belong to one and only one set. Each of these four sets represents a particular type of quantification.

D = {every,each} introduces an idea of distributivity, which we call the universal distributive quantifier.

E = {a, one, some, many, none, most of the, few, who, whom, ...} is the first-order logic existential quantifier.

Q = {a lot of, a little, a few, ...} introduces an idea of quantity, which we call the quantitative existential quantifier.

U = {the (plural), all the, all, no, ...} is equivalent to the first-order logic universal quantifier.

We don't take into account the ambiguities inherent to some determiners such as "a" in "*a dog has four legs.*" In this particular case, "a" means "*all the*". In fact, no linguistic theory can really solve this kind of ambiguity.

The range indicator of sentences in the passive voice is built from their active voice correspondant, i.e. we proceed to a re-inversion of the object and the subject.

A range indicator then results in the substitution of a determiner by the quantifier it introduces. For instance, sentence (1) is composed of the following determiners :

$$a_1 \quad every_2$$

its range indicator is : $E_1 \ D_2$

2.2. APPLICATION OF REWRITE RULES ON THE RANGE INDICATOR

Finally, a set of rewrite rules is applied to the range indicator. The goal of these rules is to generate all the relevant configurations of quantifiers from the initial range indicator. The general form of a rule R_i is :

$$R_i : X_n \ Y_m \ \text{--->} \ Y_m \ X_n \ (\text{or} \ X_m \ Y_n)$$

where : X, Y belong to {E,D,Q,U}

and n,m are integers such as n < m.

From the semantic representation point of view, this means that the original tree :

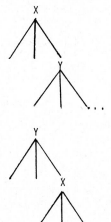

Let n, m, p be three integers such as $n < m < p$, then we have the following rewrite rules :

R_1 : $U_n E_m \longrightarrow E_m U_n$

R_1' : $U_n E_m \longrightarrow U_m E_n$

R_2 : $E_n D_m \longrightarrow D_m E_n$

R_3 : $Q_n U_m \longrightarrow Q_m U_n$

R_4 : $E_n U_m \longrightarrow E_m U_n$

R_5 : $D_n E_m \longrightarrow E_m D_n$

R_5' : $D_n E_m \longrightarrow D_m E_n$

R_6 : $Q_n D_m \longrightarrow D_m Q_n$

and if we include the negation, we have as well :

R_7 : $NOT_n X_m \longrightarrow X_m NOT_n$

      $X = D, E$ or U.

R_8 : $U_n NOT_m \longrightarrow NOT_m$ "some"$_n$

R_9 : $U_n NOT_m E_p \longrightarrow E_p U_m NOT_n$

These rules are applied from left to right to the range indicator until no more rule is applicable. The rule application order makes no difference. The algorithm always stops. It is easy to show that there is a finite number of rule applications to produce all the relevant range indicators from the original range indicator. The maximum number of rule applications is :

$$max = 13 * \sum_{i=2}^{n} (i - 1) * 5^n$$

where n is the number of determiners that appear in the input sentence.

For an unambiguous sentence, these rules produce one and only one quantifier configuration.

The final formal representation(s) contains the original determiners rather than the quantifiers E, D, Q or U. Thus, no information is lost and a distinction can be made in a further stage, if needed, between determiners such as cardinal numbers or between determiners such as : few-many-most.

2.3. EXAMPLES.

We will now examine some examples that will illustrate the application of the rules :

(7)   *"One worker collects all the magnetic tapes."*

(*Un employé ramasse toutes les bandes magnétiques.*)

The range indicator is : $E_1 U_2$, rule R_4 is applicable and the range indicator is rewritten into $E_2 U_1$. At this point, no other rule is applicable and the final representation is :

(7a) one(x,worker(x),all_the(y,magnetic_tape(y),to_collect(x,y)))

or :

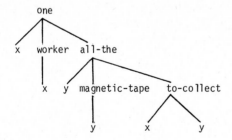

The next example is :

(8)   *"Peter invited all the lovers of a musical instrument."*

(*Pierre a invité tous les amateurs d'un instrument de musique.*)

The range indicator is U_1 E_2. Rules R_1 and R_1' are applicable and give the following representations :

(8a) a(x,musical_instrument(x),
          all_the(y,lover_of(y,x),to_invite(Peter,y)))

(8b) all_the(y,a(x,musical_instrument(x),
          lover_of(y,x)),to_invite(Peter,y))

As Pique <Piq 81> says, we prefer (8b) because we think that the sentence is intended to mean that Peter is planning some musical party, for which several musical instruments are needed.

Is we consider now :

(5)   *"All the students have not solved a problem."*

(*Tous les étudiants n'ont pas résolu un problème.*)

The range indicator is : U_1 NOT_2 E_3, three interpretations are produced :

* application of R_9 : E_3 U_2 NOT_1 (cf. interpretation 5a)
* application of R_7, R_1 and R_8 : E_3 "some"$_1$ (cf. interpretation 5c)
* application of R_7 and R_1' : U_1 E_3 NOT_2 (cf. interpretation 5b).

3 - PROCESSING OF CONJUNCTIONS

If there are conjunctions in a sentence then we introduce brackets in the range indicator. Between brackets are found all the elements tied together by a given conjunction. The brackets are indexed as if they were a single quantifier. For example, the range indicator of :

(9)   *"All the teachers and some students have a micro computer.*

(*Tous les professeurs et quelques étudiants ont un micro-ordinateur.*)

is $(U\ E)_1$ E_2.

When the rewrite rules are applied, the quantifiers included between the brackets are then considered as a single quantifier determined as follows :

$(X_1 \ldots\ldots X_n)_j$ is equivalent to Y_j ; the value of Y_j is :

X if all the X_k are the same quantifier,

D if there exists a $X_k = D$

(The distributivity of D is extended to the other determiners)

U if there exists $X_k = U$ and no $X_j = D$.

E otherwise.

The range indicator of the above example (9) is equivalent to $U_1 E_2$. Rules R_1 and R_1' are applicable. The application of the rule R_1' gives the correct representation $(U_2 E_1)$ because micro-computers are often personal computers and everybody has his own micro-computer. But, if we say :

(9')   *"All the teachers and some students use a VAX."*

The range indicator is still $U_1 E_2$, but in this case, the application of the rule R_1 gives the correct representation because a VAX is a shared-computer.

If, in a conjunction of NPs some NPs have noun complements, then,

(a) Only the first determiner of each NP (in the input reading order) is taken into account to find the equivalent quantifier to all the determiners of the NPs linked by a conjunction.

(b) The rewrite system is applied separately on each NP and then on the whole range indicator.

For instance, the sentence :

(10)   *"Some teachers in every schools and most of the business men have a micro-computer."*

(*Certains professeurs dans chaque école et la plupart des hommes d'affaire ont un micro-ordinateur.*)

has the following range indicator :

$((E_1 D_2)E_1)_1 E_2$

It is equivalent to : $(E\ E)_1 E_2$ (cf. (a)) and finally to : $E_1 E_2$. The rewrite rules are applied first on $(E_1 D_2)$ and then on $E_1 E_2$. The final range indicator is :

$((D_2 E_1)E_1)_1 E_2$

The formal representation is :

```
AND(every(x,school(x),some(y,teacher_in(y,x),
          a(z,micro_computer(z),to_have(y,z)))),
    most_of_the(x₁,business_man(x₁),
         a(z₁,micro_computer(z₁),to_have(x₁,z₁)))))
```

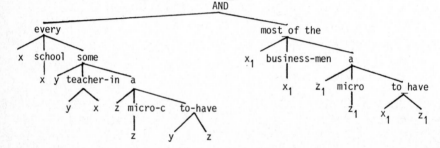

In fact, sentence (10) is represented as two separate sentences linked by a "AND".

Sentence (9') is represented by :

a(x,VAX(x),AND(all_the(y,teacher(y),to_have(y,x)),
        some(z,s̄tudent(z),to_have(z̄,x))))

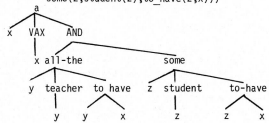

In this example, the variable x denotes the same object for teachers and students.

Another example is :

(11)   "*A lot of people have invited all my neighbours and some artists.*"

(*Beaucoup de personnes ont invité tous mes voisins et quelques artistes.*)

The range indicator is : $Q_1(U\ E)_2$. (U E) is equivalent to U and then R_3 is applicable ; the final representation is :

a_lot_of(z,people(z),AND(all_my(x,neighbours(x),to_invite(z,x))),
        some(y,artist(ȳ),to_invite(z,y))))

This sentence is intended to mean that the same set of people have invited my neighbours and some artists.

4 - PROCESSING OF RELATIVE CLAUSES

In this work we only consider the relative clauses that introduce a restriction on the set of objects denoted by the noun to which they refer. In this case, the quantifier hierarchy in a relative clause is processed independently of that of the main clause. In the logical formula, a relative clause is linked to the noun it refers to by an "AND" <Dah 77>.

In the semantic representation of a sentence that includes at least one relative clause, quantifiers are only partially ordered because quantifiers introduced in relative clauses are local and they apply only to the semantic representation of that relative clause. Note also how a relative clause can prevent some determiners to take a wider scope over other determiners. In the sentence :

   "*I spoke to a man from each south-american country.*"

rule R_2 gives wider scope to "*each*", whereas in the sentence :

   "*I spoke to a man who was representing each south-american country.*"

determiner "*a*" has wider scope over determiner "*each*" <Fod 83>.

The set of relative clauses that does not introduce a restriction is more difficult to characterize. However, it seems that these relative clauses do not have to be processed independently but rather have to be processed as a part of the main clause. For instance, in the sentence :

(12)   *"Most of the toys that all the children have are made of plastic."*

(*La plupart des jouets qu'ont tous les enfants sont en plastique.*)

The relative clause is here only a digression rather than a restriction stricto sensu. Formally, it is represented by :

    all_the(x,child(x),most_of_the(y,toy(y),
        to_have(x,y).to_be_made_of_plastic(y)))

or, according to F. Pereira's representation :

    all_the({(x,y):child(x) AND
        y = { z:toy_of(z,x)}},to_be_made_of_plastic(y))

The problem that remains is that, up to now, within the framework of computational linguistics, we are not able to decide whether a relative clause introduces a restriction or not. I think that this distinction is very difficult to make and I wonder if it is possible to specify, for each lexical item that can be concerned with this problem, that this lexical item, in a given context, introduces a restriction or not. In any case, this would reduce drastically the transportability of the parser.

5 - QUESTIONS

The rewrite rules enable us to take into account the fact that questions like :

(13)   *"Which rivers run through each european country ? "*

(*Quels fleuves traversent chaque pays européen ?*)

call for multiple answers.
"*Which*" is an element of the class denoted by the quantifier E ; the range indicator is E_1 D_2, rule R_2 is applicable :

(13a)   QUEST_ON((x,y),

    every(x,AND(country(x),european(x)),
        which(y,river(y),to_run_through(y,x))))

The variable introduced by "each" governs the variable introduced by the questionning item. (13a) can be paraphrased :

(13'a)   *"For each country, find all the rivers that run through it."*

We can here see that a determiner may move above a questionning item. The top level operator QUEST_ON indicates that the underlying sentence is a question. In addition, its first argument specifies the variable(s) on which the question runs.

6 - USING CONTEXTUAL INFORMATION TO DEAL WITH AMBIGUITIES

If a sentence is ambiguous then the determination of the correct formal representation can be done in two ways : by the user via a paraphrase or by inferences from contextual information.

The use of paraphrases raises many problems : paraphrasing the various readings of a sentence is impossible because the user runs the risk of beeing assaulted by too many sentences. Furthermore, paraphrases have to be formulated as clearly as possible for the user to be able to understand the differences between each of them. No additional ambiguity must also be added. Such paraphrases, especially to express quantifier scoping, are not obvious to formulate in an understandable manner and they risk beeing very inelegant. Very few works have been done on paraphrasing and it is now too early to say more about the linguistic and man-machine communication problems they raise.

The alternative to paraphrases is to use contextual information. Contextual information needs however to be very precise and, consequently, is sometimes very difficult to specify a priori in a knowledge base. The above examples (2a) and (2b) are a good illustration of the problem.

In a first approximation, we can say that if the context is sufficiently restrictive to determine uniquely the speaker's intentions, then appropriate formal representations can be produced for a wide range of utterances which are often considered as problematic. But, if the context is not sufficiently restrictive, the system has then to generate some kinds of paraphrases that lead to clarification dialogues.

We will now look with more detail into how contextual information can be used to select the correct representation of a natural language sentence. Most of the time, and especially if we interface a data-base, contextual information is the set of (1) the facts stored in the database, (2) the relations on these facts and (3) integrity constraints. It is then possible to verify when applying a rule of our rewrite system that the result does not contradict any fact, relation or integrity constraint. I think that the verifications to be done involve only the structure which dominates immediately the two determiners concerned by the rule. For instance, if we consider the sentence :

(13)   *"Every prime-minister of a european country has visited each south american capital."*

The quantifier scoping ambiguity of the subject noun phrase is local to this noun phrase, i.e. no additional information is needed to decide what is the correct representation. If we restrict the problem to the noun phrase :

"Every prime-minister of a country ..."

according to rules R_5 and R_5', two representations are possible. With wide scope *"a country"* is existential and with narrow scope, it is universal. If there exists the rule (under a sentence form) :

"There is only one prime-minister in each country."

Then the narrow scope for a country is the correct interpretation and only the corresponding rule can be applied.

The next example shows that the interactions with the knowledge base can be quite complicated to handle :

"Which rivers run through each european country ?"

That possible representation :

```
which(x,river(x),each(y,
    AND(country(y),european(y)),to_run_through(x,y)))
```

will be rejected if in the knowledge base we have the following facts and rules :

(a)   *"Only countries that have a common border can have common rivers."*

(b)   *"A country which is an island does not have any common border with any other country."*

(c)   *"Iceland is an island."*

(d)   *"Chypra is an island."*

From (a), (b), (c) and (d) it is possible to deduce (but this is not obvious) that *"some european countries cannot have a common river with other european countries"*. The above representation can thus be rejected because it is highly probable that the other possible representation, that has solutions, is the correct one. This approach seems to us promising but it is still under study and more details about interactions between our scoping rules and a knowledge base and the implementation in PROLOG will be published in a further paper. We think that this approach can be generalized to all modifiers : adjectives, negations, adverbs and relative clauses.

I think that, event if relevant contextual information is not available for all rules, at least it will strongly reduce the number of possible representations of an ambiguous sentence. If at a given moment two rules may be applied and if no contextual information can be used to select the appropriate one, then the ambiguous part of the sentence can be paraphrased and the user will be asked to say that what is the correct formulation. This ambiguous part of the sentence could be the structure which immediately dominates the two determiners involved in the rule, as we discussed above for the interactions with the knowledge base.

CONCLUSION

In this paper, we have described a rewrite system whose goal is to reorder the range of quantifiers so as to produce a correct logical representation of natural language sentences. The main original properties of the system are :

- to produce all the relevant interpretations of a sentence when it is ambiguous from the quantifier hierarchy point of view,

- to be free of semantic considerations.

- to take into account negations, interrogative forms, conjoined noun phrases and relative clauses.

We think that these rules can be applied to languages such as french, english, spanish or italian. However, it seems they are not directly applicable to free-order languages and to case languages. This work is adaptable to various semantic representations based on logic such as : <Fpe 83>, <Kam 83>, <Uehara K. and al., in this volume>.

Finally, we have shown how contextual information can be used during the quantifier scoping computation process to select the correct rule when two or more rules were applicable. This work has been integrated into our parser/generator of french sentences.

REFERENCES

<Col 79>   COLMERAUER A. An interesting subset of natural language. Logic programming (CLARK and TARNLUND Edts) Academic Press, London, pp. 45-66.

<Coo 83>   COOPER R. 83 Quantifier and syntactic theory. D. Reidel Pub. Co. Vol. 21.

<Dah 77>   DAHL V. Un système déductif d'interrogation de banques de données en espagnol. Thèse d'Université, Marseille-Luminy II.

<Dah 79>   DAHL V. Quantification in a three-valued logic for natural language question-answering systems. 6th IJCAI Tokyo.

<Dah 80>   DAHL V. A three-valued logic for natural language computer applications. 10th international symposium on multiple-valued logic. Univ. of Illinois.

<Dah 81>   DAHL V. Translating Spanish into logic through logic. Amer. Journ. of computational linguistics, Vol. 7, n° 3, pp. 149-164.

<Fod 81>   FODOR J.D. The mental representation of quantifiers. In processes, Beliefs and questions D. Reidel Pub. Co. S. Peters and E. Saarinen Edts.

<Hob 83>   HOBBS J.R. An improper treatment of quantification in ordinary english. Proceedings of ACL 83.

<Kam 83>   KAMP H. A theory of truth and semantic representation, in J. Groendijk and al. Formal methods in the Study of Language. Amsterdam Press.

<Kee 80>   KEEMAN E.L., FALTZ L.M. A new approach to quantification in natural language. Proc. Linguistische Arbeiten Niemeyer Edts Tubingen.

<McC 82>   McCORD M. Using slots and modifiers in logic grammars for natural language. Technical note 69-80. Univ. of Kentucky (1981) and Artificial Intelligence 1982.

<Mul 77>   MÜLLER C. Analyse linguistique des relations de champs entre quantificateurs et négation. Revue Langages n° 34, Larousse Edts.

<FPe 80>   F. PEREIRA, WARREN D. Definite clause grammars for natural language analysis. A survey of the formalism and a comparison with ATN. Artificial intelligence n° 13.

<FPe 83>   PEREIRA F. Logic for natural language analysis. SRI international technical note n° 275.

<Piq 81>   PIQUE J.F. On semantic representation of natural language sentences. Logic programming conference, Marseille 1982.

<Sai 83>   SAINT-DIZIER P. Modelling human-computer interactions in a man-machine interface. Logic Programming Workshop 83, albufeira, Portugal.

<Sai 85>   SAINT-DIZIER P. Programmation en logique et résolution des anaphores. AFCET 5ème génération.

<Woo 72>   WOODS W., KAPLAN R., NASH-WEBBER B. The LUNAR sciences natural language information system. BBN report 2378.

Natural Language Understanding and Logic Programming
V. Dahl and P. Saint-Dizier (Editors)
© Elsevier Science Publishers B.V. (North-Holland), 1985

MUTUAL BELIEF LOGIC
FOR PROCESSING DEFINITE REFERENCE

Luis Fariñas-del-Cerro
Saïd Soulhi

Langages et Systèmes Informatiques
Université Paul Sabatier
118, route de Narbonne
F - 31062 Toulouse Cedex

In this paper we define a new logic for mutual belief. Mutual belief logic appears to be an appropriate tool to using and understanding the speech act of identifying reference in conversational systems.
We define also the decision method for this logic which is an extension of classical resolution.

I. INTRODUCTION

One of the most important function of language is to identify some existing entity in the world. According to Russell (1905), proper nouns and definite descriptions can be used to refer to entities in the real world. Definite descriptions correspond to English phrases containing the definite article "the" (e.g. "The author of Waverley"). Russell used the reversal iota symbol to represent it: $(^1x) D(x)$ where D is a property. After that, he proved that this operator is eliminable if we have identity and quantifiers. Hence, by "$(^1x) D(x)$" he means that exactly one entity e satisfies D ; that is, $(\exists e)(\forall x)(D(x) \equiv (x = e))$. However, reference can present problems such as the nonexistence of referent (e.g. "The present king of France"). Therefore some logicians defined free logics, that is to say, logics without any existential presupposition.

Another difficulty of reference pointed out by Donnellan (1966) is its attributive use in which the speaker has no intention that the hearer identify a referent. For example the description

"Smith's murderer is insane (whoever he is, since only a maniac would have done such a thing)" is attributively prononced because "Smith"s murderer" does not refer to anyone, and the phrase does not describe a particular person. Our discussion has so far focused on referential reference in task-oriented conversations ; that is, it is presupposed that an entity fits the definite description and that the speaker intends to use the definite description to pick out the particular entity he is talking about.

Recent research consider reference in the context of speech acts and speakers' intentions. It's within this framework that Searle states his "principle of identification": "A necessary condition for the successful performance of a definite reference in the utterance of an expression is that either the expression must be an identifying description or the speaker must be able to produce an identifying description an demand" (Searle (1969) p.88) or (Perrault and Cohen (1981) p.218).

Perrault and Cohen (1981) reformulate this principle by expliciting the notion of context: "A necessary condition for the successful performance of a definite reference by a speaker S using a description D in a context C is that S believes that D is fulfilled in C" (Perrault and Cohen (1981) p.221). By "C" they mean a set of entities "known" to speaker and hearer and by "D is fulfilled in C" they mean that in C $({}^1x)$ D(x).

Clark and Marshall (1981) give examples which purport to show that for S to refer to a hearer H to some entity $\underline{e}$ using some description D in a context C, it issufficient that S and H mutually know that P where P is the following proposition: "the description D in the context C is uniquely satisfied by $\underline{e}$". That is:

- . S knows that P
- . H knows that P
- . S knows that H knows that P
- . H knows that S knows that P
- . S knows that H knows that S knows that P
- . H knows that S knows that S knows that P

and so on.

Perrault and Cohen (1981) show that this condition is too strong by giving examples in which two interlocutors, are talking about another man at a party, and one says to the other, "the woman with the martini is the mayor's daughter" and is understood perfectly well, even though the woman he intended to refer to was in reality holding a glass of water.

They claim that an infinite number of conjuncts are necessary for successful reference:

    (S believes that P) & ...

with only a finite number of false conjuncts.

In this paper we formulate this idea in terms of statements in a logic of belief. We choose belief system because it allows false beliefs.

II. A PROPOSITIONAL BELIEF LOGIC B4

Let Sp be a set of agents, let Pr be a set of propositional variables. The set of well formed formulas is defined to be the least set Wff such that:

    . P, Q ε Wff implies P → Q ε Wff
    . S ε Sp, P ε Wff implies [S]P ε Wff

The symbol → denotes "implication" and [S]P means "S believes P". We assume the usual definitions of conjunction, disjunction, equivalence and doxastic possibility (noted <S>). The axioms schemata for B4 are:

    A1. Axioms of ordinary propositional logic
    A2. [S]P → <S>P
    A3. [S](P → Q) → ([S]P → [S]Q)
    A4. [S]P → [S][S]P

The inference rules are:

    Modus ponens: from P and P → Q infer Q
    Necessitation: from P infer [S]P for any S ε Sp

We define the notions of proof and theorem in the usual way. A
proof of a formula A from a set S of formulas is a finite sequence
of formulas each of which is either an axiom or an element of
set S or a formula obtainable from earlier formulas by a rule
of inference. A formula A is derivable from a set $S (S \vdash A)$ iff it
has a proof from set S. A formula A is a theorem of B4 $(\vdash A)$ iff
it is derivable from the axioms alone. A set S of formulas is
consistent if no formula of the form A & $\sim$ A is derivable from S.

The meaning of formulas is defined by using the notion of a model.
For us a model is a triple:

$$M = <W, \quad R_S: S \quad Sp , \quad m >$$

where W is a non-empty set of possible worlds (we fix a reference
point in W called the actual world: K_0). R_S is a transitive relation on set W for any $S \varepsilon Sp$, and m is a meaning function that
assigns to each propositional variable p a subset $m(p)$ of W.

Given a model M we say that a formula A is satisfied by a world
K in model M (M, K sat A) iff the following conditions are satisfied:

      M, K sat P iff $K \varepsilon m(P)$ where P is a propositional variable
      M, K sat $\sim$ A iff not M, K sat A
      M, K sat A v B iff M, K sat A or M, K sat B
      M, K sat A $\wedge$ B iff M, K sat A and M, K sat B
      M, K sat A $\rightarrow$ B iff M, K sat ($\sim$ A v B)
      M, K sat A $\leftrightarrow$ B iff M, K sat (A $\rightarrow$ B) & (B $\rightarrow$ A)
      M, K sat [S]A iff for all $K' \varepsilon W$ if $(K,K') \varepsilon R$ then M, K'
          sat A
      M, K sat $<S>$A iff there is a $K' \varepsilon W$ and such $(K,K') \varepsilon R_S$
          and M, K' sat A

Given a model M, to each formula A of the language we assign a
set of worlds called the extension of A in model M (ext_M A):

$$ext_M A = \{K \varepsilon W: M, K \text{ sat } A\}$$

We admit the usual notions of truth and validity of formulas.
A formula A is true in a model M ($\models_M$ A) iff ext_M A = W. A formula
A is valid in B4 ($\models$ A) iff A is true in every model for B4.
A formula A is a semantical consequence of a set S of formulas

(S ⊨ A) iff for any model M the formula A is true in M whenever all formulas in S are true in M. A formula A is satisfiable iff M, K sat A for some model M and world K. A set S of formulas is satisfied in a model M by a world K (M, K sat S) iff M, K sat A for all A ε S. A set S is satisfiable iff M, K sat S for some model M and world K.

Hintikka (1962, 1971) showed that B4 is complete relatively to those semantic structures.

We can represent a model by a tree structure whose nodes represent worlds linked by accessibility relations. The start node is the actual world. Then S believes that P in K is equivalent to say that P is true in every world which is compatible with what S believes (see figure 1).

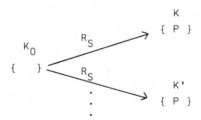

figure 1

III. AN EXTENDED BELIEF LOGIC BM4

In this part we describe an extended belief logic where mutual belief can be expressed directly in the language. We then introduce a set of modal opertors [S/H], where S and H ε Sp. The intuitive meaning of [S/H]P for any sentence P is that S and H mutually believe that P from the point of view of S. More precisely it means that S believes that P, that S believes that H believes P, that S believes that H believes that S believes that P and so on.

To express that S and H mutually believe that P, we assert:
$$[S/H]P \land [H/S]P.$$

To obtain a complete axiomatization of the system with mutual belief operators, we extend the axiomatization of B4 with the following two axioms:

A5. $[S/H]P \rightarrow [S](P \land [H]P) \land [S][H][S/H]P$
A6. $[S](P \rightarrow [S][H]P) \rightarrow ([S][P \land [H]P) \rightarrow [S/H]P)$

This new system will be called BM4.

The fixpoint axiom A5 expresses the definition of mutual belief operators, and the induction axiom A6 states that if S believes that P and believes that S believes that H believes that P and S believes that P holds and believes that H believes that P, then P is mutually believed by S and H from the point of view of S.

The meaning of formulas in BM4 is defined by using an exension of a model in B4 with the following condition:

M, K sat $[S/H]P$ iff for all $K' \in$ W such that $(K,K') \in R_S$ then M, K' sat P and for all K" such that $(K',K") \in R_H$ then M, K" sat P and so on.

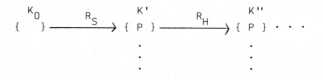

figure 2

Figure 2 shows the graphic notation used to represent mutual belief (it represent that $[S/H]P$).

The completeness and the decidability of BM4 can be obtained using filtration methods (Segerberg, 1977).

Now, in BM4, we can reformulate the principle of identification as follows:

A necessary condition for the successful performance of a definite reference by a speaker S using a description D in a context C is that $\sim$[S/H] $\sim$ [S/H]P that means: P is a mutual belief with H from the point of view of S, is compatible with mutual belief of S and H from the point of view of S. In other words, in the infinite conjunction:

$$[S]P \wedge [S][H]P \wedge \ldots$$

only a finite number of conjuncts can be false.

This means that from an alternatively finite sequence of R_S and R_H, P is a mutual belief of S and H from the point of view of S (see figure 3);

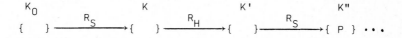

figure 3

In the same way, a necessary condition for the successful performance of a definite reference by a hearer H understanding a description D in a context C is that $\sim$[H/S] $\sim$[H/S]P

To illustrate this, consider now the following example from Perrault and Cohen (1981) :

"S and H are at a party. They watch together as water and gin are being poured in two identical glasses and given to women W1 and W2 respectively. Later S sees H see the women swap glasses but S believes that H did not see H. S then tells H: "The woman with the martini is the mayor's daughter." (Perrault and Cohen, 1981, pp.223).

In this example S has successfully referred to W2, although the description failed in [S] and [S][H] that is in K' and K" (in figure 3). Then we have:

```
[S] (W1 fulfils "TWWM" ∧ W2 fulfils "TWWW") ∧
[S][H] (W1 fulfils "TWWM" ∧ W2 fulfils "TWWW") ∧
[S][H][S/H] (W1 fulfils "TWWW" ∧ W2 fulfils "TWWM")
```

where "TWWM" means "The woman with the martini",
and   "TWWW" means "The woman with the water".

IV. DECISION METHOD

The decision method for BM4 is similar to that of propositional
temporal logic of programs. It is an extension of classical resolution to belief operators.

1. Conjunctive Normal Form (C.N.F.)

Let F be a formula, we shall say that F is in C.N.F. if it is
of the form:

$$F = C_1 \land \ldots \land C_m$$

where $m > 1$ and each C_i (clause) is a disjunction (perhaps with
only one disjunct) of the general form:

$$C_i = L_1 \lor \ldots \lor L_{n_1} \lor [S_1]D_1 \lor \ldots \lor [S_{n_2}]D_{n_2} \lor <S'_1>A_1 \lor \ldots \lor <S'_{n_3}>A_{n_3}$$

where each L_i is a literal preceded by a string of zero or more
operators $[S_i/S_j]$; each D_i is a disjunction that possesses the
general form of the clauses, and each A_i is a conjunction, where
each conjunct possesses the general form of the clauses.

2. Resolution rules

2.1. Let C_1 and C_2 two clauses. We define the operations :

  · $\Sigma(C_1, C_2)$

  · $\Gamma(C_1)$

And the properties:

  · (C_1, C_2) is resolvable (i.e. C_1 and C_2 are resolvable).

  · (C_1) is resolvable

recursively as follows:

2.1.1. Classical operations.

    a) . $\Sigma(p, \sim p) = \emptyset$ ($\emptyset$ is the empty symbol)

        And $(p, \sim p)$ is resolvable.

    b) . $\Sigma((F_1 \vee F_2), F) = \Sigma(F_1, F) \vee D_2$

        And if (F_1, F) is resolvable, then $((F_1 \vee F_2), F)$ is resolvable.

2.1.2. Belief operations.

We don't give all operations. For more details you can see (Cavalli and Farinas del Cerro, 1984)

    a) . $\Sigma([S]F, \triangle_S F') = \triangle_S \Sigma([S]F, F')$ with $\triangle_S = [S], <S>$

        And if $([S]F, F')$ is resolvable, then $([S]F, \underline{\quad S \quad} F')$ is resolvable

    b) . $\Sigma([S/H]F, \triangle_{S/H} F') = \triangle_{S/H} \Sigma(F, F')$ with $\triangle_{S/H} = [S/H]$ or $<S/H>$

        And if (F, F') is resolvable then $([S/H]F, \triangle_{S/H} F')$ is resolvable

    c) . $\Sigma([S/H]F, \triangle_S F') = \triangle_S \Sigma(F, F')$

        And if (F, F') is resolvable, then $([S/H]F, \triangle_S F')$ is resolvable

In what follows, we define the notions of resolvent, deduction and refutation:

If C_1 and C_2 are clauses and C_1 and C_2 are resolvable (or C_1 is resolvable) i.e. the empty symbol is obtained using the operation a) in 2.1.1., then a clause is called resolvent of C_1 and C_2 $((C_1))$ if it is the result of substituting :

    $\emptyset$ for every occurrence of $(\emptyset \wedge E)$
    E for every occurrence of $(\emptyset \vee E)$
    $\emptyset$ for every occurrence of $\Delta \emptyset$, where Δ is $[.]$, $<.>$ or $[./.]$.

in $\Sigma(C_1, C_2)(\Gamma(C_1))$, as times as necessary.

We note by $R(C_1, C_2)$ (or $R(C_1)$) a resolvent of C_1 and C_2 $((C_1))$.

Then the resolution and factoring rules are defined as in the classical case.

Let C_1 v C and C_2 v C' be two clauses, the resolution rules :

1) $$\frac{C_1 \text{ v } C \qquad C_2 \text{ v } C'}{R(C_1, C_2) \text{ v } C \text{ v } C'}$$

is applied if C_1 and C_2 are resolvable.

And the rule:

2) $$\frac{C_1 \text{ v } C}{R(C_1) \text{ v } C}$$

is applied if C_1 is resolvable

Let E(D v D v F) be a clause. The following factoring rule will be applied

3) $$\frac{E(D \text{ v } D \text{ v } F)}{E(D \text{ v } F)}$$

Now, we define the notion of deduction:

Let S be a set of clauses. A deduction of C from S is a finite sequence $C_1, \ldots, C_n$ such that:

- C_n is C
- C_i $(1 < i < n)$ is:
    a clause of S, or
    a clause obtained from C_j, j < i using the inference rules 2) or 3)

    or a clause obtained from C_j and C_k, j,k < i, using the inference rule 1).

A deduction of the empty clause is called a refutation.

As in (Cavalli and Fariñas del Cerro, 1984) the following completeness theorem can be obtained:

A set S of clauses is unsatisfiable iff S is refutable.

Example :

We illustrate the method by solving an example which shows that
any agent can do modus ponens on mutual belief. We should be able
to conclude that

[S/H]P ∧ [S/H](P → Q) → [S/H]Q

is a valid formula.

Since we want to prove this by refutation, we negate the conclusion and prove that

S = { [S/H]P, [S/H](~ P v Q), <S/H> ~Q } is unsatisfiable

To do this, we must prove that S is refutable. The proof steps,
can be easily represented by a tree called a deduction tree (see
figure 4).

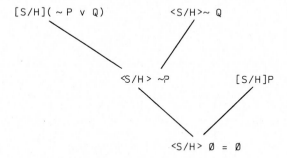

figure 4

Since the last clause is the empty clause that is derived from
S, we conclude that S is unsatisfiable.

V. RELATION TO RELATED WORKS

There is another finite representation of "mutual knowledge" proposed by (Sato 1977). The distinction between mutual belief and
mutual knowledge is that mutual knowledge is a true mutual belief.
In other words, mutual knowledge is conformable to reality. Sato
claims that mutual knowledge is what a particular individual denoted by O knows. Additional axioms are then required to define
mutual knowledge:

$$B1. \quad [O]P \rightarrow P$$
$$B2. \quad [O]P \rightarrow [O][S]P$$

This representation is too strong because $[O]P \rightarrow [S/H]P$. The
main steps of the proof are:

1. $[O]P \rightarrow [S][H]P$, from (B2) and (B1)
2. $[O]P \rightarrow (P \rightarrow [S][H]P)$,
3. $[S][O]P \rightarrow [S](P \rightarrow [S][H]P)$, from Necessitation and (A3)

and

4. $[O]P \rightarrow [S][O]P$ from (A4), (B1) and (B2)

we have

$$[O]P \rightarrow [S](P \rightarrow [S][H]P) \quad \text{from (4) and (3)}$$

In the same way we have

$$[O]P \rightarrow [S](P \wedge [H]P)$$

Then, we have

$$[S/H]P \quad \text{by (A6).}$$

Nadathur and Joshi (1983) presents another extended logic in which
they express the following idea: "in conversational situations,
if the speaker knows (or believes) that the hearer knows (or believes) that an object a satisfies the description D uniquely, then
he/she often conjectures that this is mutual knowledge (or a mutual belief) if there is no reason to doubt it" (Nadathur and
Joshi 1983, pp. 603).

VI. CONCLUSION

In this note we have given some ideas about how to analyse mutual
belief using logic tools. We have extended classical belief logic

with operators that express mutual belief relative to the beliefs of one agent about another. A mechanical proof procedure, as in Cavalli & Farinas del Cerro (1984), has been defined for BM4 and has been implemented in PROLOG on a DEC LSI-11/23.

REFERENCES:

Clark,H.H. and Marschall, C., Definite Reference and Mutual Knowledge, in: Elements of Discourse Understanding, A.K. Joshi, B.L. Webber and I.A. Sag (eds), (Cambridge University Press 1981).

Donnellan, K., Reference and Definite Description, Philosophical Review, 75 (1966) 281-304. Reprinted in: Steinberg, D. and Jakobovits, J. and al. (eds), Semantics, (Cambridge University Press, 1982).

Cavalli, A.R. and Fariñas del Cerro, L., A decision method for linear temporal logic, Proc. of 7th International Conference on Automated Deduction, Napa, California, (Springer-Verlag, 1984), LNCS n. 170.

Hintikka, J., Knowledge and belief: an introduction to the logic of two notions, (Cornell University Press, 1962).

Hintikka, J., Semantics for propositional attitudes, in: Linsky, L., ed.,Reference and modality, (Oxford University Press, London, 1971).

Kripke, S., Semantical considerations on modal logic, in: Linsky, L. (ed.), Reference and Modality, (Oxford University Press, London, 1971).

Nadathur, G. and Joshi, A.K., Mutual belief in conversational systems: their role in referring expressions, Proc. of IJCAI-8, Karlsruhe (1983).

Perrault, C.R. and Cohen, P.R., It's for your own good: a note on Inaccurate Reference, in: Elements of Discourse Understanding, Joshi, A.K., Webber, B.L. and Sag, I.A. (eds), (Cambridge University Press, 1981).

Russell, B., On denoting (1905) reedited in: Marsch,R. (ed.), Logic
and Knowledge, Allen and Unwin, New York (1956).

Sato, M., A study of Kripke-type models for some modal logics by
Gentzen's sequential method. Research Institute for Mathematical
Sciences, (Kyoto University, Japan, 1977).

Searle, J.R., Speech Acts, (Cambridge University Press, 1969).

Segerberg, K., A completeness theorem in modal logic of programs,
Note AMS,24: 6 A-552 (1977).

Natural Language Understanding and Logic Programming
V. Dahl and P. Saint-Dizier (Editors)
© Elsevier Science Publishers B.V. (North-Holland), 1985

AN INTEGRATED PARSER FOR TEXT UNDERSTANDING:
VIEWING PARSING AS PASSING MESSAGES AMONG ACTORS

Kuniaki Uehara, Ryo Ochitani
Osamu Mikami, Junichi Toyoda

The Institute of Scientific and Industrial Research
Osaka University
8-1 Mihogaoka, Ibaraki, Osaka 567
JAPAN

We present the formalism of an Integrated Parser (IP) for text
understanding. For IP, the word 'integrated' has two meanings. First, syntactic, semantic, and contextual analyses
occur as an integral part of the parsing process.   Second,
there are three distinct metaphors available in the field of
computational linguistics: procedure oriented, declaration
oriented, and actor oriented metaphors.   IP was designed to
incorporate them within a single grammar formalism. Our parsing mechanism offers simplicity, perspicuity, modularity, no
side effects, and simple but powerful computational semantics.

1. INTRODUCTION

1.1 Some Background

Prolog (Pereira 1983) is a programming language one of whose unique feature is
that programs written in it can be read either procedurally or declaratively as
Horn clauses of first-order predicate logic.   Since the syntax of Prolog is a
natural extension of that of Context-Free Grammar (CFG), several Prolog-based
grammar formalisms have been proposed for natural language processing.   In fact, a
Definite Clause Grammar (DCG) (Pereira et al. 1980) and PAMPS grammar (Uehara et
al. 1984) are the simplest formalisms among them.   These grammars, however, have
certain deficiencies to describe natural languages.

First, Pereira and Warren (Pereira et al. 1980) pointed out that DCGs can be used
for generation as well as for recognition, since the input and output arguments of
a grammar rule do not have to be distinguished in advance, but may vary from one
call to another.   Grammar rules can thus be used in a multi-purpose way. But, to
one's surprise, this characteristic gives rise to the problem that it is slightly
difficult to understand grammar rules procedurally, since the usage of variables
in a grammar rule can not be specified without looking into the details of how
they are used in the whole grammar.

Second, these grammar formalisms seem to pay little attention to understanding
groups of sentences, either in text or in dialogue, focusing instead on
understanding single sentences.   Only the system proposed by Simmons and Chester
(Simmons et al. 1982) presented a primitive approach for using Horn clauses (i.e.
Prolog programs) to relate successive sentences into a discourse structure.   The
system first maps each sentence into its syntactic structure, then translates it
into its semantic structure, and finally extracts the relationship between these
semantic structures. In this sequential process, semantic context is not utilized
to provide the syntactic component with information that can help it along.   If
input sentences include some forms of deletions, ellipses, and anaphoric
references, it is difficult to determine their correct meanings at the isolated
sentence level.

1.2 The Scope and Aims of the IP Project

This paper presents the formalism of an 'Integrated Parser' (IP) for text
understanding which runs as a single module; syntactic analysis, semantic analysis
and contextual analysis occur as an integral part of the parsing process. This
integrated scheme follows from the idea that not only general linguistic knowledge
(i.e. lexical, syntactic, and semantic knowledge) but also episodic knowledge
contained in a text must be used to parse sentences in the text.

The formalism of an IP grammar is based on that of a Lexical Functional Grammar
(LFG) introduced by Kaplan and Bresnan (Bresnan 1982), which has grown out of
ideas from current transformational linguistics and computational linguistics. An
LFG consists of both standard context-free rules and lexical items with associated
functional equations (schemata). These schemata are finally solved to produce a
functional structure (f-structure), that is, a deep structure of an input
sentence. Solving the schemata can be seen as if it transfers partial f-
structures from node to node upward in accordance with the growth of a parse tree.
We can view this control structure as message passing in Actor theory proposed by
Hewitt (Hewitt 1977). That is, we can correspond each context-free rule to an
actor. Computation during parsing is, thus, performed only by sending messages
among actors.

Another of our claims is that there are three distinct metaphors available in the
field of computational linguistics today; procedure oriented (i.e. PROGRAMMAR
(Winograd 1972) and ATN (Woods 1970)), declaration oriented (i.e. DCG and PAMPS)
and actor oriented metaphors (i.e. Object-Oriented Parser (Phillips 1983) and Word
Expert Parser (Small 1981)). These metaphors are usually embedded in completely
separated grammar formalisms. IP was designed to incorporate all three metaphors
within a single grammar formalism so as to allow users to write practical grammars
with ease.

IP has been implemented in C-Prolog (Pereira 1983) and run on an ECLIPSE
MV/8000-II.

2. AN IP GRAMMAR

The following introduction is fairly self-contained, but readers are expected to
be familiar with the basic concepts and notations of LFGs (Bresnan 1982).

2.1 Data Structure

In IP, the grammatical relation of an input sentence is represented by an f-
structure. The f-structure consists of a set of ordered pairs each of which
consists of an attribute and a specification of the attribute's value for the
input sentence. The f-structure is composed of grammatical function names,
semantic forms, and feature symbols. The f-structure is of the form:

$$
\begin{bmatrix}
\langle attribute\_1 \rangle = \langle value\_1 \rangle \\
\vdots \qquad\qquad \vdots \\
\langle attribute\_k \rangle = \langle value\_k \rangle
\end{bmatrix}
$$

An attribute is the name of a grammatical function or a feature. A value is
either a symbol, a semantic form, an f-structure, or a set of symbols, semantic
forms, or f-structures. A symbol is a primitive type of attribute's values.
There are three kinds of semantic forms. One is called an event, which is a
logical formula encoding the meaning of an input sentence. The event comprises a
predicate name followed by a sequence of one or more arguments. A predicate name
is characterized to represent its sense or meaning. An argument will be assigned

to an f-structure which specifies the grammatical function of its thematic role. The second type of semantic forms is called an individual. Individuals are also semantic forms, but do not have any arguments. The last type of semantic forms is called a class, which specifies a set for describing individuals of a particular kind. A class corresponds to a common noun in the traditional linguistics. We assume a number of predicate names --- e.g., stay-in, reach, get-on, corresponding roughly to verbs, which are not so rigidly categorized as primitive acts and states in Conceptual Dependency theory (Schank 1977), an arbitrary number of individuals --- e.g., John, New-York, corresponding to proper nouns, and a number of classes --- e.g., window, book.

$$\begin{bmatrix} \text{subject} = \begin{bmatrix} \text{num} = \text{singular} \\ \text{ind} = \text{john} \end{bmatrix} \\ \text{tense} = \text{past} \\ \text{event} = \text{open}(\begin{bmatrix} \text{num} = \text{singular} \\ \text{ind} = \text{john} \end{bmatrix}, \begin{bmatrix} \text{num} = \text{singular} \\ \text{class} = \text{window} \end{bmatrix}) \\ \text{object} = \begin{bmatrix} \text{num} = \text{singular} \\ \text{class} = \text{window} \end{bmatrix} \end{bmatrix}$$

Fig.1 An f-structure.

For example, 'subject' and 'object' in Fig.1 are grammatical functions, and 'tense' is a feature. 'Singular' and 'past' are symbols. 'Open([...],[...])' is a semantic form and the f-structure '$\begin{bmatrix} \text{num} = \text{singular} \\ \text{ind} = \text{man} \end{bmatrix}$' is its argument.

2.2 The Syntax of an IP Grammar

An IP grammar has two kinds of rules: augmented context-free rules (hereafter we will simply say grammar rules) and lexical items.

A grammar rule is of the form:

[<left-hand-side>   <right-hand-side>]

<left-hand-side> ::= <non-terminal>

<right-hand-side> is of the form:

$$\begin{bmatrix} [<\text{non-terminal\_1}> (<\text{schemata\_1}>)] \\ \cdot \\ \cdot \\ \cdot \\ [<\text{non-terminal\_k}> (<\text{schemata\_k}>)] \end{bmatrix}$$

A lexical item is of the form:

[<terminal>   [<non-terminal>   <schemata>]]

F-structures are generated by solving schemata associated with grammar rules and lexical items. A schema is either a defining schema, which defines the value of some feature, or a constraining schema, which constrains a feature whose value is expected to be defined by a separate specialization. A defining schema is either of the form:

<designator> = <designator>   (1)

or

<designator> << <designator>   (2)

(1) is an identification schema which expresses that the f-structure indicated by
the left-hand side is identified with the f-structure indicated by the right-hand
side.   (2) is a membership schema which expresses that the f-structure indicated
by the right-hand side is a set containing the f-structure indicated by the left-
hand side.

A constraining schema is of the form:

$$\langle designator \rangle == \langle designator \rangle \qquad\qquad (3)$$

$$\langle designator \rangle \qquad\qquad (4)$$

$$not(\langle designator \rangle) \qquad\qquad (5)$$

(3) is an equational constraint which constrains that the f-structure of the
right-hand side should be equal to the f-structure of the left-hand side.   (4) is
an existential constraint.   The existential constraint is satisfied when the
expression has   some value.   (5) is a negative constraint formed by adding a
negation operator to a constraining schema. The negative constraint is acceptable
only if the constraining schema without the negation operator is false.

A designator consists of a meta-variable followed by another designator, or none
or more symbols. A designator is either of the form:

$$(\langle meta\text{-}variable \rangle \ \langle designator \rangle)$$
or
$$(\langle meta\text{-}variable \rangle \ \langle symbol\_0 \rangle, \ ... \ , \langle symbol\_n \rangle)$$

Meta-variables are of just two types:

$$\langle\text{-} \quad , \quad \text{-}\rangle \qquad\qquad i)$$

$$\langle\text{=} \quad , \quad \text{=}\rangle \qquad\qquad ii)$$

A meta-variable '<-' refers to the f-structure attached to the left-hand side non-
terminal of a grammar rule.   A meta-variable '->' refers to the f-structure
attached to the non-terminal where the meta-variable '->' itself appears.   Meta-
variables '<=' and '=>' are used to characterize the 'long-distance' dependencies
found in relative clauses and questions.

2.3 The Semantics of an IP Grammar

As was mentioned above, an IP grammar is founded on three readings of grammar
rules. Consider, for instance, the following grammar rule:

$$[S \ [[NP \ (\langle\text{-}subject = \text{-}\rangle)],[VP \ (\langle\text{-} = \text{-}\rangle)]]]$$

From the point of view of the S-dominated NP node, the schema '<-subject = ->'
says that the value of the subject attribute of S is the f-structure of NP.   The
schema '<- = ->' says that the f-structure of S is equal to the f-structure of VP.
First of all, we can read this rule declaratively as:

    "An S is an NP followed by a VP, where the value of the subject attribute
    of the S is the f-structure of the NP and the value of the S is the f-
    structure of the VP."

or procedurally as:

    "To construct the f-structure of an S, first construct the partial f-
    structure of an NP whose attribute is subject, then construct the partial
    f-structure of a VP, and finally mix them into a single f-structure of

the S."

Furthermore, in another point of view, we can understand this control structure as message passing in Actor theory proposed by Hewitt: actor oriented reading. In Actor theory, an actor is organized as a computational entity which has aspects of both procedures and data. Actors are not primarily partitioned into procedures and separate data. All of the action of an actor comes from passing messages between actors. Actors interpret the uniform message form locally. The actor oriented paradigm says that the surface structure chosen by a grammar (i.e. parse tree) is taken to be the skeleton for a program whose substantive components are actors. Each node of the tree, that is, each non-terminal of the grammar rule, is associated with an actor. Meta-variables specify the flow of message between actors, that is, meta-variables provide a mechanism for message sending and receiving. The grammar rule indicates the flow of control between actors, or we can say that the right-hand side of the rule indicates the sequence of behaviors actors can take.

According to Actor theory, we can re-interpret meta-variables. A meta-variable '<-' would be read as a form of the verb "send". For example, if the designator '<-subject' appears at the left-hand side of a schema, it would be read as:

"send the receiver an f-structure with the attribute subject."

If it appears at the right-hand side, it would be read as:

"send the receiver a request to get an f-structure with the attribute subject."

A meta-variable '->' is read as 'receive'. For example, '->pcase' can be read as:

"receive from the sender an f-structure with the attribute pcase."

In the actor oriented reading, the above grammar rule is read as:

"receive an f-structure of an NP and send it to an S with the attribute subject, then receive an f-structure of a VP and send it to the S."

The actor oriented paradigm is well suited to applications where the description of entities is simplified by use of uniform protocols. If we are adding the idea of Actor theory to our grammar formalism, we can produce a better practical way of writing complex grammars.

3. THE CONTROL STRUCTURE OF IP

Each actor is one component of IP. An actor consists of an internal state and set of operations (patterns). The internal state of an actor can be modified when the actor receives a message, which invokes one of the patterns. An actor's internal state can be manipulated only by evaluating its patterns.

3.1 Realization of Actors

There are two types of actors in IP; one is an actor corresponding to a grammar rule (grammatical actor), the other is an actor corresponding to a lexical item (lexical actor). A grammatical actor consists of two parts: a 'script' which describes what should be done when the actor receives a message, and a set of 'acquaintances' which are the other actors that the actor knows about.

The grammatical actor is of the form:

[<actor_name>   <script>]

where <actor_name> is the left-hand side of a grammar rule. A 'script' part shows
a set of schemata which indicate how to construct an f-structure. <Script>
consists of a set of right-hand sides of the grammar rules whose left-hand sides
are the same non-terminal. Each element of the script is called a pattern. The
script is of the form:

[<pattern_1>],
.
.
.
[<pattern_n>]

<pattern_i> ::= <right-hand-side>

A lexical actor has a script which specifies its syntactic features and semantic
forms in terms of patterns. The lexical actor is of the following form:

[<actor_name> [<non-terminal> <schemata>]]

where <actor_name> is a terminal.

3.2 Activated Patterns and Inactivated Patterns

In Actor theory, communication between actors is assumed to be done in parallel.
However, since achieving parallelism within our implementation would consume more
space during parsing and require more difficult implementation technique, IP
parses sentences in a traditional top-down serial way with automatic backtracking.
Hewitt's Actor model does not make any reference to the sequencing of patterns
within the script of an actor. The sequencing information, however, is necessary
for IP to parse sentences. It constitutes crucial control information for IP.
When an actor has some applicable patterns, it chooses the first pattern,
evaluates the schemata of the first element of the pattern, modifies the actor's
internal state, and sends a message to the grammatical actor of the first element.
The selected pattern is called an activated pattern. All the other patterns are
turned out to be inactivated and wait to be executed until the chosen one fails to
be sent to another actor. These patterns are called inactivated patterns. The
receiver, an actor to which the message was sent, also evaluates its pattern
according to the received message, modifies its internal state, and returns the
result of the transmitted message to the sender, an actor which sent the message.
The sender, in turn, evaluates the second schemata of the activated pattern and
performs the same sequence of behaviors as was mentioned above.

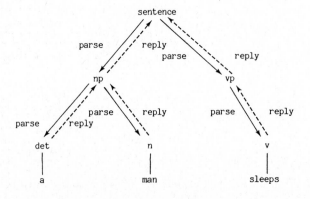

Fig.2 The flow of messages in IP.

There are two cases in which the parsing process fails; one is the case that the actor cannot construct a proper f-structure of the input sentence, the other is the case that there are no more patterns waiting to be activated. In these cases, the most recently activated actor abandons the computation made by transmitting a message, chooses an alternative among inactivated patterns, and evaluates the chosen one.

3.3 The Internal Representation of F-structures

In an IP grammar, the correspondence between constituents and elements of an f-structure is not one-to-one. A single element, for example, will play roles in different parts of the f-structure simultaneously. It is rather tiresome to represent identical constituents within a single f-structure. Furthermore, the conventional 'literal' representation of f-structures may consume a large amount of space. IP reduces these redundancies by using the 'shared structure' technique for the internal representation of f-structures. The data structure used by IP is a kind of network, consisting of segment f-structures which are collections of attribute-value pairs. Each segment f-structure has as its identifier a unique name (indicated by f_n for any number n). Some values of the segment f-structure are really pointers to other segment f-structures. They could be drawn as links to those other segment f-structures if they were shown in a visual way. Fig. 3 indicates that the segment f-structure f_1 has its segment f-structure f_2 whose attribute is subject.

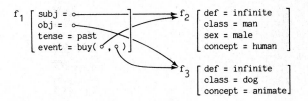

Fig.3 An example of segment f-structures

In our implementation, these segment f-structures are represented as internal states of the corresponding actors. The 'shared structure' technique facilitates very rapid creation and discard of f-structures at the sacrifice of somewhat slower access to its components, since reference to the components of an f-structure entails extra work to trace down any chains of segment f-structures.

3.4 The Evaluation of Schemata

The evaluation of schemata can be divided into two types. This difference in evaluation accurately reflects the conceptual distinction represented by the two types of schemata.

1) Defining Schemata: When an actor receives a message, each meta-variable '<-' is replaced by the identifier for the 'parent' segment f-structure. The actor then creates a unique identifier and assigns it to each meta-variable '->'. These identifiers, in turn, are used as pointers to other segment f-structures.

2) Constraining Schemata: The evaluation of constraining schemata is different from that of defining schemata. Constraining schemata are evaluated by finding the real values of their designators. If a designator has a meta-variable '<-', the actor searches up its superiors in the parse tree, until its finds the value of the designator. If the designator has a meta-variable '->', the actor searches down the tree.

Since IP parses each prefix of 'w' ('w' is an input sentence) before reading any of the input beyond prefix (i.e. on-line parser), some of the values of constraining schemata may have not been determined when an actor tries to evaluate them. These undetermined schemata are recorded in a message and their evaluation is postponed until they are assigned values (delayed computation).

3.5 A Message

Once an actor, A, transmits a message to another actor, B, the computation proceeds by following the script of B using the message from A. To do this, the message must have fairly rigid form. This provides the basis for meaningful communication between actors. The message consists of four parts:

1) f-structure: An identifier for the 'parent' segment f-structure.

2) trail list: Trail list is used as a push-down list. It is used to store the names of actors which need to be re-activated on backtracking.

3) hold list: Hold list is used to analyze the phenomenon which in generative transformational grammars would be called left extraposition. A possible candidate for an extraposed constituent is attached to a meta-variable '=>', and is recorded in the hold list. The corresponding meta-variable '<=' picks up the constituent from the hold list in the transmitted message and embeds it into the hole left by the missing constituent. This enables the actor to simulate the HOLD-VIR mechanism in an ATN.

4) constraining schema list: Constraining schemata whose meta-variables could not be instantiated so far are recorded in the constraining schema list. When an actor receives a message, it always checks to see if some of the elements in the constraining schema list are computable or not. This list gives the actor the power to perform the delayed evaluation.

4. TEXT UNDERSTANDING IN IP

Early researchers in natural language processing concentrated almost exclusively on individual sentences. Recently there has been much effort to pay attention to whole texts instead of individual sentences. Most previous natural language understanding systems have been made up of two or three components. These systems first map a single sentence in a text into its syntactic structure, then use semantic knowledge to determine the meaning of the sentence, and finally build a contextual structure of the text from semantic structures. However, this paradigm of modularity seems to be an illusion, since these components cannot freely communicate with each other. Thus, the semantic or contextual component cannot provide the syntactic component with information that can help it along. IP, on the other hand, runs as a single module: syntactic, semantic, and contextual analyses occur as an integral part of the parsing process. We will, hereafter, discuss text understanding of IP.

4.1 Prediction and Presupposition

Before focusing our discussion on text understanding, we start by reviewing some basic concepts, making clear our terminology in the process. An event means either an action that people carry out or a simple change of state. As was mentioned above, we represent the event as a logical formula consisting of a predicate name followed by one or more arguments. A state is defined as a property or condition of an object or a stable relationship among a set of objects. Actions are defined as intentional human acts that change from one state to the next in some way that would not have come about otherwise (Rumelhart 1975).

As a basic assumption, we begin with the premise that when one reads a sentence in a text and understands its meaning, one can easily make the prediction about what kind of events are coming next. That is, we assume that the next sentence can be predicted from the current one. The prediction can be invaluable as a guide to the parser in such difficult problem areas as resolving referents and selecting meanings of ambiguous words, which will be discussed later. Furthermore, we also suppose that when one tries to understand the sentence, one makes sure that some presuppositions have already been fulfilled in the contextual memory, which is the representation of the previously understood sentences in the text. Assume that S1 refers to the sentence currently being processed, S0 to be a previous one, and S2 to be a next one. If the event of S0 can match with the presupposed event of S1 or the predicted event of S1 can match with the event of S2, then we will say that S0 (S1) has a coherent relation to S1 (S2) (Hobbs 1979).

We will now slightly extend the system organization so as to realize our ideas in IP. After the analysis of a single sentence, the 'Sentence' actor, i.e. the top node of a parse tree, sends created events to the superior actor, named 'Context'. The contextual memory, thus, is represented by the internal state of 'Context' actor. Both prediction and presupposition are encoded implicitly within the structure of a lexical actor in terms of semantic forms, called a predicted event and presupposed event respectively. In Fig.4, we show some examples of these events.

(1) John went to a pet shop.

```
presupposed_event = come(john,(<-place),pet_shop)
event = go(john,pet_shop)
predicted_event = stay_in(john,pet_shop)
```

(2) There he bought a dog.

```
presupposed_event = stay_in(he,pet_shop)
event = buy(he,dog)
predicted_event = pay(he,(<-obj),money)
                  get(he,dog)
```

Fig.4 Events extracted from sentences.

Sentence (1) has the predicted event that John will stay in the pet-shop, and the presupposed event that John came to the pet-shop from somewhere. Sentence (2) has the presupposed event that John stays in the pet-shop and the predicted events that John will pay some money to get a dog, and that he will get it. The predicted event of (1) can be matched against the presupposed event of (2), thus both sentences are coherent.

4.2 Selecting Meanings of Ambiguous Words

Fig.5 shows a schematic view of a lexical actor for a verb.

```
⎡<terminal> ⎡<non-terminal>   (<schema> ⎤⎤ } condition
⎢           ⎢                      .    ⎥⎥ } presupposed event
⎢           ⎢                      .    ⎥⎥ } event
⎣           ⎣                 <schema>) ⎦⎦ } predicted event
```

Fig.5 A schematic view of a lexical actor for a verb.

The condition part consists of a set of constraining schemata which are conditions for the application of the lexical actor.   Lexical actors are highly specific and a single word may have several different entries corresponding to its various meanings.   Conditions are used to select the correct meaning depending on the context in which the word appears.   The presupposed event part includes some semantic forms which must have been satisfied previously.   The event part specifies the semantic form corresponding to each meaning of the word.   The predicted event part contains the semantic forms which will be inferred after the analysis of the current sentence.   Fig.6 shows the lexical actor of the word 'eat'.

$$
\begin{bmatrix} eat \begin{bmatrix} Verb & \begin{bmatrix} ((<\text{-object kind}) == food \\ predicted\_event = is\text{-hungry}((<\text{-subject})) \\ event = eat((<\text{-subject}),(<\text{-object})) \\ predicted\_event = is\text{-satisfied}((<\text{-subject}))) \\ ((<\text{-object kind}) == metal \\ (<\text{-}(\text{->}pcase)) == into \\ event = corrode((<\text{-subject}),(<\text{-object}))) \end{bmatrix} \end{bmatrix} \end{bmatrix} \begin{matrix} \\ \} \ condition\_1 \\ \\ \\ \} \ condition\_2 \\ \\ \\ \end{matrix}
$$

Fig.6   The lexical actor of the word 'eat'.

In this example, the lexical actor of 'eat' is highly specialized.   It is applicable to the use of 'eat' in sentences like 'The man eats an apple' where the condition part of the word 'eat' should contain the condition that the object must be a kind of food.   The presupposed event indicates that the subject is hungry. The predicted event says that the subject will be pleased.   The event means that the subject eats the object.   Though, to analyze the sentence 'Acids eat into metals,' the condition part must contains the condition that the object must be a metal.   The event means that the subject corrodes the object.

4.3 Anaphora and Its Referent

Events are also useful to deal with simple cases of anaphora and ellipsis.   Even if the sentences S0 and S1 are coherent by a continuity of state-action tracks understood in terms of events, some arguments in events may be partially undefined or omitted.   These partially undefined parts occur because of anaphora and ellipsis.   To understand a text, we must fulfill these partially undefined parts. The values of these arguments may be determined when the event matches against some predicted event.

In many systems anaphora is handled differently from other processing.   These systems usually create a list of possible anaphoric referents before encountering a pronoun.   When an anaphoric reference is found, one of them is chosen on the basis of syntactic knowledge, such as number and gender agreements, and on semantic knowledge which checks to see if the referent can fit into the rest of the sentence.

To illustrate how IP finds an anaphoric referent, consider the Wilks's classical example.

The soldiers fired at the women and we saw some of them fall.

To find the anaphoric referent of "them", it does not suffice to make use of only general linguistic knowledge since both soldiers and women can fall.   The only way to disambiguate the anaphoric referent of 'them' is by searching the sequence of events (i.e. contextual memory) while the sentence is parsed.   After the analysis of the first sentence, the contextual memory will include the following events:

```
presupposed_event = have([ def = definite ],[concept = weapon])
                         [ noun = soldier  ]
                         [ num = plural    ]
                         [ concept = human ]

event = fire_at([ def = definite ],[ def = definite  ])
                [ class = soldier]  [ class = woman   ]
                [ num = plural   ]  [ num = plural    ]
                [ concept = human]  [ sex = female    ]
                                    [ concept = human ]

predicted_event = injury([ def = definite ])
                         [ class = woman   ]
                         [ num = plural    ]
                         [ sex = female    ]
                         [ concept = human ]
                    die([ def = definite ])
                        [ class = woman   ]
                        [ num = plural    ]
                        [ sex = female    ]
                        [ concept = human ]
                   fall([ def = definite ])
                        [ class = woman   ]
                        [ num = plural    ]
                        [ sex = female    ]
                        [ concept = human ]
```

The event of the second sentence is:

```
event = see([ num = plural   ],[num = plural],(<-vcomp_event))
            [ concept = human ]

vcomp_event = fall([num = plural])
```

The third predicted event of the first sentence can match with the vcomp-event of
the second one. The matching process is very similar to the unification algorithm
in logic programming.   The most significant difference is that uninstantiated
parts of IP's structure are either omitted or implicitly specified by some
schemata.   The function of IP's matching process is to find appropriate
substructures by matching a partially instantiated f-structure against the well-
formed one.   In this example, we can get the following vcomp-event after the
execution of the matching process:

```
vcomp_event = fall([ def = definite ])
                   [ class = woman   ]
                   [ num = plural    ]
                   [ sex = female    ]
                   [ concept = human ]
```

Thus, we can easily infer that 'them' refers to 'women'.   Note that the proper
treatment of quantified noun phrases, such as 'some of them', is difficult to
handle semantically.   We will, therefore, not go into the analysis of the phrase
any more detail.

Consider another text:

   1)   John took a train to New York.

   2)   He got off it at Grand Central.

From sentence 1), IP infers the predicted event that John will get off the train at somewhere in New York:

$$get\_off(\begin{bmatrix} num = sg \\ ind = john \\ sex = male \\ concept = human \end{bmatrix}, \begin{bmatrix} def = infinite \\ class = train \\ num = sg \\ concept = cargo \end{bmatrix}, \begin{bmatrix} ind = New\_York \\ part\_of = USA \\ concept = place \end{bmatrix})$$

While processing the second sentence, IP builds the following event:

$$get\_off(\begin{bmatrix} num = sg \\ sex = male \end{bmatrix}, [num = sg], \begin{bmatrix} ind = Grand\_Central \\ part\_of = Manhattan \\ concept = place \end{bmatrix})$$

IP, finally, finds the predicted event of sentence 1) partially matches with the event of sentence 2). From these events we can find that the word 'he' should be identified as referring to 'John'. The 'train' is found to be the referent of 'it'.

In order to match the predicted event to the event completely, IP must know the fact that Grand Central is located in New York. This mechanism can be performed simply by associating a hierarchy with actors (property inheritance). This hierarchy supports a very convenient form of default reasoning and increases the brevity and modularity of an IP grammar. In addition, it should provide a more general and powerful approach to resolving anaphora and ellipsis. This 'fuzzy' matching process is basically intersection search of Quillian's semantic network (Quillian 1968). The process first attempts to match two arguments X and Y using the standard matching process. If the matching fails, it traces along the superpart actors from the two lexical actors corresponding to X and Y, i.e. in the above example, these lexical actors are 'New York' and 'Grand Central', until an intersection is found. If the intersection is found, the 'fuzzy' matching succeeds. We must leave to a separate paper the details of the 'fuzzy' matching algorithm.

4.4 A More Complicated Example

First of all, We show a more complicated text in Fig.7. The story was taken from the Japan Times of December 1, 1981.

   (1)   Mrs. Miura was shot in Los Angeles on Nov. 18, 1981.
   (2)   Mrs. Miura was wounded in the head.
   (3)   She entered the university hospital.
   (4)   She received intensive medical treatment there.
   (5)   The woman had not recovered consciousness since the incident.
   (6)   She eventually died of a lesion of the brain without regaining consciousness.

Fig.7 A simple text.

In Fig.8, we show a fragment of an IP grammar to illustrate the notation. The grammar covers sentence (1) in the above text.

```
⎡ sentence ⎡[s          (<- = ->)] ,                  ⎤⎤
⎢          ⎣[endsymbol  (<- = ->)]                    ⎥⎥
⎢ s        ⎡[np         (<-subj = ->)] ,              ⎤⎥
⎢          ⎢[vp         (<- = ->)] ,                  ⎥⎥
⎢          ⎣[ppr        (<-adjunct = ->)]             ⎦⎥
⎢ np       ⎡[lm         (<-left_mod = ->)] ,          ⎤⎥
⎢          ⎣[noun       (<- = ->)]                    ⎦⎥
⎢ np       [[noun       (<- = ->)] ]                  ⎥
⎢ vp       ⎡[v          (<- = ->)] ,                  ⎤⎥
⎢          ⎣[vp1        (<-vcomp = ->)]               ⎦⎥
⎢ vp       [[v          (<- = ->)] ]                  ⎥
⎢ vp1      [[vp         (<- = ->)] ]                  ⎥
⎢ lm       [[adj        (<- = ->)] ]                  ⎥
⎢ ppr      [[pp         (<-(->pcase) = ->)] ]         ⎥
⎢ ppr      ⎡[pp         (<-(->pcase) = ->)] ,         ⎤⎥
⎢          ⎣[ppr        (<- = ->)]                    ⎦⎥
⎢ pp       ⎡[prep       (<- = ->)] ,                  ⎤⎥
⎣          ⎣[np         (<- = ->)]                    ⎦⎦
```

a)   Grammatical actors

```
[ mrs          [adj   ((<-sex) = female)] ]
⎡ miura        ⎡noun  ((<-ind) = miura                              ⎤⎤
⎢              ⎢      (<-left_mod,sex) = (<-sex)                    ⎥⎥
⎢              ⎣      (<-concept) = human)                         ⎦⎥
⎡ los_angeles  ⎡noun  ((<-ind) = los_angeles                       ⎤⎤
⎢              ⎣      (<-concept) = place))                        ⎦⎥
⎡ nov_18_1981  ⎡noun  ((<-ind) = nov_18_1981                       ⎤⎤
⎢              ⎣      (<-concept) = date)                          ⎦⎥
⎡ was          ⎡v     ((<-tense) = past                            ⎤⎤
⎢              ⎢      (<-vcomp,participle) = past                  ⎥⎥
⎢              ⎢      (<-vcomp,subj) = (<-subj)                    ⎥⎥
⎢              ⎢      (<-event) = (<-vcomp,event)                  ⎥⎥
⎢              ⎣      (<-predicted_event) = (<-vcomp,predicted_event)) ⎦⎥
⎡ shot         ⎡v     ((<-participle) = past                       ⎤⎤
⎢              ⎢      (<-event) = shot((<-by_obj),(<-subj))        ⎥⎥
⎢              ⎢      (<-predicted_event) = [ injury((<-subj)),    ⎥⎥
⎢              ⎢                             die((<-subj)),        ⎥⎥
⎢              ⎣                             fall((<-subj))])      ⎦⎥
[ in           [prep  ((<-pcase) = in)] ]
[ on           [prep  ((<-pcase) = on)] ]
[ '.'          [endsymbol ((<-sentence) = assertion)] ]
```

b)   Lexical actors

Fig.8   Examples of the IP grammar.

The analysis of sentence (1) with the IP grammar depicted above produces the following f-structure.

```
┌                                                                           ┐
│ sentence = assertion                                                      │
│ subj = ┌ sex = female    ┐                                                │
│        │ ind = miura     │                                                │
│        │ sex = female    │                                                │
│        └ concept = human ┘                                                │
│ tense = past                                                              │
│ vcomp = ┌ participle = past                                           ┐   │
│         │ subj = ┌ sex = female    ┐                                  │   │
│         │        │ ind = miura     │                                  │   │
│         │        │ sex = female    │                                  │   │
│         │        └ concept = human ┘                                  │   │
│         │ event = shot([], ┌ sex = female    ┐ )                      │   │
│         │                  │ ind = miura     │                        │   │
│         │                  │ sex = female    │                        │   │
│         │                  └ concept = human ┘                        │   │
│         │ predicted_event = injury( ┌ sex = female    ┐ )             │   │
│         │                           │ ind = miura     │               │   │
│         │                           │ sex = female    │               │   │
│         │                           └ concept = human ┘               │   │
│         │                    die( ┌ sex = female    ┐ )               │   │
│         │                         │ ind = miura     │                 │   │
│         │                         │ sex = female    │                 │   │
│         │                         └ concept = human ┘                 │   │
│         │                   fall( ┌ sex = female    ┐ )               │   │
│         │                         │ ind = miura     │                 │   │
│         │                         │ sex = female    │                 │   │
│         └                         └ concept = human ┘                 ┘   │
│ adjunct = ┌ in = ┌ pcase = in          ┐ ┐                                │
│           │      │ ind = los_angeles   │ │                                │
│           │      └ concept = place     ┘ │                                │
│           │ on = ┌ pcase = on           ┐│                                │
│           │      │ ind = nov_18_1981    ││                                │
│           └      └ concept = date       ┘┘                                │
│ event = shot([], ┌ sex = female    ┐ )                                    │
│                  │ ind = miura     │                                      │
│                  │ sex = female    │                                      │
│                  └ concept = human ┘                                      │
│ predicted_event = injury( ┌ sex = female    ┐ )                           │
│                           │ ind = miura     │                             │
│                           │ sex = female    │                             │
│                           └ concept = human ┘                             │
│                    die( ┌ sex = female    ┐ )                             │
│                         │ ind = miura     │                               │
│                         │ sex = female    │                               │
│                         └ concept = human ┘                               │
│                   fall( ┌ sex = female    ┐ )                             │
│                         │ ind = miura     │                               │
│                         │ sex = female    │                               │
└                         └ concept = human ┘                              ┘
```

Fig.9 An f-structure of sentence (1).

Fig.10 shows the representation of the coherent relation between six sentences. Sentence (1) has the event which means that Miura was shot by someone, and three predicted events that Miura will be injured, that Miura will be dead, and that Miura will fall. Sentence (2) has the event which means that Miura was injured. The predicted event of sentence (1) can match with the event of sentence (2), thus we can find that these two sentences are coherent. Both pre-required events of sentence (4) can match with the event of sentence (2) and the predicted event of sentence (3), respectively. We can thus find that the word 'she' refers to 'Miura'. It is difficult to infer a negative event such as sentence (5). There are no predicted events that can completely match with the event of sentence (5). The predicted event of sentence (4) can only be matched against the event of sentence (5) without the negative operator. The dashed line between them show an 'implicit' coherent relation.

Fig.10 Representation of the coherent relation in the text.

5. IP GRAMMARS AND SOME RELATED GRAMMARS

Now we shall discuss the relationship between IP grammars, DCGs, and Augmented
Phrase Structure Grammar (APSG) (Heidorn 1972), which Heidorn took as a basis for
the text processing system EPISTLE.

Firstly, these grammars are based on the same grammar formalism, i.e. CFG. In the
course of parsing with IP grammars and DCGs, non-terminals are replaced by the
sequence of non-terminals that are matched by unification, though the unification
process of IP is superficially different from the one used in logic programming.
An APSG uses explicit constructors and selectors instead of unification.

Secondly, the data structure of a DCG is more or less described in terms of
functional notation (i.e. compound terms) or list notation. The data structure of
IP is in effect a hierarchy of a set of ordered pairs each of which consists of an
attribute and the value of the attribute.   The data structure of IP bears some
similarities to that of APSG.   Like an f-structure, the data structure used by
APSG consists of 'records' which are collections of attribute-value pairs.   It
seems fair to say that the record can be viewed as a special case of the f-
structure.   From another point of view, the data representation technique by use
of f-structures is similar to slot-filler technique which is used in Frame theory
proposed by M. Minsky (Minsky 1975). The fillers of slots can be associated with
attribute values, whereas slot identifiers with attribute names.

Finally, IP grammars and DCGs parse sentences in a left-to-right, top-down, serial
way. APSGs use a strictly left-to-right, bottom-up, parallel-processing algorithm
in which all rules that can be applied to an input sentence at a particular time
are applied.   Certain deficiencies with DCGs have been inherited by the IP
grammar.   For example, in the process of backtracking it is difficult to describe
default behavior. Debugging in DCGs is very difficult for lack of a distinction
between failures and errors.

There are, however, limitations to IP's applicability. IP can understand a simple
text which requires low-level inferences.   IP must have some classes of knowledge
structures, such as frames, plans, points, and scripts, in order to understand
texts 'in depth' in the sense used by Dyer (Dyer 1981).   Furthermore, though IP
was built on Prolog, IP cannot utilize the power of Prolog fully.   IP, for
example, can only partially make use of Prolog's pattern matching.   This problem
would be overcome by translating from a grammar to a Prolog program as was
discussed in (Reyle et al. 1983), or by augmenting the pattern matching mechanism
of the Prolog interpreter as was proposed in (Kornfeld 1983).   However, these
limitations do not argue that our approach is not adequate for text understanding.
Our parsing mechanism offers simplicity, perspicuity, modularity, no side effects,
a simple but powerful computational semantics and, furthermore an integrated
approach to text understanding.

REFERENCES

1) Bresnan, J. (ed.), The Mental Representation of Grammatical Relations (MIT
    Press, Cambridge, Mass., 1982).
2) Dyer, M. G., In-Depth Understanding (MIT Press, Cambridge, Mass., 1983).
3) Heidorn, G. E., Natural Language Inputs to a Simulation Programming, Naval
    Postgraduate School Technical Report, No. NPS-55HD72101 (1972).
4) Hewitt, C., Viewing Control Structures as Patterns of Passing Messages, Artif.
    Intell. 8 (1977) 323-364.
5) Hobbs, J. R., Coherence and Coreference, Cognitive Science 3 (1979) 67-90.
6) Kornfeld, W. A., Equality for Prolog, Proc. of the 8th IJCAI (1983) 514-519.
7) Minsky, M., A Framework for Representing Knowledge, in P. Winston (ed.), The
    Psychology of Computer Vision (McGraw-Hill, New York, 1975).
8) Pereira, F. C. N. et al., Definite Clause Grammar for Language Analysis,

Artif. Intell. 13 (1980) 231-278.

9) Pereira, F. C. N., C-Prolog User's Manual, Version 1.2a, EdCAAD, Department of Architecture, University of Edinburgh (1983).

10) Phillips, B., An Object-Oriented Parser for Text Understanding, Proc. of the 8th IJCAI (1983) 690-692.

11) Quillian, M. R., Semantic Memory, in M. Minsky (ed.), Semantic Information Processing (MIT Press, Cambridge, Mass., 1968).

12) Reyle, U. et al., A Prolog Implementation of Lexical Functional Grammar, Proc. of the 8th IJCAI (1983) 693-695.

13) Rumelhart, D. E., Notes on a Schema for Stories, in D. G. Bobrow and A. Collins (eds.), Representation and Understanding (Academic Press, New York, 1975).

14) Schank, R. C., Scripts, Plans, Goals, and Understanding (Lawrence Eribaum, Hillsdale, N.J., 1977).

15) Simmons, R. F. et al., Relating Sentences and Semantic Networks with Procedural Logic, Comm. of the ACM 25 (1982) 527-547.

16) Small, S., Viewing Word Expert Parsing as Linguistic Theory, Proc. of the 7th IJCAI (1981) 70-76.

17) Uehara, K. et al., A Bottom-up Parser Based on Predicate Logic, Proc. of the 1984 International Symposium on Logic Programming (1984) 220-227.

18) Wilks, Y., An Intelligent Analyzer and Understander of English, Comm. of the ACM 18 (1975) 264-274.

19) Winograd, T., Understanding Natural Language (Academic Press, New York, 1972).

20) Woods, W. A., Transition Network Grammar for Natural Language Analysis, Comm. of the ACM 13 (1970) 591-606.

Natural Language Understanding and Logic Programming
V. Dahl and P. Saint-Dizier (Editors)
© Elsevier Science Publishers B.V. (North-Holland), 1985

Facilities of the BUP Parsing System

Yuji MATSUMOTO,
Electrotechnical Laboratory
Ibaraki, 305, Japan

Masaki KIYONO,
Matsushita Electric Industrial Co., Ltd.
Tokyo, 105, Japan

and

Hozumi TANAKA
Tokyo Institute of Technology
Tokyo, 152, Japan

ABSTRACT

The BUP Parsing System [1] is a bottom-up parsing system written in Prolog. It is intended for natural language analysis. Grammar rules and dictionary entries are written in an "epsilon-free" DCG formalism (a DCG formalism [2] that does not contain empty production rules). The BUP translator transforms the grammar rules and the dictionary entries into Prolog clauses. The resulting clauses together with some additional Prolog clauses combine to form a bottom-up parsing program. This can be viewed as a compilation of context-free grammar rules into a Prolog program.

This paper introduces the basic concept of the BUP system and some of the utility programs that are currently available for supporting the development of parsing programs. In addition to the BUP translator, the system includes utilities for morphological analysis, an idiom handler, and a tool for automatic segmentation of Japanese sentences. These facilities are neatly embedded in the framework of our system.

1. Introduction

The aim of this paper is to introduce the current facilities of the BUP parsing system [1]. The BUP system, is a general parsing system for natural languages, and is currently used for analysis of English and Japanese text.

DCGs (Definite Clause Grammars) of Pereira and Warren [2] give a clear grammatical formalism for natural languages. A DCG is directly transformed into a Prolog program which comprises a top-down backtracking parser for context-free grammars. Although the formalism is very clear, the derived parsing system has problems due to its reliance on a top-down backtracking algorithm. The parser cannot deal with left recursive rules, for they may cause an infinite loop; it cannot be an efficient parser because of its naive parsing strategy; and it is not easy to know when to consult the dictionary, since the dictionary is put on the same level as the grammar rules.

The basic component of the BUP system is a set of Prolog clauses called BUP clauses, which are obtained through a uniform transformation from grammar rules written in DCGs. We can say, therefore, that the BUP system gives another procedural semantics to DCGs.

A parsing system must have many flexible facilities to analyze a broad area of a language. Two such facilities are the automatic segmentation and idiom handlers. For example, text in some languages like Japanese do not include word separators, such as spaces. Parsing systems for such languages must take word inflection into account while partitioning sentences into their components. Another special problem is unusual word patterns (idioms) which often occur in sentences in many languages.

This paper introduces the basic concept of the BUP system and presents two utility programs that cope with the automatic segmentation and idiom handling problems mentioned in the previous paragraph.

2. A Brief Introduction to the BUP Parsing System

In the BUP system, users first describe grammar rules and dictionary entries using DCGs. Empty production rules are prohibited in our system, but most such rules can be included in the grammar rules with some modifications [1]. Next context-free grammar rules written in DCG formalism are then transformed into Prolog clauses (called BUP clauses) by the BUP translator [3]. For example, the following context-free grammar rules:

```
1)   sentence(s(NP,VP)) -->
          noun_phrase(NP),verb_phrase(VP).
2)   noun_phrase(np(john)) --> [john].
```

are transformed by the BUP translator to become:

```
1')  noun_phrase(Goal,[NP],Info) --> {link(sentence,Goal)},
          goal(verb_phrase,[VP]),
          sentence(Goal,[s(NP,VP)],Info).

2')  dict(john,noun_phrase,[np(john)]) --> [john].
```

We will not describe the system in detail here. Dictionary entries in the system are DCG clauses where the first element of the body is a list (i.e. a terminal symbol). All other clauses are treated as grammar rules. The informal meaning of BUP clause 1') is stated as follows: When a noun_phrase is found, first we check whether the non-terminal symbol 'sentence' can link to the current goal 'Goal' as a descendant. This process checks whether it is worth using this grammar rule in this context or not. If this check is successful the next thing to do is to find a verb_phrase. And we would get a sentence, if all of these are successful. The predicate 'link' is computed and all of the instances are asserted during the transformation. This predicate works as the top-down expectation just like the 'oracle' of LINGOL [4] and Extended LINGOL [5]. BUP clauses like 2') are dictionary entries. In this case, it says that 'john' is a noun_phrase.

We must define the predicate 'goal'. Additional clauses are necessary to terminate the procedure:

```
3) goal(Goal,Args,[Word|X],Z) :-
      dict(Word,Cat,Args1,[Word|X],Y),link(Cat,Goal),
      P=..[Cat,Goal,Args1,Args,Y,Z],call(P).
```

```
4) cat(cat,I,I,X,X).     (for every non-terminal symbol 'cat')
```

The predicate 'goal' first consults the dictionary and obtains a non-terminal symbol ('Cat'). Next 'goal' checks whether the obtained non-terminal symbol can link up to the current goal, and makes a call whose predicate name is that non-terminal symbol (Thus we have now identified a phrase in the text which belongs to that non-terminal). Clause 4) says that the process terminates immediately if the current goal is equal to what has just been found.

All of the above Prolog clauses combine to form a parsing program. This is a basic view of the BUP parsing system.

A slight modification of 'goal' improves the efficiency of the parsing algorithm a great deal. The idea is to avoid useless repetitions by saving partial successes and failures. The predicate 'goal' is rewritten as follows:

```
    goal(Goal,Arg,X,Y) :-
      wf_goal(Goal,_,X,_),!,wf_goal(Goal,Arg,X,Y);
      fail_goal(Goal,X),!,fail.
    goal(Goal,Arg,X,Z) :-
      dictionary(Cat,Arg1,X,Y),link(Cat,Goal),
      P=..[Cat,Goal,Arg1,Arg,Y,Z],call(P),
      assertz(wf_goal(Goal,Arg,X,Z)).
    goal(Goal,Arg,X,Z) :-
     ( wf_goal(Goal,_,X,_);
      assertz(fail_goal(Goal,X)) ),!,fail.

    dictionary(Cat,Arg,X,Y) :-
      wf_dict(_,_,X,_),!,wf_dict(Cat,Arg,X,Y).
    dictionary(Cat,Arg,[Word|X],Y) :-
     ( dict(Word,Cat,Arg,[Word|X],Y) ;
      morpheme(Cat,Arg,[Word|X],Y) ),
      assertz(wf_dict(Cat,Arg,[Word|X],Y)),
      fail.
    dictionary(Cat,Arg,X,Y) :-
      wf_dict(Cat,Arg,X,Y).
```

In the above clauses, 'wf_goal', 'fail_goal', and 'wf_dict' are predicates used for asserting partial information, which correspond to the partial successes, partial failures, and the successful dictionary entries. The predicate 'morpheme' performs the morphological analysis and returns the original form of the word and the information about the inflection.

3. Facilities of the System

This section describes two major facilities of the BUP system, the automatic segmentation and the idiom handler.

3.1 Combining Automatic Segmentation with Morphological Analysis

Preliminary analysis of Japanese sentences poses an especially difficult problem: the division of sentences into words. Although it seems better to segment input sentences beforehand, it is difficult even for a Japanese to segment a sentence correctly. We have combined the processes of automatic segmentation and morphological analysis. The segmentation algorithm isolates a word from the beginning of the input based on the longest successful matching. When the word has an inflection, the type of inflection and the suffix are examined using the following 'morpheme' predicate:

```
morpheme(Cat,N_Arg,[Bunso|Bun],Bun1) :-
    name(Bunso,B_List),
    reverse(B_List,B_List_R),
    wakachi(B_List_R,[],R_List,Word,Cat,Arg),
    gobi_shori(Word,Cat,Arg,R_List,Bun,N_Arg,Bun1).

wakachi([Char|W_List_R],Rest,[Char|Rest],Word,Cat,Arg) :-
    reverse(W_List_R,W_List),
    name(Word,W_List),
    dict(Word,Cat,Arg,[Word],[]).
wakachi([Char|W_List_R],Rest,[Char|Rest],Word,doshi,Arg) :-
    onbin_shori(W_List_R,Arg).
wakachi([Char|W_List_R],Rest,R_List,Word,Cat,Arg) :-
    wakachi(W_List_R,[Char|Rest],R_List,Word,Cat,Arg).
```

The predicate 'wakachi' takes one character from the given word and consults the dictionary. If the consultation fails, 'wakachi' then examines the possibility of euphonic changes (using the predicate, 'onbin_shori'), causing unusual formation of verb inflections. This process is executed repeatedly. Dictionary entries of inflectional words are indexed by their stems. Thus the inflectional analysis ('gobi_shori') is performed once a stem of a word has been isolated by 'wakachi'. Fig. 1 shows a sample analysis of a Japanese sentence. As is seen by the program, a partially segmented sentence is analyzed more efficiently than a sentence not segmented. A partially segmented input sentence, "tarou wa hanako wo siranakatta youda", takes a total of 938 msec. to execute.

3.2 Idiom Handling

Natural languages have many idiomatic expressions (idioms). By an idiom we mean a particular sequence of words and/or phrases, not necessarily consecutive, with a peculiar semantic interpretation. Although such a sequence may fit some of the grammar rules, we call it an idiom because of its peculiar interpretation. We choose not to represent idiomatic expressions using grammar rules, as the number of grammar rules directly affects the efficiency of the parsing system. Thus we construct an idiom dictionary, whose every element is invoked by a particular word. So, idioms are registered and referred to only by their head words. A typical idiom is expressed as follows (we

```
Input a sentence.
|: tarouwahanakowosiranakattayouda.
  (Tarou seemed not to know Hanako.)


937  msec.
No. 1
```

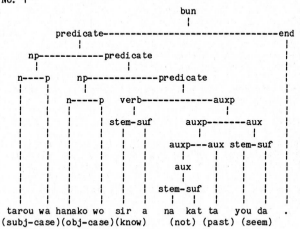

```
                                   bun
                                    |
              predicate----------------------------------end
                   |                                      |
        np-------------predicate                          |
        |                 |                               |
     n----p      np-------------predicate                 |
     |    |      |              |                         |
     |    |   n-----p    verb-------------auxp            |
     |    |   |     |      |               |              |
     |    |   |     | stem-suf      auxp-------aux        |
     |    |   |     |  |    |         |         |         |
     |    |   |     |  |    |     auxp---aux stem-suf     |
     |    |   |     |  |    |      |     |   |    |        |
     |    |   |     |  |    |     aux    |   |    |        |
     |    |   |     |  |    |      |     |   |    |        |
     |    |   |     |  |    |   stem-suf |   |    |        |
     |    |   |     |  |    |    |    |  |   |    |        |
     |    |   |     |  |    |    |    |  |   |    |        |
     tarou wa hanako wo  sir  a   na  kat ta  you da    .
    (subj-case)(obj-case)(know)   (not) (past) (seem)
```

```
Total Time = 1576  msec.

number of wfgoal was :      28.
number of failgoal was :    11.
number of wfdict was :      22.
```

Fig. 1   A Sample Analysis Tree of a Japanese Sentence

      (Words in parentheses are not the system output)

refer to this clause as an 'idiom clause'):

    idiom(word,category,receive_var,return_var) --> body.

The first argument, 'word', is the key word which invokes this idiom.
The morphological analysis ensures that even when idiomatic words in a
given sentence are inflected, the proper idiom clauses are identified.
The second argument, 'category', stands for the name of the grammar
category that the idiomatic expression belongs to. The third
argument, 'receive_var', represents the information of the key. The
fourth variable, 'return_var', gives the complete information for the
idiom when the call to the idiom clause has succeeded. All the idiom
clauses comprise the idiom dictionary.

We now show some kinds of idiomatic expressions and how they are
represented in the idiom dictionary.

(1) idioms made up of words only:

The body of such idiom clauses consists only of terminal symbols.
However, we provide a predicate 'word' to handle words that may be
inflected. Examples are:

a) idiom(as,postmod,_,[Syn,Sem,[postmod,'as well']]) -->
        [well].
b) idiom(computer,n,_,[Syn,Sem,[n,[n,computer],Tree]]) -->
        word(system,_,n,[Syn1,Sem1,Tree]).

The first example a) includes the non-inflected words, 'as' and
'well'. In the second example b), 'system' can appear in the plural
form. The first argument of the predicate 'word' is the base form of
the word and the third is the name of its grammar category. The
second is for returning the information of suffix, which is not used
here.

(2) idioms including phrases:

When an idiom includes not only simple words but some phrases, it
can use the 'goal' predicate and any Prolog predicate to indicate the
properties of the phrases.

a) idiom(by,adv,_,[Syn,Sem,[adv,[prep,by],Tree]]) -->
        goal(pron,[Syn1,Sem1,Tree]),
        { type_of(Syn1,reflexive) }.
b) idiom(look,v,Arg1,Arg) -->
        (goal(np,Arg2) ; []),[up],
        { look_up(Arg1,Arg2,Arg) }.

The first example treats a phrase consisting of 'by' followed by a
reflexive pronoun. The second example shows an idiom 'look up', that
can have a noun phrase between its components.

(3) idioms including phrases not belonging to specific categories

Let us consider the following example:

```
idiom(not,Goal,_,[Syn,Sem,[Goal,[not,not],[only,only],Tree1,
        [but,but],[also,also],Tree2]]) -->
    [only],
    goal(Goal,[Syn1,Sem1,Tree1]),[but,also],
    goal(Goal,[Syn2,Sem2,Tree2]).
```

Two phrases (indicated by 'goal') that appear in this example are not specified by a certain grammar category. Instead, this idiom clause indicates that they belong to the same grammar category (The variable 'Goal' ensures this property) as does the whole sequence.

If we choose to restrict these phrases to one of the grammar categories, noun phrase, adjective phrase or prepositional phrase, this clause may be rewritten as below:

```
idiom(not,Goal,_,[Syn,Sem,[Goal,[not,not],[only,only],Tree1,
        [but,but],[also,also],Tree2]]) -->
    [only],{ member(Goal,[np,adjp,pp]) },
    goal(Goal,[Syn1,Sem1,Tree1]),[but,also],
    goal(Goal,[Syn2,Sem2,Tree2]).
```

Partial success results can be saved during the idiomatic analysis to avoid repetitive computation as in the previous cases of dictionary look-up and morphological analysis. Failure to find idioms is noted to avoid useless repetition. These optimizing memorizations are taken into our system just like in the case of 'goal'. The predicate 'dictionary' is modified as follows:

```
dictionary(Cat,Arg,X,Y) :-
    wf_idiom(_,_,X,_),!,
        wf_idiom(Cat,Arg,X,Y);
    fail_idiom(X),!,
        word(_,_,Cat,Arg,X,Y).
dictionary(Cat,Arg,[Word|Y],Z) :-
    idiom(Word,Cat,_,Arg,Y,Z),
        assertz(wf_idiom(Cat,Arg,[Word|Y],Z)),
        fail;
    word(Rword,_,Cat1,Arg1,[Word|Y],_),
        Rword\==Word,
        idiom(Rword,Cat,Arg1,Arg,Y,Z),
        assertz(wf_idiom(Cat,Arg,[Word|Y],Z)),
        fail;
    wf_idiom(_,_,[Word|Y],_),!,
        wf_idiom(Cat,Arg,[Word|Y],Z);
    assertz(fail_idiom([Word|Y])),
        fail.
dictionary(Cat,Arg,[Word|Y],Y) :-
    wf_dict(Word,Cat,Arg,_,_).
```

This 'dictionary' predicate differs from the previous one (in Section 2) in that it refers to the idiom handling. Thus this new 'dictionary' uses a 'word' predicate that actually acts the same as the previous 'dictionary' predicate. (Note: 'word' has already appeared in the definition of idioms). 'Word' has two arguments in addition to the arguments of the previous 'dictionary'. These additional arguments, the first and the second, unifies with the original form and with the suffix of the first word of the current

|: He looks it up.

216 msec.
No. 1

|: He looks up the dictionary.

293 msec.
No. 1

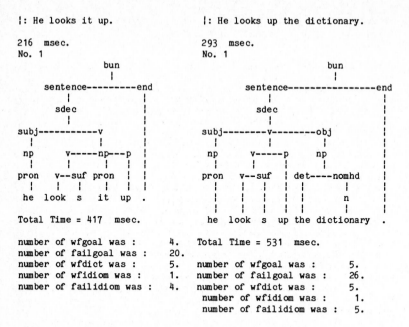

Total Time = 417 msec.

number of wfgoal was :   4.
number of failgoal was :   20.
number of wfdict was :   5.
number of wfidiom was :   1.
number of failidiom was :   4.

Total Time = 531 msec.

number of wfgoal was :   5.
number of failgoal was :   26.
number of wfdict was :   5.
number of wfidiom was :   1.
number of failidiom was :   5.

Fig. 2   Sample Parsing Trees

|: This algorithm is not only clear but also efficient.

634 msec.
No. 1

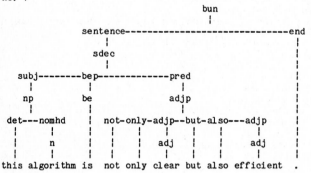

Total Time = 1017 msec.

number of wfgoal was :   12.
number of failgoal was :   30.
number of wfdict was :   11.
number of wfidiom was :   1.
number of failidiom was :   8.

Fig. 3   A Sample Parsing Tree

input (the first element of the list given as the value of the fifth argument).

Note that the last clause for 'dictionary' only calls 'wf_dict'. This is because 'word' in the second clause of 'dictionary' has already searched for every variation of the first word of the current input by backtracking, and all of them have already been asserted. Some sample analyses of idioms are shown in Figs. 2 and 3.

4. Discussions and Conclusions

We have presented some of the facilities of the BUP parsing system. This bottom-up parsing system is more powerful than top-down realization of DCGs in that it is as efficient as Earley's [6] and Pratt's [4] algorithms, and that it does not fall into infinite loops even when left-recursive rules are included. The facilities described here have been achieved by slight modifications to the auxiliary predicates, 'goal' and 'dictionary'. The majority of the programs and the basic parsing strategy can be used with widely differing grammatical structures. Thus the system is a highly versatile facility for parsing many different natural languages, most notably Japanese and English.

Weak points in the system are that empty production rules are prohibited, and that cycles of grammar rules (sets of grammar rules which make a self recursive loop) may cause an infinite loop. The problem of cycles, which we have not yet discussed, is actually a special case of left recursive rules. Cycles can be rewritten without greatly changing the size of grammar rules and thus without greatly affecting the efficiency.

Future research on syntactic problems will consider undefined words, ellipses, parenthetical expressions, and movements.

In languages such as English and other Indo-European languages, undefined words can be easily identified after morphological analysis, even though no dictionary entry occurs. However, in a language like Japanese, where sentences usually do not delineate words with spaces or other separators, the identification of undefined words is very troublesome. Even if a sentence includes an undefined word, a part of the word may be recognized as a different word because of a wrong segmentation. Although the identification of undefined words might be performed by an exhaustive search, we need more sophisticated methods for the identification so as not to lose the efficiency.

Pereira's analysis of extraposition grammars [7] is inspiring. Most of his idea on left extrapositions, a major problem in the phenomenon of movements, can be incorporated into the original BUP system. We hope to adjust the memorization feature of the revised version so as to implement left extraposition with this optimization.

Bottom-up strategies are better than top-down strategies for the problems of ellipses and parenthetical expressions (For a discussion of these problems, see [8]). We plan to attack such phenomena using the BUP system.

The entire system is implemented both in DEC-10 Prolog [9] ,[10] on DEC 2060 and in C-Prolog [11] on VAX-11/780. The execution time shown in the examples is the CPU time of the compiled version of DEC-10 Prolog on the DEC 2060. The interpreted versions on the DEC 2060 and VAX-11/780 require respectively about five times and seven times as much execution time as the compiled version on the DEC 2060.

Acknowledgments

The authors wish to express their thanks to Mr. Kazuhiro Fuchi, Director of the ICOT Research Center for his encouragement. We thank the members of Dr. Tanaka's Lab at the Tokyo Institute of Technology, the natural language processing group at ICOT Research Center, and the Machine Inference Section of ETL for their discussions and comments. Thanks are also due to Monica Strauss for her various comments on this manuscript.

References

[1] Matsumoto, Y., et al., BUP: A Bottom-Up Parser Embedded in Prolog, New Generation Computing, vol.1, no.2, pp.145-158, 1983.
[2] Pereira, F.C.N. and Warren, D.H.D., Definite Clause Grammar for Language Analysis--A Survey of the Formalism and a Comparison with Augmented Transition Networks, Artificial Intelligence, 13, pp.231-278, 1980.
[3] Matsumoto, Y., Kiyono, M. and Tanaka, H., BUP Translator (in Japanese), Bulletin of Electrotechnical Laboratory, vol.47, no.8, pp.67-85, 1983.
[4] Pratt, V.R., LINGOL--A Progress Report, Proc. of 4th IJCAI, pp.422-428, 1975.
[5] Tanaka, H., Sato, T. and Motoyoshi, H., Extended LINGOL --A Programming System for Natural Language Processing (in Japanese), IECE Japan, J60-D, Dec. 1977.
[6] Earley, J., An Efficient Context-Free Parsing Algorithm, C.ACM, 13, Feb. 1970.
[7] Pereira, F.C.N., Extraposition Grammars, AJCL, vol.7, no.4, pp.243-256, October-December, 1981.
[8] Hayes, P.J., Flexible Parsing, AJCL, vol.7, no.4, pp.232-242, October-December, 1981.
[9] Pereira, L.M., Pereira, F.C.N. and Warren, D.H.D., User's Guide to DECsystem-10 Prolog, Edinburgh, 1978.
[10] Bowen, D.L. (eds.), DECsystem-10 Prolog User's Manual, DAI Occasional Paper no.27, Edinburgh, 1982.
[11] Pereira, F., C-Prolog User's Manual version 1,2a, EdCAAD, Edinburgh, 1983.

Natural Language Understanding and Logic Programming
V. Dahl and P. Saint-Dizier (Editors)
© Elsevier Science Publishers B.V. (North-Holland), 1985

Object-Oriented Parser in the Logic Programming Language ESP

Hideo Miyoshi and Koichi Furukawa

Institute for New Generation Computer Technology(ICOT)
Mitakokusai Building, 21F
1-4-28, Mita, Minato-ku, Tokyo, 108, Japan

In this paper we propose an object-oriented parsing mechanism
for logic programming language ESP. In this object-oriented
parser, each program component is abstracted as a class, and access
between the two classes is performed by a message-passing
mechanism. Since grammatical categories are also abstracted as
classes, the intrinsic grammatical features which are implemented
as predicate arguments in DCG, are described as instances of
category classes. This helps to simplify Horn clause grammar rule
description. Being implemented in the logic programming language
ESP, the fundamental mechanism of DCG is also applicable to our
parser.

1. Introduction

The logic programming language Prolog is based on first-order predicate
logic and has features that are especially useful for symbol computation. DCG
(Definite Clause Grammar) [1], embedded in DECsystem-10 Prolog [2], is a good
formalism for analyzing a context-free language, and XG (Extraposition Grammar)
[3] and MG (Metamorphosis Grammar) [4] are good choice for analyzing a type-0
language. In DCG, each context-free grammar rule is represented as a Prolog
Horn clause , and each grammar category in a rule is treated as a predicate in
the clause. Therefore, the elements of a context-free grammar are translated,
one-to-one, into those of a Prolog program. Context-sensitive information can
be handled easily in arguments of Prolog predicates. Furthermore, Prolog
predicates can be arbitrarily inserted into grammar rules. These capabilities
facilitate the use of the parser in combination with such auxiliary routines as
semantic checking. Consequently, several systems for natural language
processing applications, (for example a database query system), have been
implemented in Prolog [3, 5, 6]. However, when a large-scale natural language
processing system is implemented using these formalisms, the number of grammar
rules, syntactic and semantic features, and constraints inevitably increase. If
all of these features and constraints are embedded in the grammar rule as the
arguments of a category or Prolog predicate call, the grammar rule will become
too complex. This will decrease the readability of the grammar and make
modifications difficult.

On the other hand, object-oriented methodology has recently begun to look
very attractive in this regard, and several object-oriented programming systems
have been developed, such as SIMULA [7], Smalltalk-80 [8], and Loops [9]. Since
the object-oriented notion of data abstraction provides the function of
information hiding and locality, the internal data structure is hidden from the
outside modules and only a specifically defined message can be used to access
the data [10]. These facilities provide the user with methods to develop
programs that are highly reliable and understandable, and can be easily
modified. So far, several natural language processing systems have been

developed using the object-oriented mechanism [11].

To remedy the defects of DCG or XG mentioned above, we propose an object-oriented parsing mechanism to be integrated into the logic programming language, and we have implemented an experimental small-scale parser. The main features of this parser are as follows:

(1) Implementation in ESP [12]

As described in section 2, ESP has two aspects: a logic programming language, and an object-oriented language. Therefore, basic methodologies that have already been established in the logic programming framework, such as DCG, can be used. We can also abstract the program components using the object-oriented mechanism. By doing this, the grammar rules can be simplified.

(2) Abstraction of Grammatical Categories

Each grammatical category (nonterminal symbol) is abstracted as a class. A category class has features representing intrinsic grammatical information of the category for example syntactic information. These features are implemented as the slots of a category class. While these features are implemented as the arguments of a category in DCG formalism, an instance which contains those features is embedded in the category as one argument in our program. The number of the arguments in the grammar rule can be reduced using this mechanism.

(3) Using Inheritance Mechanism

In order to define the slots of the grammatical categories which are in X-bar phrasal level [13], the inheritance mechanism is used. HFC(Head Feature Convention) in Generalized Phrase Structure Grammar (GPSG) [14] by Gazdar is easily implemented by this method.

Example.

$$S \longrightarrow VP \longrightarrow VERB$$
$$(\bar{\bar{V}}) \qquad (\bar{V}) \qquad (V)$$

Class 'VP' inherits class 'S'.
Class 'VERB' inherits class 'VP'.

An overview of the programming language ESP is given in section 2. In section 3, the object-oriented parsing mechanism and its implementation in ESP are presented.

2. Programming Language ESP

In this section, we give an overview of the programming language ESP. ESP is a logic programming language based on Prolog; it is intended for use on the Sequential Inference Machine (PSI) [15] currently being developed at the ICOT research center. The main features of ESP are as follows:

- Unification, as the basic parameter passing mechanism

- Backtracking, as the basic control structure

- Various built-in predicates

- Object-oriented calling mechanism

2.1 Object

An object in ESP represents an axiom set, and consists of a class object and an instance object. The axiom set to be used in a certain call can be specified by giving an object as the first argument of a call. An object may have slots, each of which has its own name and value.

2.2 Class and Inheritance

An object class, or simply a class, defines the characteristics common to a group of similar objects, i.e., objects that differ only in their slot values. An object belonging to a class is said to be an instance of that class. A class definition consists of nature definitions, slot definitions, and clause definitions. The nature definition defines the inheritance relationship between the classes. ESP provides a multiple inheritance mechanism like that of the Flavor system [16]. All class definitions whose names are given in the nature definition are inherited. The slot definition defines the slot used in the class. Clause definitions are used for defining Prolog-like clauses. The syntax of the class definition is shown in Figure 2.1.

```
<class definition> ::=
    "class" <class name>
        [ <macro bank declaration> ]
    "has"
        [ <nature definition> ";" ]
        { <class slot definition> ";" }
        { <class clause definition> ";" }
  [ "instance"
        { <instance slot definition> ";" }
        { <instance clause definition> ";" } ]
  [ "local"
        { <local clause definition> ";" } ]
    "end" "."
```

Figure 2.1 Syntax of the Class Definition in ESP

In Figure 2.1, "X" indicates a terminal symbol, X. { X } indicates an arbitrary number of appearances of X (including zero) . [X] indicates X or void, i.e., that X is optional. There are two kinds of slots definitions: one is for slots of the class itself, called class slots; the other is for slots of the class instance, called instance slots. This is also true of clause definitions. A local clause is a non-object-oriented local predicate used only in one class.

3. Implementation

In this section, we present the implementation of the object-oriented parser in ESP. The program components are described in 3.1. In 3.2 and 3.3, the examples of a simple program and a parsing result are given.

3.1 Program components

This program consists of the following five components.

(1) Set of Phrase Structure Rule Classes

Basically, the methods of analyzing the left-hand-side category of a context-free grammar rule are described in each phrase structure rule class. The method generates an instance of a category class during parsing. Some classes send messages for dictionary looking up to a dictionary class, or send messages for constraint checking to a constraint class.

(2) Dictionary Class
The dictionary looking up methods are described in this class. The methods also perform a feature instantiation to the instance of a lexical category class.

(3) Set of Category Classes
The slot definitions in each category class describe the intrinsic grammatical features of categories. The structure of a category feature is a two dimensional tree, as in GPSG.

(4) Set of Constraint Classes
The method for grammatical constraint checking is described in each constraint class. At present, HFC (Head Feature Convention) and CAP (Control Agreement Principle) in GPSG are implemented.

(5) Set of Feature Classes
The feature class defines the feature structure which will be instantiated to the slot of the instance of a category class.

The parsing model for this object-oriented parser is shown in Figure 3.1.

3.2 Example Program
An example of a program that analyzes a simple noun phrase based on this object-oriented parsing model is presented here.

(1) Set of Phrase Structure Rule Classes
Figure 3.2 shows the set of phrase structure rule classes. The method in the class 'np_rule' analyzes the phrase structure generated by the following rule:

$$NP \rightarrow DET \quad NOUN$$

The method calls ':head_of' and ':control' are the messages to the constraint classes 'hfc' and 'cap' respectively. The methods in the classes 'det_rule' and 'noun_rule' are used to consult a dictionary of determiners and nouns.

(2) Dictionary Class
Figure 3.3 shows the dictionary class. The class 'dict' has methods to look up the words 'these' and 'men'. The body part of the method performs the feature instantiation to the instance of a lexical category classes.

(3) Set of Category Classes and Set of Feature Classes
Figure 3.4 shows the class definition of grammatical category 'np', 'det', and 'noun'.
Figure 3.5 shows the class definition of the set of feature classes. The semantics of the class definition 'np' is as follows:
The instance of the class 'np' has a slot 'head', and its slot value is an instance of the feature class 'noun_head_feature' in Figure 3.5.

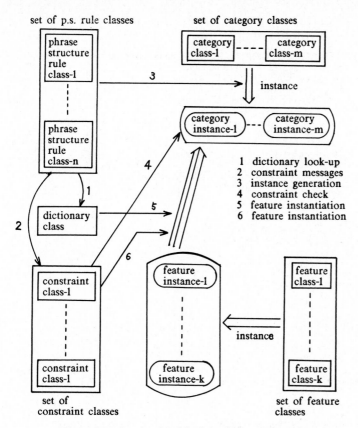

set of p.s. rule classes   set of category classes

1 dictionary look-up
2 constraint messages
3 instance generation
4 constraint check
5 feature instantiation
6 feature instantiation

set of
constraint classes

set of feature
classes

Figure 3.1   Parsing Model of the Object-Oriended Parser

The feature class 'noun_head_feature' has two slots, namely 'gender' and 'agreement'. The slot value of 'agreement' is an instance of the feature class 'noun_head_agreement_features'. The class 'noun_head_agreement_features' has a slot 'number'. By the mechanism mentioned above, the instance of the class 'np' can have a complex feature structure in its slot, as shown in Figure 3.6.

```
              gender
    head <
              agreement — number
```

Figure 3.6 Feature Structure of an Instance of a
            Class 'np'

By the same mechanism, the instance of the class 'det' has the following

```
%-------------------------------------------------
% np_rule class definition
class np_rule has
        :np(O, np(DETs, NOUNs), X0, X, NP) :- :new(# np, NP),
            :det(# det_rule, DETs, X0, X1, DET),
            :noun(# noun_rule, NOUNs, X1, X, NOUN),
            :head_of(# hfc, NOUN, NP),
            :control(#cap, NOUN, DET) ;
end.


%-------------------------------------------------
% det_rule class definition
class det_rule has
        :det(O, det(DETs), X0, X, DET) :- :new(# det, DET),
            :dict(# dict, DETs, X0, X, DET)
end.


%-------------------------------------------------
% noun_rule class definition
class noun_rule has
        :noun(O, noun(NOUNs), X0, X, NOUN) :- :new(# noun, NOUN),
            :dict(# dict, NOUNs, X0, X, NOUN) ;
end.
```

Figure 3.2 Set of Phrase Structure Rule Classes

```
%-------------------------------------------------
% dictionary class definition
class dict has
        :dict(D, these, [these|X], X, DET) :-
            DET!head!agreement!number := plural ;
        :dict(D, men, [men|X], X, NOUN) :-
            NOUN!head!agreement!number := plural,
            NOUN!head!gender := male ;
end.
```

Figure 3.3 Dictionary Class

```
%---------------------------------------------
% category class
% np class definition
class np has
instance
     attribute
        head is noun_head_features;
end.
%---------------------------------------------
% category class
% det class definition
class det has
instance
     attribute
        head is det_head_features;
end.
%---------------------------------------------
% category class
% noun class definition
class noun has
        nature
           np;
end.
```

Figure 3.4 Set of Category Classes

```
%---------------------------------------------
% feature class
% noun_head_feature class definition
class noun_head_features has
instance
   attribute
      gender,
      agreement is noun_head_agreement_features;
end.
%---------------------------------------------
% feature class
% noun_head_agreement_features class definition
class noun_head_agreement_features has
instance
   attribute
      number;
end.
%---------------------------------------------
% feature class
% det_head_features class definition
class det_head_features has
instance
   attribute
      agreement is det_head_agreement_features;
end.
%---------------------------------------------
% feature class
% det_head_agreement_features class definition
class det_head_agreement_features has
instance
   attribute
      number;
end.
```

Figure 3.5 Set of Feature Classes

feature structure (Figure 3.7):

head — agreement — number

Figure 3.7 Feature Structure of an Instance of a
Class 'det'

By the nature definition 'nature np;' in the class definition of the category 'noun', the class definition of the 'np' is inherited to the class 'noun'. Therefore, an instance of the class 'noun' has the same feature structure as the instance of the class 'np'.

(4) Set of Constraint Classes

Figure 3.8 shows the constraint classes used in this program. The class 'hfc' is an implementation of Head Feature Convention (HFC), which is the terminology used in GPSG, such that mother and head in a context free grammar rule carry the same feature. The class 'cap' is an implementation of the GPSG Control Agreement Principle (CAP) in GPSG. CAP is a relation holding between sisters in a rule, such that, if A controls B, then the agreement feature of A is the same as that of B. Figure 3.9 shows an illustrative example of HFC and CAP [13].

In Figure 3.9, an arrow indicates the control relation, and a bold line indicates the HFC.

3.3 Parsing Mechanism

In this section, we show the parsing mechanism by the example program presented in section 3.2. The program parses the input noun phrase 'these men'. The top level goal is given by

':- :np(#np_rule,N_St,[these,men],[],NP).'.

The parsing is performed in the following steps.

STEP 1.

The instance of a class 'np' is generated by the goal ':new(#np, NP)', and assigned to NP. The value of leaves of feature 'head' are not assigned yet(Figure 3.10 (a)).

STEP 2.

The instance of a class 'det' is generated, and assigned to DET. Then, the dictionary for det is consulted and the value of head feature of DET is assigned 'plural'(Figure 3.10 (b)).

STEP 3.

The instance of a class 'noun' is generated, and assigned to NOUN. By the nature definition, NOUN has the same feature structure as NP. By the method in the dictionary class, the head feature of NOUN is assigned, 'male' for gender and 'plural' for number(Figure 3.10 (c)).

STEP 4.

The method in the class 'np' calls the constraint class 'hfc' and 'cap'. In the class 'hfc', slot value of NOUN is assigned to NP. The constraint class 'cap' checks the equality of agreement feature between DET and NOUN(Figure 3.10 (d)).

The term which indicates the phrase structure (Figure 3.11) is instantiated

```
%---------------------------------------------
% HFC class definition
% Head Feature Convention
%    If A is the head of B then HEAD(A) = HEAD(B)
class hfc has
       :head_of(HFC, HEAD, PARENT) :-
           PARENT!head := HEAD!head ;
end.


%---------------------------------------------
% CAP class definition
% Control Agreement Principle
%    If A controls B then AGR(A) = AGR(B)
class cap has
       :control(CAP, CONTROLLER, CONTROLLEE) :-
       agr_equal(CONTROLLER!head!agreement,
                 CONTROLLEE!head!agreement) ;
local
       agr_equal(A, B) :-
          A!number == B!number ;
       agr_equal(A, B) :-
          A!number == void ;
       agr_equal(A, B) :-
          B!number == void ;
end.
```

Figure 3.8 Set of Constraint Classes

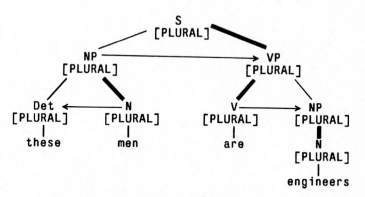

Figure 3.9 An Example of HFC and CAP

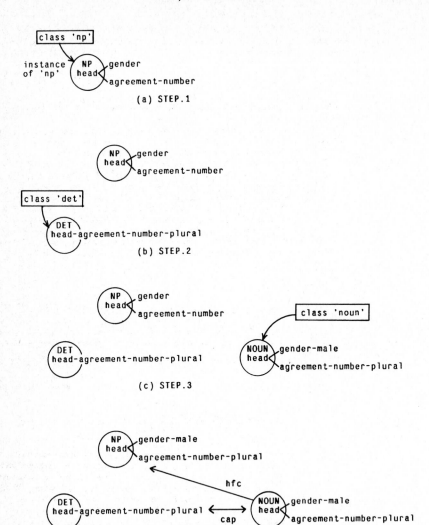

Figure 3.10   Parsing Step

to the second argument of ':np', and the instance of 'np' that has the feature structure shown in Figure 3.12 is instantiated to the fifth argument of ':np'.

```
├np
  ├det
  |  ├these
  ├noun
     ├men
```

Figure 3.11 Phrase Structure
of 'these men'

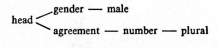

Figure 3.12 Feature Structure of
the Instance of 'np'

4. Summary

The object-oriented parsing mechanism and its implementation in the logic programming language ESP was presented. Each program component, as well as grammatical categories, are abstracted as class objects. Access between program components is performed by a message-passing mechanism. The abstraction of grammatical categories helps to reduce the number of arguments in a rule, and enables the user to update category features without changing the grammar rules. The inheritance mechanism is used to fix the features of a category class. This framework is thought to be suitable for implementing a complex feature system such as GPSG.

Acknowledgements

The authors are thankful to H. Yasukawa of ICOT for his helpful discussions. The authors would also like to thank to Dr. G. Gazdar of Univ. of Sussex and Dr. T. Gunji of Osaka Univ. for their helpful comments on GPSG, and Dr. T. Chikayama of ICOT for his useful comments on ESP. The authors are grateful to the Dr. K. Fuchi, Director of the ICOT Research Center, for providing the opportunity to conduct this research.

[References]

[1] Pereira, F. and Warren, D.; Definite Clause Grammar for Language Analysis - A Survey of the Formalism and a Comparison with Augmented Transition Networks, Artificial Intelligence, 13 (1980) 231-278.

[2] Pereira, L. and Pereira, F. and Warren, D.; User's Guide to DECsystem-10 Prolog, Dev. de Informatica, LNEC, Lisbon and Dept. of AI, University of Edinburgh (September 1978).

[3] Pereira, F.; Logic for Natural Language Analysis, Technical Note 275, SRI International (January 1983).

[4] Colmerauer, A.; Metamorphosis Grammars, Natural Language Communication with Computers, Bolc, L.(ed.) (Springer-Verlag, 1978).

[5] Dahl, V.; On Database Systems Development through Logic, ACM Transactions on Database Systems, Vol.7, No.1 (March 1982) 102-123.

[6] McCord, M. C.; Using Slots and Modifiers in Logic Grammars for Natural Language, Artificial Intelligence, 18 (1982) 327-367.

[7] Nygaard, K. and Dahl, O. J.; The Development of the SIMULA Languages, ACM SIGPLAN Notices, Vol.13, No.8 (August 1978) 245-272.

[8] Goldberg, A. and Robson, D.; Smalltalk-80: The Language and its Implementation (Addison-Wesley Publishing Company, 1983).

[9] Bobrow, D. G. and Stefik, M.; The LOOPS Manual (Preliminary Version), XEROX PARC Knowledge-based VLSI Design Group Memo, KB-VLST-81-13, (1983).

[10] Sado, K. and Yonezawa, A.; A Tutorial on Abstract Data Type Oriented Languages (in Japanese), Journal of Information Processing, Vol.22, No.6 (June 1981).

[11] Phillips, B.; An Object-Oriented Parser for Text Understanding, Proceedings of the Eighth International Joint Conference on Artificial Intelligence (1983) 690-692.

[12] Chikayama, T.; ESP Reference Manual, ICOT Research Center Technical Report, No.44 (February 1984).

[13] Jackendoff, R.; Introduction to the X-bar Convention, Indiana University Linguistics Club (October 1974).

[14] Gazdar, G. and Pullum, G. K.; Generalized Phrase Structure Grammar: A Theoretical Synopsis, Indiana University Linguistics Club (August 1982).

[15] Nishikawa, H., Yokota, M., Yamamoto, A., Taki, K., and Uchida, S.; The Personal Inference Machine(PSI): Its Design Philosophy and Machine Architecture, ICOT Research Center Technical Report No.13 (June 1983).

[16] Weinreb, D. and Moon, D; Lisp Machine Manual, 4th ed., Symbolics, Inc. (1981).

Natural Language Understanding and Logic Programming
V. Dahl and P. Saint-Dizier (Editors)
© Elsevier Science Publishers B.V. (North-Holland), 1985

NOUN PHRASES IN LEXICAL FUNCTIONAL GRAMMAR

Werner Frey

Institut fuer Linguistik/Romanistik
Universitaet Stuttgart
Stuttgart, West Germany

This paper contains LFG-rules to handle some simple and complex noun phrases. The analysis of simple and partitive noun phrases is compared with the one given by Jackendoff who uses the framework of X-bar theory. The analysis of comparative constructions like the one in
´As many of the girls as Peter thinks that he loves love John´
is compared with the one given by Gazdar who showed for the first time that it is possible to give a nontransformational treatment of the long distance binding involved in such a noun phrase.
The underlying goals of this paper are (1) to show that LFG constitutes a supportive tool for formulating grammatical insights and for keeping tabs on the interaction of the various rules which are proposed, and (2) to indicate that the f-Structure, which is the crucial level of representation in LFG, is the right starting point for formulating rules for constructing a full semantic representation of the input.

INTRODUCTION

It is commonly accepted that noun phrases play a very important role in natural language. However the amount of linguistic literature on the internal structure of NPs is surprisingly small. The reason is that linguistic syntax was guided by the transformational framework for a long time and only few of the transformations seems to be relevant for this micro structure. The background has changed since Lexical-Functional Grammar (LFG) [14] and Generalized Phrase Structure Grammar (GPSG) [10] have shown how to describe without the use of transformations different complex phenomena which were previously thought to require such a powerful formalism. On the other hand the formal semantics of natural language is concerned to a large extend with noun phrases. Stemming from the work of Barwise/Cooper [1] a large number of investigations on the semantics of NPs have been conducted under the header "generalized quantifier". Kamp´s Discourse Representation Theory [12] [13] can be seen to be up to now mainly a theory on the semantics of tense and of determiners. Both approaches use a rather simple syntactic base. Therefore I think it is worthwile to study the syntax of NPs using a powerful yet nontransformational formalism like LFG.
Although the above remarks could possibly be enough motivation for a linguist, some additional comments are in order for an audience of logic programmers.
Sometimes one hears statements which seem to indicate that there is a sharp distinction between logic programmers and computer linguists who are guided by a linguistic theory, the former being free in formulating appropriate rules to cover the data of natural language, the latter being hampered by a strict formalism which complicates everything. This opinion is based on the idea that the freer the formalism, the easier it is to formulate rules to describe the data. Finding a formalism which is not more powerful than necessary is an

important area of research in its own right.

Also it is well-known that for efficient parsing a tractable number of context-free phrase structure rules should be used. But also, an appropriate (and restricted) formalism can help to find the right generalizations. To quote Bresnan on this topic "If the formal theory contains the appropriate concepts and representations, then linguistic principles and grammatical descriptions expressed within it will immediately generalize along the right dimensions, simplifying both descriptive rules and theoretical postulates. An inappropriate formal theory will require a host of auxiliary concepts and definitions, and may obscure the underlying regularities that optimal grammars must express. " ([3], p.282)

Furthermore it is obvious that a transparent formalism for writing the grammar rules is necessary to keep control and clarity when the grammar becomes larger. Such a formalism also offers a universal framework for expressing and communicating linguistic principles. It is therefore no accident that Pereira [16] and Dahl [5], although two logic programmers, decided to design a metagrammar in which the rules are first formulated and then compiled or interpreted to get a PROLOG program. It is important to note that these metagrammars are in fact based on a specific linguistic theory of the natural language constructions in question. Therefore, we should, I believe, not compare e.g. LFG systems with definite clause grammar programs; rather we should compare LFG with Pereira's Extraposition Grammar, and we should do it with linguistic argumentation.

Just as it is possible to write a compiler for Extraposition Grammar, it is possible to write a compiler for LFG. The latter was done at our institute (see [6]). The syntax rules which are formulated below were compiled into a PROLOG program with this compiler, which is written in PROLOG II.

Chapter 0 will give a brief introduction to LFG. Chapter 1 is concerned with simple NPs, chapter 2 with partitive, pseudopartitive, and noun complement constructions Chapter 3 deals primarily with comparative deletion and comparative subdeletion.

0. Lexical Functional Grammar

LFG provides each sentence with two descriptions, a description of constituent structure (c-structure) and a description of functional structure (f-structure). C-structures are generated in the usual way by context-free phrase structure rules (PSRs). F-structures , which are the interface between c-structure and semantic interpretation, are constructed using functional information associated with PSRs and with lexical entries.

An example for a PSR annotated with functional equations is : [1]

(i)   S -->   NP   (^SUBJ) = v
                     VP   ^ = v

The equations here convey that the NP is the subject of its mother, S, and that all the information about the VP is also information about the S in the functional structure. To be more precise: f-structures are functions which associate to an attribute a value, which may itself be an f-structure. The first equation expresses that the function F1 corresponding to the S-node has for the attribute SUBJ a value which is the f-structure built up beneath the NP-node. The second one says that further attribute-value pairs of F1 will be found beneath VP, or in other words, the function corresponding to the VP-node is F1.

To see how the relevant aspects of the system work , let us consider the syntax and lexical representation of:

(A) This girl likes this cat

The lexical entries for the words of the sentence will contain the following equations:

```
likes: V,   (^PRED)='LIKE<(SUBJ)(OBJ)>'      girl: N,   (^PRED)='GIRL'
            (^SUBJ AGR NUM)=SG                           (^AGR NUM)=SG
            (^SUBJ AGR PERS)=3                           (^AGR PERS)=3
            (^TENSE)=PRESENT

cat:   N,   (^PRED)='CAT'                     this: DET, (^SPEC)=THIS
            (^AGR NUM)=SG                                (^AGR NUM)=SG
            (^AGR PERS)=3
```

The value of the 'PRED' of 'likes' is called a semantic form. This semantic form subcategorizes the grammatical functions SUBJ and OBJ. In addition to (i) the relevant rules are: [2)]

```
(ii)   VP  -->   V        ^ = v
                 NP       (^OBJ) = v


(iii)  NP  -->   DET      ^ = v
                 N        ^ = v
```

First, these rules generate the usual c-structure for (A). Then the c-structure is indexed. The next step is the instantiation of the functional equation schemata with the indices of the tree. The instantiation is done as follows: $\hat{\ }$ appearing in an equation attached to a node Xi refers to the mother node of Xi. 'v' appearing in the same equation refers to Xi itself. The instantiation procedure yields a series of equations whose solution is the f-structure. By following the steps just mentioned the following f-structure is induced for sentence (A):

```
| SUBJ        | PRED       'GIRL'    | |
|             | SPEC        THIS     | |
|             | AGR   | NUM  SG |    | |
|             |       | PERS 3  |    | |
|             |                      |
| PRED        'LIKE<(SUBJ)(OBJ)>'    |
|             |                      |
| TENSE       PRESENT                |
|             |                      |
| OBJ         | PRED       'CAT'     | |
|             | SPEC        THIS     | |
|             | ARG   | NUM  SG |    | |
|             |       | PERS 3  |    | |
```

This f-structure is to be read as having pointers from the f-structures subcategorized by the semantic form to the argument position of this semantic form.

The f-structure satisfies all the equations derivable from (i)-(iii) and the lexical entries; furthermore it fulfils certain conditions which are imposed on f-structures to be well-formed. The two most important conditions on f-structures are:

(a) Every grammatical function subcategorized by the semantic form must appear in the f-structure.

(b) Every subcategorizable grammatical function contained in the f-structure must be subcategorized by a semantic form.

It should be noted that LFG provides another description tool not appearing in the example above. It is possible to expand rule (i) with a constraint like:

```
        VP       ^ = v
                 (^TENSE)
```

An instatiation of such a constraint is satisfied just in case the expression has some value in the final f-structure. The TENSE schema thus expresses the requirement that S-clauses must have tensed verbs.

In LFG, syntactic binding or constituent control is effected through the instantiation of another set of equations, the linking equations. These employ the new variables => and <=, whose use is illustrated in (iv):

(iv) S´ --> NP (^FOC) = v
v = (S => NP)

S ^ = v

NP --> e ^ = (<= NP)

The binding effected by the (=>) and (<=)metavariables is not strictly local, as is the binding effected by ^ and v. If no further constraints are imposed, the presence of a => (the so-called controller) indicates that the index at the node carrying the => must be set equal to the index at a node carrying a <= (the so-called controllee) somewhere in the domain c-commanded by the node carrying the =>. An expression of the form (R => C) is to be read as follows: R is the root node of the domain in which the controllee is to be found and C is the category (plus features) of the controllee.

Consider the topicalized version of sentence (B)

(B) This cat this girl likes ___.

With (iv) we get the following c-structure for (B)

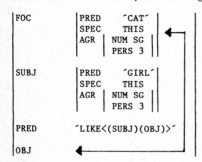

The "long-distance metavariables" => and <= get instantiated with the same actual variables. This, and solving the equations yields:

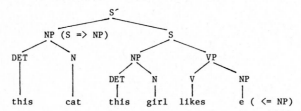

The arrow indicates that the FOC and OBJ functions have as their value the same f-structure.

As discussed in [14] the domain in which the instantiation of metavariables can occur must be constrained. A first constraint was already noted: the controller (to be more precise: the node which the controller is attached to) must c-command the controllee. The island constraints with respect to c-control

[17] are expressed by so-called ´bounding nodes´. These are the root nodes of
the islands and they are ´boxed´ in the Kaplan/Bresnan notation.
For example one has to prevent ´moving´ an NP out of a relative clause.   (This
is an instance of a complex NP constraint.) Thus, for the sentence

(C) I know the man who adores this woman

the topicalized version is ungrammatical

(D) * This woman I know the man who adores ___.

This is reflected in LFG by the following rule for relative clauses

(v)   NP   -->   NP   ^ = v
                     bounding S´   (^R-ADJ) = v

In order for ´this woman´ to be associated with the gap in (D) the c-control
path would have to cross the bounding S´ node of (v). This is forbidden by
Kaplan/Bresnan´s Bounding Convention, and (D) is therefore rejected   as
ungrammatical.
If one assumes that in English all S nodes are bounding nodes (´boxed´), then
the Bounding Convention would also block the derivation of the grammatical
sentence

(E)   This woman I don´t believe that Harold likes ___.

The effect of the box can be circumvented by means of the linking equation
(=>)= (<=), which links two distinct c-control domains. Thus we have the
following rule which gives the right treatment for (E)

(vi)   S´   -->   that
                   bounding S   ^ = v
                                (<=) = (S =>)

1. Simple Noun Phrases

The syntax for simple NPs has to account for -among others- the following facts:

(1) some books, *the some books, the many books, *some/many his books, *many
    three books, John´s three books

Jackendoff [11] offers the following analysis:

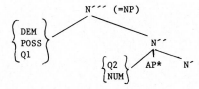

The categories expand as follows:

DEM: demonstrative pronouns, interrogative pronouns, ´the´, (possibly)´a´,
        ´some´(singular)
POSS: possessives
Q1:   ´each´, ´all´, ´no´, ´every´,...
Q2:   ´many´, ´few´, ´several´, ´much´, ´little´
NUM: numerals, a few, a little, a dozen

To block undesired results, Jackendoff proposes the following constraint: An NP specifier may contain at most one demonstrative, one quantifier, and one numeral. Jackendoff calls it "a highly plausible constraint". But no motivation is given other than to block Q1 Q2 combinations (eg. *all many). Its plausibility is questionable in that it suggests that some NP specifier could be completely filled, i.e. contain a demonstrative, a quantifier, and a numeral. None can.

In order to avoid such a constraint I will allow different phrase structure rules for NPs. Furthermore I will slightly diverge from two other features of Jackendoff's analysis. Because I am not committed to his strong version of X-syntax theory it is possible to introduce a category dominating DEM and POSS which I call RP, thereby avoiding Jackendoff's partitive constraint (see below). Second, Jackendoff did not consider that the elements of his category Q2 share certain structural properties with adjectives:

(2) The problems with this approach are many/*some

(3) These are as difficult/many/*some problems as you'll ever encounter

(The sentences are taken from [15])
I do not want to go as far as Klein who analyzes 'many, few, much, little' as ordinary adjectives differentiated from the others only by the feature 'quant'. The reason is the word order: 'many' has to precede the ordinary adjectives. Therefore, I will use the category QP, introduced by Bresnan [2] and dispensed with by Klein, to analyze the elements of Jackendoff's second quantifier group. Crucial is that the elements of Q will behave like ordinary adjectives when we come to semantics. Adjectives map individuals into truth valences. The elements of Q map sets of individuals into truth valences. 'Many' will be true of a set just in case the set has many members. For simple NPs we have the following three structures:

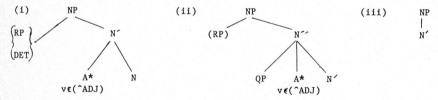

DET is Jackendoff's Q1, R contains: the, this, that ,his, John's, NPposs,... (In the terminology of the 'generalized quantifier' approach the R's are not quantifiers in the mormal sense; rather they function to restrict the host set o '. 'These books' takes the set of books and then restricts this set to just the intersection of indicated things and books. 'John's books' names the set of books down to just those which stand in some relation to John. In terms of Kamp's Discourse Representation Theory, the elements of R give rise to picking up an already introduced discourse referent.)

The trivial equation is attached to every node of the structures besides to the adjective A. This means that a feature specification introduced by an item has to be unified by the specialization introduced by some other item. Note that the phrases in (1) are correctly generated.

We are rather liberal in allowing categories. For example, QP and RP expand into the genuine specifier and an optional modifier preceeding it. For example the phrase 'all the women' has the structure

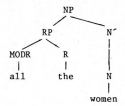

There is some evidence in German (and stronger in Dutch) for considering the ´all´ of ´all the women´ to be a distinct lexical item from that of ´all women´: ´alle Frauen´, ´*alle die Frauen", ´all die Frauen´.
Heavy use is made of the feature ´definiteness´. This feature is helpful for generating only the well-formed DEG Q co-occurrences; e.g. ´too many´, ´*exactly many´, ´exactly three´. This is achieved by associating e.g. ´DEF = - ´with ´too´, and ´DEF = +´ with ´exactly´.
The interrogatives ´which´ and ´what´ are analyzed as elements of DET, differentiated from the others by the feature marking them as question words. However, some problems remain with the interrogatives. We do not account for the fact that they can occur with NUMs; and by the discussion of the partitives below we can not block ´* what of the books?´.
It is well known that there are dependencies between an NP specifier and its head being a count or mass noun. Because of the fact that every category appearing in the rules introduced up to now has attached the trivial equation, we can account for the regularities by assigning the feature ´count´ in the usual manner, e.g.: the lexical entry of ´much´ includes ´COUNT = -´ just like the noun ´soup´, the entry of ´few´ includes ´COUNT = +´, just like the noun ´book´. The entries of ´the´, ´no´, ´any´, ´all´ are unspecified for this feature.
The structures offered up to now prohibit the following ungrammatical phrases, (but are not able to produce the grammatical ones) for the following data:

(4) $\begin{Bmatrix} each \\ no \\ some \end{Bmatrix}$ $\begin{Bmatrix} three \\ *many \\ *several \\ *few \end{Bmatrix}$ books

I will treat ´each three books´ as an instance of the noun complement constructions for which a structure will be proposed below.
Structure (iii) is for the generation of bare plurals. Carlson [4] argues convincingly that it is incorrect to treat bare plurals as having a null determiner O which is simply the plural form of ´a´. The semantic treatment that he sketches treats bare plurals as similiar to proper nouns. To reflect in the syntax the parallelism that Carlson sees in the semantics, we simply allow the rule NP -> N as a category and type-altering rule.

Rules for simple NPs:

(I)   NP   ->   N´   ^ = v
                                 (^AGR NUM) = PL.

(II)   NP   ->   (RP   ^ = v)
                     N´´   ^ = v

(III)   NP   ->   { RP   ^ = v }
                     { DETP   ^ = v }
                       N´   ^ = v

(IV)   N´´   ->   QP   ^ = v

some lexical entries:

N,   man: (^COUNT)= +   MR   men: (^COUNT)= +
             (^AGR NUM) = SG   ==>   (^AGR NUM)= PL
             (^PRED)= ´MAN´   (^PRED)= ´MAN´

      people:(^COUNT)= +
             (^AGR NUM)= PL
             (^PRED) = ´PEOPLE´

      wine: (^COUNT)= −   Redundancy Rule:
             (^PRED) = ´WINE´   (^COUNT)= − => (^AGR NUM)= SG

R,   these: (^AGR NUM)= PL
             (^R) = +
             (^DEM) = THIS

DET, every: (^COUNT)= +   all: (^COUNT)= +
             (^AGR NUM)= SG   (^AGR NUM)= PL
             (^DET) = ´EVERY´   (^DET)= ´ALL´

      both: (^COUNT)= +   no: (^DET)= NO
             (^AGR NUM)= PL
             (^DET)= ´BOTH´

Q,   much: (^COUNT)= −   three: (^COUNT)= +
             (^DEF) = −   (^AGR NUM) = PL
             (^QUANT)= ´MUCH´   (^DEF) = +
                                                (^QUANT)= ´THREE´

      many: (^COUNT)= +
             (^AGR NUM)= PL
             (^DEF)= −
             (^QUANT)= ´MANY´

2. Partitives, pseudopartives, and noun complements

In transformational grammar the same deep structure is constructed for ´many girls´ and ´many of the girls´. As Selkirk [18] points out this is not correct:

The partitives allow a mass, this means non-count, specifier phrase to co-occur with a lower noun phrase containing a singular count noun, for example:

(5) She doesn´t believe much of that story

(6) *She doesn´t believe much story

In simple noun phrases all specifier elements are required to agree with the head noun in their specification of syntactic features. In partitives this condition on agreement is inapplicable and ´much of that story´ is therefore possible. Compare also ´one of the girls´ where we have singular and plural co-occuring.
Therefore we have to introduce a grammatical function (I call it SELS) which forbids the percolation of the features of the embedded NP. This function is not subcategorizable; this means it is never mentioned in semantic forms of lexical items.

Rules for partives

```
(V)    NP  ->      DET          ^ = v
                   QP           ^ = v

                   NP´          (^SELS) = v

(VI)  NP´ ->       of
                   bounding NP  ^ = v
                                (v R)
```

With this structural difference between ´many girls´ and ´many of the girls´ we can account for the behavior of extraposition from the NP in its application to these different phrase types. Consider:

(7) How many of the answers to this classical problem have been found?

(8) How many answers to this classical problem have been found?

However:

(9) *How many of the answers have been found to this problem?

(10) How many answers have been found to this problem?

The NP nodes under NP´ constitute an island. Therefore we have to prevent any movement out of it.   This explains why the NP of the NP´ rule is a bounding node.
The constraint that a R is present in the lower noun phrase is designed to capture the ungrammaticality of

(11) *three of some girls

(12) *two of too many books (vs. two of her many books)

(13) *nine of many of the girls (vs. nine of the many girls)

This constraint corresponds to Jackendoff´s Partitive Constraint.   However Jackendoff´s constraint is a semantic filtering rule. His formalism does not make it possible to state it as such a simple syntactic restriction as we can. (Of course the necessity of a R in the partitive NP should be explained on semantic grounds, but Jackendoff does not do that either.)
Note that: In partitive noun phrases relative clauses may ´modify´ both the lower and upper phrase. For example:

(14) That one of the girls that were arrested together who is willing to talk...

If we assign to nonrestricted relative clauses a source immediately under the NP node, it follows that the structure we have assigned to partitives can have two relative clauses.

In the partitives above the ´higher´ specifier (in the c-structure) governs the form of the verb if the NP is in subject position. Therefore the trivial equation is attached to this specifier. However the situation is different with measure nouns occurring in partitives. Consider

(15) A bunch of those flowers were/ was thrown out on the back lawn

(The example is from [18]) According to the form of the verb, sentence (15) contains a partitive or a noun complement construction. If the verb is plural, the subject is a partive NP; if the verb is singular we have a noun complement

construction.   This means that in such partives the embedded NP is the head of
the construction. To get a structure similiar to the one above but with another
head we use the rule

(VII)   NP ->   bounding NP ($^{\wedge}$QUANT) = v
                                (vMEAS) =c +

                NP$^{\wedge}$ ($^{\wedge}$SELS) = v
                                ($^{\wedge}$AGR) = (vAGR)

($^{\wedge}$(vMEAS) =c +$^{\wedge}$ requires a measure noun to be the head of the NP.)
Before we come to noun complements we should consider pseudopartitives like $^{\wedge}$a
number of books$^{\wedge}$.   Selkirk [18] argues convincingly that a construction like
this one has a different structure from real partitives. The main evidence is
provided by extraposition.

(16) He gave a rather large number of his/0 books to Mary.

(17) He gave a rather large number to Mary of his/*0 books.

The pseudoparitive gets a structure in analogy to the ones for simple NPs.

(VIII) N$^{\wedge}$ -> bounding NP   ($^{\wedge}$QUANT) = v
                                     not($^{\wedge}$R)
                 of
                 N $^{\wedge}$ = v
                                     (vAGR NUM) = PL

With the rules (VII), (VIII) we account for (17) because there is no
extraposition of a N node.

To propose rules for noun complements first consider the following examples:

(18) Kim gave a book only to Sandy

(19) Kim gave a book to only Sandy

The synonymity of these two sentences indicates that the PP has the same meaning
as the dominant NP, ie. the only function of the preposition is to indicate the
position of the NP in the argument list of the verb.   This leads to the
following rule:

(IX)   PP -> P $^{\wedge}$ = v
              NP $^{\wedge}$ = v
(here P is the minor category, NP being the head)

        to: P, ($^{\wedge}$PCASE) = TO-OBJ

The analogous situation appears in

(20) the destruction of the city by the barbarians

Here, too, the prepositions do not contribute anything to semantics, they only
serve for the assignment to the predicate-argument structure. This can be
proved by the impossibility of formulating the relative clause:

(21) *the destruction which is of the city

We assign to the noun $^{\wedge}$destruction$^{\wedge}$ a semantic form which corresponds directly
to the semantic form of the verb $^{\wedge}$destroy$^{\wedge}$, i.e.

N, destruction: (^PRED) = ´DESTRUCTION <(BY-OBJ)(OF-OBJ)>´

We need the additional rule:

(X)   N´   ->   N   ^ = v
                      PP*   (^(vPCASE)) = v

We get the following f-structure for the NP under discussion (details ommitted)

```
| PRED     ´DESTRUCTION<(BY-OBJ)(OF-OBJ)>´  |
|                                           |
| BY-OBJ | PRED  ´BARBARIAN´ |              |
|                                           |
| OF-OBJ | PRED  ´CITY´ |                   |
```

If we want to analyze the subject of

(22) a group of students is outside the door´

in the same way we need the following lexical entry for ´group´

N, group: (^PRED) = ´GROUP<(OF-OBJ)>´
          (^AGR NUM) = SG

(the entry for ´group´ appearing in partitives looks like:

N, group: (^PRED) = ´GROUP´
          (^MEAS) =c +
          (^AGR NUM) = SG   )

Note that by the rule (X) for noun complements, N is the head of the construction. This explains the singular form of the verb in (22). The different rules (VII) and (VIII) correspond to the different semantics of measure noun partitive and measure noun complement constructions.

It remains to account for the grammatical phrase of (4) above. The semantic of the sentence and the singular form of the verb in

(23) every three weeks with you is like heaven

indicates that ´every three weeks´ is similar to the complement constructions with measure nouns above.
To mirror this I will treat ´three´ in addition to its status as QUANT as a noun. Note that its number as a noun is singular. It constitutes the head of the construction. I propose the rule and the lexical entry:

(XI)   N´ -> N   v = ^
                        (vNUMB) =c +
                N´   (^ARG) = v

        N, three: (^PRED) = ´THREE<(ARG)>´
                     (^AGR NUM) = SG
                     (^NUMB) = +

To finish this chapter I would like to treat another type of a PP construction. Consider the NP

(24) The books on the rack.

Here it is possible to use a relative clause construction

(25) The books which are on the rack

The preposition ´on´ is similar to a verb whose subject is given by the NP which is modified by the PP. We use the rules:

(XII)   NP   ->   bounding NP   (^HEAD) = v

                      PP   ^ = v
                                       (vSUBJ) = (^HEAD)

(XIII) PP   ->   P   ^ = v
                       NP   (^OBJ) = v
   (in this rule P is the head)

          ON: P,   (^PRED) = ´ON <(SUBJ),(OBJ)>´

3. Two comparative constructions

For a long time comparatives had been thought to require a transformational analysis. Gazdar has shown that this is not the case [9]. Note first that Comparative Deletion and Subdeletion hold over unbounding contexts, this means that the compared constituents upon which Comparative Deletion and Subdeletion are defined can be separated by contexts of arbitrary length.
That these are instances of long distance dependencies is shown by sentences like:

(26) As many of the girls as the man thinks that he loves ___ sleep

(27) As many of the girls as the man claims that John thinks
     that he loves ___ sleep.

As was already mentioned, complex NPs like relative clause constructions prevent the unbounding removal of their parts. Therefore the occurrence of such a construction in Comparative Deletion context yields an ungrammatical sentence:

(28) *As many of the girls as I met a man who loves ___ sleep

(29) *As many girls as I met a man who loves ___ sleep

The comparative clause itself constitutes an island, consider:

(30) *I wonder who as many of the girls as ___ loves ___ sleep.

(30) is ungrammatical because there is an extraction out of the comparative clause.

Gazdar [9] gives the following analysis for the sentence

(31) as many of the books as John thinks that he has

(We use his categories and notation; a/b is to be read as follows: in every subtree of type a/b there will occur a node labelled b/b which immediately dominates a null element.)

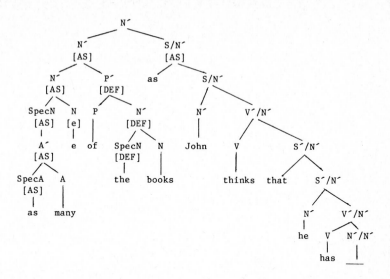

It seems difficult for the semantic interpretation to find the right filler for the gap in the comparative clause because the tree provides three different subtrees with the appropriate label. Unfortunately, in [9] no semantic rules are given.

The f-structure of LFG, by mapping parts of surface structures onto semantic arguments, forces the grammar writer to be very careful about filling gaps. The following rules construct the appropriate f-structure corresponding to the gap of comparative deletion.

```
(XIV)  NP   ->      NP           ^ = v
                                 (^MODq) = AS
                                 (^SELS) = (S´ => [+se])

            bounding S´          (^COMPA) = v
                                 (v KONJ) = AS.


(XV)   NP  ->       e            (^SELS) = ( <= [+se])
                                 (^QUANT) = X.
```

We get the following structure

134   *W. Frey*

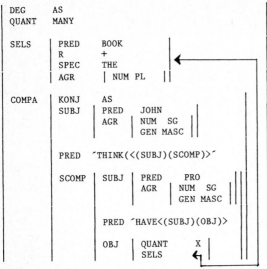

```
DEG      AS
QUANT    MANY

SELS  |  PRED   BOOK
      |  R      +
      |  SPEC   THE
      |  AGR    | NUM PL

COMPA |  KONJ   AS
      |  SUBJ   | PRED   JOHN
      |         | AGR    | NUM  SG
      |         |        | GEN MASC

         PRED   'THINK(<(SUBJ)(SCOMP)>'

         SCOMP | SUBJ   | PRED    PRO
               |        | AGR     | NUM  SG
               |        |         | GEN MASC

                 PRED   'HAVE<(SUBJ)(OBJ)>'

                 OBJ    | QUANT    X
                        | SELS
```

'QUANT = X' is the reference point of comparison. Note that the information necessary for semantic interpretation is locally available. In other words, the rules which are to be defined for recursive generation of ,e.g. Discourse representation structures, can be defined in such a manner that they operate on one local f-structure.
An instance of subdeletion is the construction

(32) As many girls as John thinks that he has _ books sleep.

Perhaps one wonders why a deletion should be necessary, because the comparative clause 'he has books' appears to be intact. The argument for the deletion of a QUANT is the following. Consider

(33) *Jack loves as many girls as he sleeps

The ungrammaticality of this sentence follows from the fact that a QUANT is not available in the clause, because the intransitive verb 'sleep' does not take direct objects. Therefore, there is nothing to delete and the sentence is ungrammatical.
To get for subdeletion structure similar as for deletion the following rule of subdeletion is used

(XVI) NP -> NP   ^ = v
                         (^MODq) = AS
                         QP = (S' => QP)

           bounding S'   (^SELS1) = v
                         (v KONJ) = AS

(XVII) QP -> e   QP = (<= QP)
                         (^QUANT) = X.

Finally we have to be aware of fact that the QUANT deleted by subdeletion cannot in general be moved from constituents it modifies by extraposition rules. The following is ungrammatical:

(34) *How many did she sell ____books to you.

The use of the controller (=> QP) is hence highly restricted.
Note that the rules do not generate the string

(35) *As many of the girls as the man loves the books

Because of the fact that in the above discussion the movement of elements   plays
an importatnt role, I would like to finish with a short remark on Pereira´s
extraposition grammar (XG), a formalism especially developed to handle left
movement.   A XG-rule is of the general form:

(a)   U1 ... U2 ... etc ... Un-1 ... Un   --->   V

with U1 a non-terminal symbol, Ui ,i>1, terminal or non-terminal, and where V is
a usual right side of a definite clause grammar rule and ´...´ denotes some
unknown constituents. The informal content of the rule is: Any sequence of
symbols of the form

(A) U1 X1 ... Xn-1 Un   with arbitrary Xi´s can be rewritten into

(B) V X1 X2 ... Xn-1.

This means that the Ui , i>1, are the extraposed elements, they must be
generated by other rules in order to apply rule (a) correctly.   For example XG
contains the following rules:

           relative   -->   relmarker S

           relmarker ... trace --> relpronoun

the relative of the sentence "the man that John saw laughed" gets the   following
analysis in XG

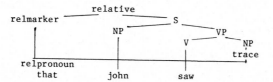

XG is in comparison with LFG far less restrictive:
(i) In XG there is no restriction demanding that the extraposed element has to
c-command its gap. In fact it is not possible to state this restriction because
the extraposed elements are associated with the left hand side of a rule.
(ii) Ui, i>1, of rule (a) can be a dummy terminal
Let us focus on (ii). It means that one can postulate elements as extraposed
which do not appear in the input string. As a consequence Pereira states a rule
which makes it possible for every preterminal category to select its item from
the list of extraposed elements.   Furthermore Ui can belong to an arbitrary
category. Consequently we have for every category C the rule (in LFG notation):

C   -->   e   ^ = (<= C)

In toto this means that transformations are allowed. The ease with which rules
for extraposition can be written in XG has the negative effect that nearly
everything goes.   This   neglects   the   success   which   is   achieved   by
nontransformational and highly restricted grammars like LFG or Gazdar´s GPSG.

footnotes

1) The LFG rules are noted throughout the paper in a format our compiler accepts. The slight difference to Kaplan/Bresnan´s notation should cause no trouble.
2) We use here the familiar analysis of noun phrases which will be modified below.

References

[1]   Barwise,J./Cooper,R. (1981),"Generalized Quantifiers and Natural Language", in: Linguistics and Philosophy, vol.4 pp. 159-219.

[2]   Bresnan,J.W. (1973),"Syntax of the Comparative Clause Construction in English", in: Linguistic Inquiry. pp. 275-343.

[3]   Bresnan,J.W. (1982),"Control and Comlementation", in: Bresnan,J.W.(ed), The Mental Representation of Grammatical Relations, MIT Press, Cambridge, Massachustts.

[4]   Carlson,G.N. (1977), "A Unified Analysis of the English Bare Plural", in: Linguistics and Philosophy, vol.1 pp. 413-457

[5]   Dahl,V. (1983), Treating Coordination in Logic Grammars, AJCL 9 (2) pp. 69-91.

[6]   Doerre,J./Eisele,A., Ein Compiler fuer LFG, working paper, Dept. of Ling., Univ. of Stuttgart (1984).

[7]   Frey,W./Reyle,U. (1983 a),"A PROLOG Implementation of Lexical Functional Grammar", in: Proceedings of the Eights International Conference on Artificial Intelligence, IJCAI 1983 VOL. II, Karlsruhe

[8]   Frey,W./Reyle,U. (1983 b),"A PROLOG Implementation of Lexical Functional Grammar as a Base for a Natural Language Processing System", in: Proceedings of the First Meeting of the Association for Computational Linguistics. Europe, Pisa

[9]   Gazdar,G. (1980),"A Phrase Structure Syntax for Comparative Clauses", in: Hoekstra,T.,et al (eds.),Lexical Grammar, Publications in Language Sciences 3,Foris-Dordrecht. pp.165-179.

[10]   Gazdar,G. (1982)," Phrase Structure Grammar", in: P.Jacobson/G.K.Pullum (eds.), The Nature of Syntactic Representation, D.Reidel Publishing Company. pp.131-186.

[11]   Jackendoff,R. (1977), X-bar Syntax: A Study of Phrase Structure. Linguistic Inquiry Monograph Two. MIT Press, Cambridge, Massachusetts.

[12]   Kamp,H. (1981a),"A Theory of Truth and Semantic Representation", in: Groenendijk,J.A.,T.U.V.(ed.), Formal Semantics in the Study of Natural Language, Vol.I, Amsterdam.

[13]   Kamp,H. (1981b),"Evenements, representations discursives et references temporelles", in: Languages, 64 pp.39-64

[14] Kaplan,R./Bresnan,J. (1982),"Lexical Functional Grammar: a Formal System for Grammatical Representation", in: Bresnan,J.(ed.) The Mental Representation of Grammatical Relations, MIT Press.

[15] Klein,E. (1980), "Determiners and the Category Q", School of Social Sciences, University of Sussex.

[16] Pereira,F. (1981), "Extraposition grammars", AJCL 7(4), 1981

[17] Ross,J.R. (1967), "Constraints on Variables in Syntax", PhD thesis, MIT. Published by Indiana University Linguistics Club, Bloomington , Indiana.

[18] Selkirk,E. (1977),"Some Remarks on Noun Phrase Structure", in: Culicover,P.W. et al (eds.), Formal Styntax, Academic Press, New York, San Francisco London. pp.285-316.

Natural Language Understanding and Logic Programming
V. Dahl and P. Saint-Dizier (Editors)
© Elsevier Science Publishers B.V. (North-Holland), 1985

P U Z Z L E   G R A M M A R S

PAUL   SABATIER

C.N.R.S. - L.A.D.L.
Université Paris 7
Tour Centrale 9E
2 place Jussieu
75005 Paris

ABSTRACT

We present a formalism, Puzzle Grammars (ZGs) for describing natural languages. In a ZG, a language is defined by means of key-trees (the elements of the puzzle) instead of rewrite rules. According to the Anchorage Principle based on unification of roots and leaves of key-trees, new key-trees can be obtained from the assemblage of others. Constraints can be attached to key-trees and are evaluated as soon as the necessary and sufficient values for the checks are known. In order to analyse/generate sentences, Strategic Rules select key-trees in a given ZG and govern the order and the mode of assemblages. We present a technique for implementing ZG in Prolog and illustrate it by an example of a program.

ACKNOWLEGMENTS

The idea of Puzzle Grammars was born during discussions with Alain Colmerauer at the Centre Mondial d'Informatique in Paris in 82-83. I thank him for these stimulating discussions. This paper was written when I was Visiting Researcher in Japan thanks to a grant from the INRIA (France) and Makoto Nagao's hospitality at Kyoto University. I am grateful to Annie Gal, Hideki Hirakawa, Richard Kittredge, Hideo Miyoshi, Jun Nakamura, Patrick Saint Dizier, Morris Salkoff, Celestin Sedogbo, Jun Tsujii and Hideki Yasukawa for their comments on a preliminary version of this paper.

1.   INTRODUCTION

In the framework of Logic Programming [12], several formalisms have been proposed for analysing/generating languages: Metamorphosis Grammars [3], Definite Clauses Grammars [18], Extraposition Grammars [17]. For an overview, see [7]. These formalisms can be gathered under the concept of "Logic Grammars" or "Term Grammars". The following features distinguish these grammars from the classical ones:

- symbols are terms: atoms, predicates (with variables) and variables; instead of simple atoms.

- the rewriting of symbols involves unification instead of simple replacement.

- conditions can be expressed in a rule, and executed as procedure calls. They generally formulate conditions on the value of variables occurring in the rule.

In case a symbol is a predicate, its arguments can be used for specifying and propagating from rule to rule:

- contextual constraints on the rewriting of particular symbols.

- arbitrary translations we wish to attach to the analysed/generated string.

The power, the efficiency and the clarity of these formalisms have been shown in [18]. They have been implemented in Prolog [20] and successfully used in several natural language systems: [5], [6], [2], [21], [30], [19], [15], [16], [29].

In this paper, we point out some limitations of these formalisms and introduce a new one, Puzzle Grammar (ZG). ZGs can be viewed as an alternative to logic grammars and rewrite systems in general.

2. DEPENDENCIES AND GENERALIZATIONS

In a langage (formal or natural) an occurrence of a symbol may depend on (or "constrain by") the context, i.e. the occurrence of other symbols (more or less distant in the string). In logic grammars, context sensitivity (or "contextual constraints") can be expressed by means of the arguments of the symbols, instead of special rules. Constraints are specified in the arguments and propagated towards the symbols they operate on. For example, the formal context-sensitive language:

$$a^n \quad b^n \quad c^n \qquad (n>0)$$

can be described by means of the following logic grammar with the nonterminal symbols S, A(-), B(-) and C(-) and using arguments for expressing the dependency (1 is an atom, the integer; successor($\underline{n}$) is a functor that can be read as "the successor of $\underline{n}$"; $\underline{n}$ is a variable).

S -> A($\underline{n}$) B($\underline{n}$) C($\underline{n}$)

A(1) -> [a]

A(successor($\underline{n}$)) -> [a] A($\underline{n}$)

B(1) -> [b]

B(successor($\underline{n}$)) -> [b] B($\underline{n}$)

C(1) -> [c]

C(successor($\underline{n}$)) -> [c] C($\underline{n}$)

(For convenience, we have dropped the arguments of the symbols that express the concatenation. Terminal symbols are in square brackets. "nil" denotes the empty string. Variables are underlined. In a same rule, variables with the same name stand for the same object.).

Context-sensitive rules are needed to describe context-sensitive languages, like in the example above. The main interest of using context-sensitive rules for describing a context-free language is to allow the expression of generalizations on the language. The obtained generalizations will make easier further (sequential or parallel) treatments and translations (like semantic ones, for example).

As an exemple, let us assume the following fragment of a context-free grammar for some French relative clauses:

    sentence -> np vp

    np -> det noun relative

    relative -> [que] np verb

    relative -> [qui] vp

    relative -> nil

    vp -> verb np

If, in a further treatment, we want to assign to relative clauses, interpretations similar to those attached to complete sentences, it will be easier to do it if relative clauses have been previously described as sentences. We can describe French relative clauses as sentences (by means of the general symbol "sentence") and state that the subject or the object of the verb is empty (depending on the nature of the relative pronouns "qui" or "que"). And for that purpose, we can imagine a classical grammar with context-sensitive rules. Or we can write the following logic grammar:

    (R1) sentence($\underline{s}$,$\underline{o}$) -> np($\underline{s}$) vp($\underline{o}$)

    (R2) np(full) -> det noun relative

    (R3) np(empty) -> nil

    (R4) relative -> [que] sentence(full,empty)

    (R5) relative -> [qui] sentence(empty,full)

    (R6) relative -> nil

    (R7) vp($\underline{o}$) -> verb np($\underline{o}$)

The first argument of sentence(-,-) carries the nature (the atom "full" or "empty") of the np(-) subject restricting its rewrite; and the second argument, the nature ("full" or "empty") for the np(-) object via vp(-).

Compared to classical grammars, we do not need here special and complex rules (context-sensitive ones) for expressing dependencies and generalizations both. Arguments of symbols are sufficient.

On principle, in these formalisms, a symbol can bear arguments only for specifying and transmitting constraints between symbols. That is the case for the symbols sentence(-,-) and vp(-) in our example. The following schema illustrates this phenomenon:

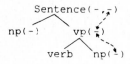

This method is very efficient but rules lose their clarity in case of non trivial grammars. In particular, when we want to relate (long) distant dependent symbols. Extraposition Grammars [17] have been introduced in order to make the expression of such relations easier. Restriction Grammars [11] and Contextual Grammars [22] are attempts for facilitating the expression of constraints and verifying them by using primitives to traverse the derived syntactic trees. But from a general point of view, we think that rewrite systems (classical ones or logic grammars) are not suitable for clearly describing such technical phenomena.

It has also been shown that some natural language specific phenomena like coordinate and elliptical structures are easier to analyse/generate from a metalevel ("off-rules") as it has been done in the framework of logic grammars: for coordination [25], [8]; for ellipsis, [16].

Since rewrite systems fail to describe clearly such natural phenomena, a general model must be thought out from these linguistic data. By developing ZGs we want to offer to the linguist a declarative, clear, simple and powerful tool for writing non trivial grammars (like String Grammars or Lexicon Grammars) for natural language systems (interfaces, machine translation, text generation, etc.). We think that a rewrite system is too procedural. The linguist wants a formalism in which he can both express very detailed restrictions on the nature of the sentences and make interesting generalizations in the descriptions associated to the analysed/generated sentences. With ZGs, the linguist describes a language by means of basic trees and formulates constraints on these trees.

3.   WELL-FORMEDNESS AND EFFICIENCY

When we conceived Puzzle Grammar formalism we had also in mind some ideas concerning the implementation of logic grammars in Prolog. For efficiency, logic grammar rules can be translated into directly executable Prolog clauses, according to a given strategy (top-down: [3], [18], [17]; or bottom-up: [27], [9] [13], [28], [14]. In that case, the rewrite mechanism and the rules of the grammar are expressed within a single formalism. Because of the strategy of Prolog, it is impossible to control the rewrite strategy. Partial and flexible analyses (able to point out the parsable substrings of a not completely parsable sentence) are difficult to implement.

In order to control a rewrite strategy we must separate the grammar from the rewrite mechanism. The grammar deals with the linguistic data (and the representations we want to associate with these data); the strategy deals with the manner to use these data for analysing/generating sentences. The concept of well-formed expression is central to grammars; the concept of efficiency, to strategies. We can change, test and choose the ideal strategy without modifying the grammar. If incorrect sentences are analysed/generated, we can change the grammar without modifying the strategy.

If grammar rules and strategies are separated, we can also consult the grammar as a database for answering "meta" questions and commands like:

> "What are the verbs?"
> "What are the structures of a noun?"
> "Give me 3 different yes-no questions with "Bob" as subject and the verb "to give"!

Puzzle Grammars are a formalism for describing natural languages; Strategic Rules are a formalism for defining strategies for analysing/generating sentences using puzzle grammars. Analysis/generation of sentences is viewed as assembling the elements of a puzzle according to a strategy (or strategies).

4. PUZZLE GRAMMARS

The basic idea of ZGs is very simple. In a ZG, a language is described by means of basic key-trees (the elements of the puzzle) instead of rewrite rules. (Of course, for any key-tree, there is a corresponding set of rewrite rules). Constraints can be attached to any key-tree.

According to the Anchorage Principle based on unification of roots and leaves of key-trees, new key-trees can be obtained from the assemblage of other ones.

A puzzle grammar ZG is a set of couples

$$ZG = \{ (K1,C1), (K2,C2), \ldots, (Kn,Cn) \} \ (n>0)$$

where

(1) Ki is a basic key-tree (i=<n)

(2) Ci is a conjunction or a disjunction of constraints on Ki. Ci can be empty.

The couple (Ki,Ci) is called a piece (the i-th) of ZG.

A string S is in ZG if there is a key-tree K whose ordered list of leaves is S. K can be a basic key-tree (i.e., a key-tree defined in the grammar) or obtained from assemblages of other key-trees.

The order of the assemblages are governed by the Strategic Rules.

Key-trees, the Anchorage Principle for assembling them, and constraints are now discussed.

4.1. KEY-TREES

A key-tree K is a tree:

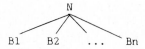

where

> (1) N is an atom or a predicate (whose name is not a variable)
>
> (2) Bi (1=<i=<n) is either:
>
>> - a terminal: any atom, predicate or variable
>> (Terminals are enclosed by square brackets).
>>
>> - a nonterminal: any atom or predicate (whose name is
>> not a variable).
>>
>> - the empty string, labelled "nil".
>>
>> - a key-tree.

N is a node of K. If no node dominates N, N is also called the root of K. If Bi is not a key-tree (i.e. Bi is a terminal, a nonterminal or the empty string), Bi is called a leaf of K.

These are examples of basic key-trees:

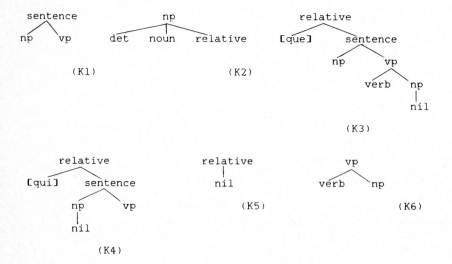

Instead of 7 rewrite rules (R1-R7), a ZG will present 6 key-trees (K1-K6).

A key-tree is either simple or complex. It is simple if and only if each of its leaves is directly dominated by the root of the key-tree. Kl, K2, K5 and K6 are simple key-trees. If a leaf is not directly dominated by the root, the key-tree is called complex. K3 and K4 are complex key-trees. Capturing descriptive generalizations by means of complex basic key-trees is one of the interests of ZGs.

As in logic grammars, symbols of key-trees can have arguments for expressing and propagating constraints. Of course, symbols with arguments are necessary for describing a context-sensitive language. In the case of a context-free language, they are necessary if we want to relate two symbols whose one of which is embedded in a recursive rule. But if it is possible and clearer to formulate constraints by means of complex key-trees (like k3 or K4) without arguments for symbols, ZGs provide sufficient formalism to do that.

In the following set of key-trees, the arguments of symbols are used for expressing very simple constraints:

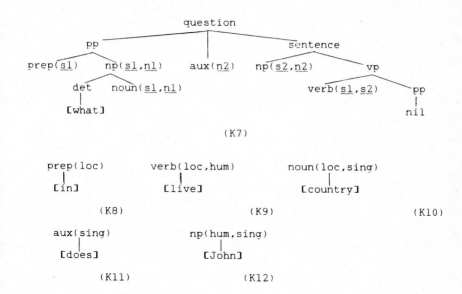

(K7)

(K8)   (K9)   (K10)

(K11)   (K12)

If we wish to associate directly (without resorting to further treatment to do it) translations to the analysed/generated string, arguments of symbols (as in logic grammars) can also be used for specifying and building any kind of translation. We do not insist on this point. ZGs facilitate the expression of descriptive generalizations (by means of complex basic key-trees) in order to make further (sequential or parallel) treatments and translations easier.

4.2. ASSEMBLING KEY-TREES A key-tree can be obtained by successive assemblages of key-trees, according to the Anchorage Principle.

Two key-trees K1 and K2 are assemblable by anchorage if:

- S1 is a leaf of K1

- S2 is a root of K2

- S1 and S2 are unifiable

After unification of S1 and S2 and the instantiation of the variables concerned by the unification, the result of the assemblage is a new key-tree K3 constituted by K1 whose leaf S1 has been replaced by K2. S1 and S2 constitute the anchorage point of the assemblage of k1 and K2.

For example, K13 is obtained by the assemblages of the basic key-trees K7, K8, K9, K10, K11 and K12:

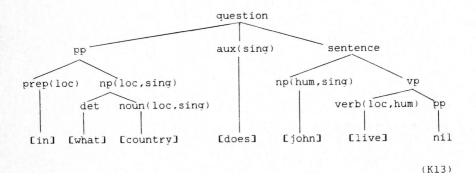

(K13)

4.3. CONSTRAINTS ON KEY-TREES

Constraints can be attached to key-trees. They restrict assemblages, and are formulated by means of predicates, as in logic grammars. They are calls to general computational functions. They express restrictions on the value(s) of certain variables occurring in the key-tree to which they are attached. They provide for the linguist a very clear and fast manner for formulating restrictions.

The conjunction or the disjunction of constraints are noted within braces "{ }". The infix operator "," (comma) denotes conjunction; and "or", disjunction. "{}" denotes the empty set of constraints, always fulfilled.

This is an example of a complete ZG (key-trees and their constraints) with 6 pieces (P1-P6):

(P1)

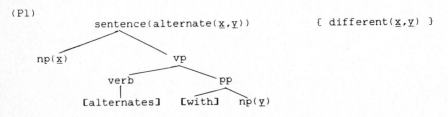

(P2)

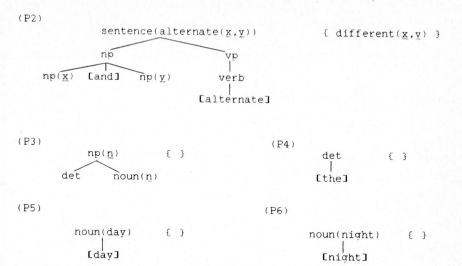

The sentences:

    the day alternates with the night
    the night alternates with the day
    the day and the night alternate
    the night and the day alternate

can be analysed/generated by this ZG. Sentences like:

    the day alternates with the day
    the night and the night alternate

will be refused/blocked because of the constraint different(-,-). This constraint is an example of a general function that must be given to the linguist as a primitive one (in Prolog II, it is a built-in predicate; see Section 6). in(-,-), out-of(-,-) are examples of other primitive constraints. The linguist formulates and defines complex ones by means of primitive ones.

In the implementation, a constraint is evaluated as soon as the necessary and sufficient values for the computation are known. When he formulates a constraint, the linguist needs not to be preoccupied with the moment it will be evaluated. (This technical aspect is solved by using a general coroutine procedure. We give some details in Section 5).

5. ABOUT STRATEGIC RULES

In this paper, we present ZGs formalism. Strategic Rules will be discussed in details later [23]. Strategic Rules deal with the method to follow to assemble key-trees for analysing/generating sentences. Working as an expert system, they will ensure efficient, "intelligent" and flexible parsings. They will select interesting key-trees in the given puzzle grammar and govern the order and the mode (top-down, bottom-up, sequential, parallel, deterministic, nondeterministic, left-to-right, right-to-left, etc.) of the different assemblages. In particular, they will play an important role for analysing/generating coordinate and elliptic sentences.

6.   PUZZLE GRAMMARS IN PROLOG, AN EXAMPLE.

At the present time, Prolog II [4] is the ideal candidate for implementing Puzzle Grammars (and Strategic Rules), in particular on three fundamental points that concern (1) the operation of unification involved in the anchorage principle, (2) the representation of key-trees, and (3) the evaluation of the constraints attached to the key-trees.

(1) The operation of unification. Prolog is a programming language based on the generalization of this operation. On this point, the implementation of ZGs in Prolog is a trivial exercice.

(2) Key-trees. In Prolog II, names of predicates can be predicates, and can be also denoted by variables, by means of the bracketed "< >" expression. This notation is very useful for representing key-trees whose nodes are predicates. In our actual implementation, each key-tree K is translated into a Prolog II predicate:

```
< - , - , - >
  a   b   c
```
where

>   (a) is the root of K (an atom or a predicate), the name of the predicate.
>
>   (b) is the skeleton of K: K in which each leaf that is a nonterminal symbol (atom or predicate) is replaced by a variable.
>
>   (c) is the revised list (L1', L2', ..., Ln') of the ordered list of K leaves (L1, L2, ..., Ln).
>
>   If Li (1=<i=<n) is
>
>   - [X] (a terminal, where X is an atom or a predicate), then Li' is the predicate <X>.
>
>   - a nonterminal NT (NT is an atom or a predicate), then Li' is the predicate <NT,v> where v is the same variable in K skeleton standing for the key-tree whose root will be NT.
>
>   - nil (the empty string), then there is no corresponding Li'.

(3) The evaluation of the constraints on key-trees. Prolog II provides facilities for coroutines by means of the built-in predicate

    freeze(v,p)

read as: "delay the execution of the goal p until the variable v (occurring in p) is instantiated". The built-in predicate:

```
      different(-,-)
```

for testing inequalities of terms involves such a coroutine.

Freeze(-,-) and different(-,-) are very useful for evaluating the constraints attached to key-trees as soon as the values for the computation are known.

We give here an example of a Prolog II program for running the ZG formed by the pieces Pl to P6. Here, we have defined (and implemented) no specific strategic rules. Each piece Pi (Pi = (Ki,Ci)) is translated into a Prolog II clause.

If Ci = {}, the corresponding clause is:

```
      <-,-,-> -> ;
```

If Ci = { Dl, D2, ..., Dn } (n>0)

where Dm = different(-,-) (1=<m=<n)

the clause is:

```
      <-,-,-> -> Dl D2 ...  Dn ;
```

The pieces Pl-P6 are translated into the following Prolog II clauses
Pl'-P6':

(Pl')

```
   < sentence(alternate(x,y)),
     <sentence(alternate(x,y)),fl,vp(verb(alternates),pp(with,f2))>,
     <np(x),fl>.<alternates>.<with>.<np(y),f2>.nil >
  -> different(x,y) ;
```

(P2')

```
   < sentence(alternate(x,y)),
     <sentence(alternate(x,y)),np(fl,and,f2),vp(verb(alternate))>,
     <np(x),fl>.<and>.<np(y),f2>.<alternate>.nil >
  -> different(x,y) ;
```

(P3')

```
   < np(n),
     <np(n),fl,f2>,
     <det,fl>.<noun(n),f2>.nil >
  -> ;
```

(P4')   < det, det(the), <the>.nil >   -> ;

(P5')   < noun(day), <noun(day),day>, <day>.nil >   -> ;

(P6')   < noun(night), <noun(night),night>, <night>.nil >   -> ;

These are the 3 clauses for a trivial top-down, depth-first, sequential, nondeterministic strategy of assemblage:

```
   assemble(l,nil,l)  -> ;
```

```
assemble(t.11,<t>.12,10)  ->
   assemble(11,12,10) ;

assemble(11,<k-root,k-tree>.14,10) ->
   <k-root,k-tree,12>
   assemble(11,12,13)
   assemble(13,14,10);
```

For analysing the sentence:

the day alternates with the night

one will formulate the question:

```
assemble(the.day.alternates.with.the.night.nil,
         <sentence(r),k-tree>.nil,
         nil).
```

and the answer will be:

r = alternate(day,night)

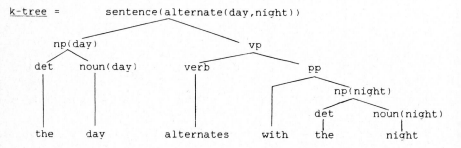

```
k-tree =         sentence(alternate(day,night))

            np(day)                        vp

       det      noun(day)       verb              pp

                                                      np(night)

                                                 det      noun(night)

       the       day        alternates    with   the       night
```

7. THE FUTURE

An application consisting in writing into the ZG formalism existing
French String Grammar [24] and subsets of French Lexicon Grammars [1],
[10] is in progress.

The conception of a compiler for translating automatically a ZG into a
Prolog II formalism is under study. (We also hope that one day it
will be possible to draw and modify key-trees on a graphical tablet or
with a similar tool).

8. REFERENCES

[1] Boons J.P., Guillet A., Leclere C., La structure des phrases
    simples en francais, Droz, 1976.

[2] Coelho H., A program conversing in Portuguese providing a library
    service, Ph. D. Dissertation, University of Edinburgh, 1979.

[3] Colmerauer A., Les grammaires de metamorphoses, Groupe

Intelligence Artificielle, Universite Aix-Marseille 2, 1975. Metamorphosis grammars, in Natural language communication with computers, Bolc L. ed., Springer Verlag 1978.

[4] Colmerauer A., Prolog in 10 figures, Proc. of IJCAI, 1983.

[5] Colmerauer A., Kanoui H., Pasero R., Roussel P., Un systeme de communication homme-machine en francais, Groupe Intelligence Artificielle, Universite Aix-Marseille 2, 1973.

[6] Dahl V., Un systeme deductif d'interrogation de banques de donnees en espagnol, These, Groupe d'Intelligence Artificielle, Universite Aix-Marseille 2, 1977.

[7] Dahl V., Current trends in logic grammars, Proc. of Logic Programming Workshop, University of Lisbon, 1983.

[8] Dahl V., McCord M., Treating coordination in logic grammars, Computing Sciences Department, Simon Fraser University, 1983. (To appear in American Journal of Computational Linguistics).

[9] Filgueras M., A kernel for a general natural language interface, Proc. of Logic Programming Workshop, University of Lisbon, 1983.

[10] Gross M., Lexicon-grammmar and the syntactic analysis of French, Proceedings of IJCAI, 1984.

[11] Hirschman L., Puder K., Restriction grammars in Prolog, Proc. of International Logic Programming Conference, Groupe Intelligence Artificielle, Universite Aix-Marseille 2, 1982.

[12] Kowalski R., Logic for problem solving, Elsevier North Holland, 1979.

[13] Matsumoto Y., Tanaka H., Hirakawa H., Miyoshi H., Yasukawa H., BUP: a bottom-up parser embedded in Prolog, New Generation Journal, Vol. 1, Springer Verlag, 1983.

[14] Matsumoto Y., Kiyono M., Tanaka H., Facilities of the BUP parsing system, in this book.

[15] McCord M., Using slots and modifiers in logic grammars for natural language, Artificial Intelligence, Vol. 18, 1982.

[16] Oliveira E., Pereira L., Sabatier P., ORBI: an expert system for environmental resources evaluation through natural language, Proc. of International Logic Programming Conference, Groupe Intelligence Artificielle, Universite Aix-Marseille 2, 1982.

[17] Pereira F., Extraposition grammars, American Journal of Computational Linguistics, Vol. 7, 1981.

[18] Pereira F. Warren D., Definite clause grammars for language analysis, a survey of the formalism and a comparison with augmented transition networks, Artificial Intelligence, Vol 13, 1980.

[19] Pique J.F., Sabatier P., An informative, adaptable and efficient natural language consultable database system, Proc. of ECAI,

1982.

[20] Roussel P., PROLOG: manuel de reference et d'utilisation, Groupe Intelligence Artificielle, Universite Aix-Marseille 2, 1975.

[21] Sabatier P., Dialogues en francais avec un ordinateur, These, Groupe Intelligence Artificielle, Universite Aix-Marseille 2, 1980.

[22] Sabatier P., Contextual grammars in Prolog, Proc. of Logic Programming Workshop, University of Lisbon, 1983.

[23] Sabatier P., Strategic rules for puzzle grammars, in preparation.

[24] Salkoff M., Une grammaire en chaine du francais, Dunod, 1973.

[25] Sedogbo C., A meta-grammar for handling coordination in logic grammars, in this book.

[26] Stabler E., Deterministic and bottom-up parsing in Prolog, Proc. of the AAAI Conference, 1983.

[27] Uehara K., Toyoda J., A pattern matching directed parser: PAMPS, ACL/LSA Meeting, 1981.

[28] Uehara K., Ochitani R., Kakusho O., Toyoda J., A bottom-up parser in predicate logic: a survey of the formalism and its implementation technique, Proc. of International Symposium on Logic Programming Altlantic City, 1984.

[29] Walker A., Porto A., KB01: A knowledge based garden store assistant, Proc. of Logic Programming Workshop, University of Lisbon, 1983.

[30] Warren D., Pereira F., An efficient easily adaptable system for interpreting natural language queries, Department of Artificial Intelligence, University of Edinburgh, 1981; and in American Journal of Computational Linguistics, (Pereira F., Warren D.), Vol. 8, 1982.

Natural Language Understanding and Logic Programming
V. Dahl and P. Saint-Dizier (Editors)
© Elsevier Science Publishers B.V. (North-Holland), 1985

A META GRAMMAR FOR HANDLING
COORDINATION IN LOGIC GRAMMARS

Célestin SEDOGBO
Groupe BULL
68, Route de Versailles
78430 LOUVECIENNES
FRANCE

Works by Colmerauer, Dahl and Pereira have shown that logic grammars using Horn clauses are efficient for natural language
processing.
Coordination is one of the most important problems in natural language processing ; in this framework we propose a meta grammar for
the treatment of coordination using definite clause grammars, which makes coordination transparent to the linguist. The treatment
is based on the similarity of conjoined parse trees. The Meta-
grammar is accessible through the special predicate "CONJ". "CONJ"
is then used to qualify the right hand side of rules which possibly involve coordination. The structure produced is an unreduced
surface parse tree which can be directly used for the semantic
interpretation.

1 INTRODUCTION

Coordination is one of the most important problems in natural language
processing: it can involve many strings in the grammar, and phenomena like ambiguity and ellipsis can occur in conjoined strings. A elegant and proper way of
handling coordination is to define a meta treatment which is able to make coordination transparent to the grammar writer.

In [Woods 73], a special facility SYSCONJ has been developed for augmented transition networks (ATNs). Reduced coordination (i.e. John drove his car through and
completely demolished a plate glass window) can be parsed by the system. There are
some problems with SYSCONJ : the processing of conjunction is inefficient and
costly, because the method is highly non determinististic and at the same time is
not generally adaptable to conjoined strings. [DAHL & Mc CORD,83], propose a system for handling coordination in logic grammars. Coordination is handled through a
formalism called "Modifier Structure Grammars" (MSGs), by an interpreter. Conjunction is treated as a demon and is not mentioned explicitly in a MSG grammar. This
treatment is the first one written in logic grammars, but some acceptable sentences are not recognized. The system also provides a semantic representation. Despite the qualities of the system, some acceptable sentences are not recognized
because of the way the parsing history is kept.

An interesting work must be mentioned here : [HUANG, 83], suggested a set of rules
named C.S.D.C. (conjunct scope determination constraints) for solving the coordination problem. C.S.D.C. rules are incorporated into an ATN parser. Many linguistic works have precised the grammatical constraints ([ROSS,67], [GAZDAR,81]) for
constructions involving coordination. According to HUANG's point of view, these
constraints are not sufficient for a proper treatment of the conjunct scope
problem. C.S.D.C. rules are defined from a procedural point of view and involve
syntactical, semantic, symmetry and closeness constraints. The method is deterministic and powerful, but is inefficient in the treatment of reduced conjunctions

(i.e. "american history and literature" and "american history and physics" are
not discrimated).

We intended initially to foward a new approach to the string grammar of the French
language, which would allow a finely detailed analysis of a sentence , and which
takes in account that an automatic analysis of a sentence aims towards its
understanding. We were thus lead to integrate the processing of coordination into
our Prolog II [VAN CANEGHEM,82] implementation of the string grammar. The approach
we took to resolve the coordination problem is linked to the nature of string
grammars ; furthermore we have only considered the aspects of coordination problems in the French language.

In this paper , we present a meta treatment using Definite Clause grammars (DCGs)
and based on the similarity of conjoined parse trees. The metagrammar has been incorporated to a string grammar parser [SEDOGBO,84] successfully. The meta-grammar
is accessible through a special predicate "CONJ" which is used to qualify the
right hand side of   rules involving coordination.

In this work, we try to propose a treatment which we think is linguistically
relevant, non deterministic (and also non combinatorial).

2 A SUMMARY OF THE COORDINATION PROBLEM

Coordination can involve a large number of strings ; [SALKOFF,79], proposes a general form of conjoined strings in a string grammar.

Let us summarize the concepts of string grammars : the full formalism is in
[SALKOFF,73], [SAGER,81]. A string grammar is a natural language grammar which assumes that every sentence of the language is composed of a kernel called center
string, and modifiers (adjunct strings).
Thus,in the following sentence :
"John drinks a coffee in his room" the center string is :
"John drinks a coffee" and "in his room" is the adjunct string built from the
preposition "in" and the nominal string "his room" built from the noun "room" modified to the left by the determiner "his". A center string "C" has the form :

$$C = \S \; sn \; \S \; tv \; \S \; on \; \S \qquad\qquad (2.1)$$

where

    sn= the subject string
    tv= the verb string
    on= the object string
    $\S$ = the sentence adjunct string

 Suppose that during the parsing of a string, the parser arrives at the i-th element :

    $Sj = X1 \; X2 \; .... \; Xi$

 and that at this point the current word is "et" (i.e and); for the string which
can be conjoined to Sj there are the following options :

$$S'j = et \; X'i$$
$$S'j = et \; X'i-1 \; \; X'i \qquad\qquad (2.2)$$
    .
    .
$$S'j = et \; X'1 \; \; X'2 \; .... \; X'i$$

where X'k and Xk are of the same syntactical category.
Then, if during the parsing of :

"pierre mange rapidement une pomme"
(Peter quickly eats an apple)   (2.3)
.   .   .
sn   vn   on

the parser encounters "et", then the following options could be generated:

et on   (et une bonne poire) (and a good pear)
et vn on   (et boit une biere) (and drinks a beer)   (2.4)
et sn vn on   (et Paul va à Paris) (and Peter goes to Paris)

However, it happens that the same conjoined sequence can be connected to a conjoined string in many ways on the parse tree ; so for the sentence :

"Paul considère l'hypothèse sur N1 et N2 "
(Paul considers the hypothesis on N1 and N2)

(where N1 and N2 are two nominal strings) ,The parser may generate two analysis:

(1) paul considère (l'hypothèse sur N1) et N2
        (the meaning is: Paul considers two things)

(2) Paul considère l'hypothese sur (N1 et N2)
        (Peter considers the hypothesis on two things)
A full discussion is in [SEDOGBO,83].

2.1 COORDINATION IN THE CENTER STRING

Coordination in the center string can be complete :

Jean mange une poire et Paul boit un peu de bière   (2.5)
(John eats a pear and Peter drinks some beer)

Sometimes, strings (subject string,verb string,or object string) can be reduced to
zero (i.e are missing)). The element reduced to zero is identical with the same
element in the first center string : we represent the element reduced to zero by
Oc :

Jean aime Marie et Paul Oc son chien
(John loves Mary and Paul Oc his dog)

(2.6)

Jean mange une poire et Paul Oc Oc aussi
(John eats a pear and Paul Oc Oc too)

We call (2.6) the unreduced surface structures.

Let us consider the following example :

"Jean confond mais Max distingue ces beaux spots"
    (John mixes up but Max distinguishes these fine spots)
The object of "confond" is "ces beaux spots", but is unknown till the conjoined
center string "Max distingue ces beaux spots" is parsed ; the object string is
then anticipated. We represent the anticipated ele ment with the special symbol
Oc. The coordination rules in the center string are defined in the following
manner: if C and C' are two conjoi   ned center strings where C = sn tv on,then
C' has one of the following structures:

a. C'= Oc   tv'   on'
b. C'= Oc   Oc   on'

```
      c.  C'= sn' Oc   on'                    (2.7)
      d.  C'= sn' Oc   Oc  (adv)
      e.  C'= Oc  Oc   Oc  (adv)
      f.  C'= sn' tv'  on'
      g.  C'= Oc  Oc   Oc  (adv)
```

Anticipated elements can occur only in the object string of a center string conjoined with another one.

A restriction in the grammar verifies that the options (d) and (e) occur only if
the sentence adjunct string to C' is of the required struc-ture (i.e a manner adverb : too, quickly , ... etc).

2.2 COORDINATION IN THE OTHERS STRINGS

If the string parsed is Sj=Xi , and if the current word is "et" for instance ,
then the string Sj' conjoined to Sj has the structure: S'j= Xi' where Xi and Xi'
are produced by the same phrase (they are of the same syntactical category).Here
are some examples :

```
    "le (sage et  doux) homme  dort "    [the ( wise and kind ) man  sleeps]
            adj     adj
```

```
    "les(hommes et femmes) sont amoureux" [the ( men and women) are in love]
          N         N
```

```
    "l'homme que (Marie aime et jean déteste) est mon frère"
                  cn/np           cn/np
```

    [the man who (Mary loves and John hates) is my brother]

```
    "jean (aime et deteste) Marie"          [John (loves and hates) Mary]
          tv       tv
```

```
    "(Deux ou trois) personnes étaient dans cette chambre"
     qt      qt
```

    [(two or three) persons were in this room]

in our notation :

```
            adj :   is the category of the adjectives
            N   :   is the category of the nouns
            cn/np : is a center string with a nominal string missing in
                    the subject string or in the object string
        and qt :    is the categoy of quantifiers (i.e two,5,some , etc...)
```


3 THE META-GRAMMAR

Our treatment is based on the observation that the parse trees for the conjoined
strings are similar. So we assume that in (2.2),Sj and S'j have similar
structures.Let us consider the sentence: "Jean confond mais Max distingue ces
beaux spots". The parse trees of the conjoined center strings are :

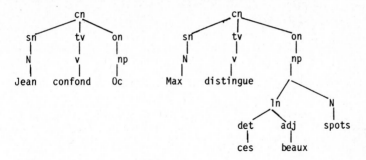

Figure 1: similar parse trees in center strings

where the parse trees nodes "cn","np", and "ln" are respectively the center
string, the nominal phrase, and the left adjunct to the noun..
We define a Metagrammar accessible through a special predicate "CONJ" which controls the similarity of conjoined parse trees. How does "CONJ" work ?

The syntax of CONJ is :

       CONJ(p(s,x,y))
    with :
    p : a grammatical rule
    s : the parse tree
    x : the input string
    y : the output string

CONJ is a one place predicate which indicates that the rule "p" can produce conjoined strings.Coordination here is not treated as in Dahl's system ; there is no
interruption of the parser . CONJ controls the parser and always tries to parse a
conjoined structure according to the similarity definitions.

3.1 SIMILARITY DEFINITIONS

(1) two parse trees T and T', parsed as center strings are similar :

      a. if the parsing results in them having roots with the same name

      b. if the sons of these roots with the same name also have the same
        name respectively.
  and c. if the constraints mentioned in 2.1 are respected.

(2) for other strings, two parse trees T and T' are also considered as
      similar, if in the result of the parsing process, their roots have
      the same name ; but for these strings, no leaves of T or T' must
      have the value Oc (i.e. no element of T or T' may be missing).

3.2   THE IMPLEMENTATION

 Metamorphosis grammars (MGs) are the first logic grammar formalism providing a
good basis for natural language analysis ; they have been proposed by
[COLMERAUER,78]. In MG, a rule has the form :

      A x --→ b

where

      A : a non terminal logic symbol of the grammar
      x,b : strings of non-terminal or terminal logic symbols

The restriction to rules of the form :

$$A \dashrightarrow b$$

(which is to be read as : A is true if b is true), is called a definite clause
(DCG) [PEREIRA,80]).

We have implemented the meta-grammar by using DCGs.

This is the definition of "CONJ" for the center string :

```
CONJ(center(s,x0,x2)) -->
    center(s1,x0,x1)
    rest-conj(center(s1,x0,x1),s,x1,x2) ;

rest-conj(center(s1,t,x1),s1,x0,x0) --> ;

rest-conj(center(s1,t,x1),conj(s1,cj(e),s3),x1,x3) -->
    conjunction(e,x1,x2)
    creature-bis
    center(s2,x2,x3)
    similar(s1,s2)
    creature'
    rest-conj(center(s2,x2,x3),s3,x3,x4);
```

where:
    creature-bis : allows the parsing of missing elements
    creature: forbids the parsing of missing or anticipated elements
    similar(s1,s2) : checks that the two trees s1 and s2 are similar
    s,s1,s2,s3: the parse trees
    xi,xn : input or output strings

We give the full metagrammar for a grammar of the french language in appendix.

3.3 HOW TO USE "CONJ"

The use of "CONJ" is based on the observation that the extra symbol Oc that we name "hole" in our implementation indicates whether a string of the grammar is allowed to be missing. In order to use "CONJ", the grammar user must write his grammar
without thinking about coordination. An interpreter will be used to qualify automatically the right hand side of the non trivial rules (this means that rules allow the parsing of conjoined strings) except those literals (of the right hand
side of the non trivial rules) corresponding to syntactic categories which cannot
involve coordination. He must add also extra assertions of the form :

```
noun-phrase(np(hole),x0,x0) -->;
```

(which can be interpreted as: a nominal phrase can be missing, or be reduced to
zero in conjoined strings) for all the syntactical rules involving coordination.
The grammar writer defines his lexicon without thinking about coordination; he
must later add supplementary assertions of the form:

```
adjective(adj(hole),x0,x0) -->;
```

(which is to be read as: an adjective can be a missing element or an element reduced to zero in conjoined strings) for all grammatical categories involving
coordination.

Let us now illustrate the use of "CONJ" , by giving a simple grammar for the sentence : "le garçon et son chien vont à la ville" (the boy and his dog go to the
city".
First we write the grammar without thinking about coordination problems:

```
        center(cn(t1,t2,t3),x0,x3)  -->
            subject(t1,x0,x1)
            verb(t2,x1,x2)
            object(t3,x2,x3);

        subject(sn(t1),x0,x1) -->
            nounphr(t1,x0,x1);

        nounphr(np(t1,t2),x0,x2) -->
            det(t1,x0,x1)
            noun(t2,x1,x2);

        prepophr(pn(t1,t2),x0,x2) -->
            prep(t1,x0,x1)
            nounphr(t2,x1,x2);

        object(on(t1),x0,x1) -->
            prepophr(t1,x0,x1);

        det(art(le),le.x0,x0) -->;
        det(art(la),la.x0,x0) -->;
        det(art(son),son.x0,x0) -->;
        noun(Noun(garçon),garçon.x0,x0) -->;
        noun(Noun(chien),chien.x0,x0)-->;
        noun(Noun(ville),ville.x0,x0) -->;
        prep(pp(à),à.x0,x0) -->;
        verb(tv(vont),vont.x0,x0) -->;
```

    figure 2 : a simple grammar with lexicon

Now, we embody the meta-grammar; thus , the grammar becomes :

```
        center(cn(t1,t2,t3),x0,x3)-->
            CONJ(subject(t1,x0,x1))
            CONJ(verb(t2,x1,x2))
            CONJ(object(t3,x2,x3));

        subjet(sn(t1),x0,x1) -->
            CONJ(nounphr(t1,x0,x1));

        nounphr(np(t1,t2),x0,x2)-->
            CONJ(det(t1,x0,x1))
            CONJ(nounphr(t1,x1,x2));
        nounphr(np(hole),x0,x0)-->;

        prepophr(pn(t1,t2),x0,x2) -->
            CONJ(prep(t1,x0,x1))
            CONJ(noun(t2,x1,x2));
        prepophr(pn(hole),x0,x0) -->;
```

```
object(on(t1),x0,x1) -->
   CONJ(prepophr(t1,x0,x1));
object(on(hole),x0,x0) -->;

det(art(le),le.x0,x0)-->;
det(art(la),la.x0,x0) -->;
det(art(son).son.x0,x0) -->;
noun(Noun(garçon),garçon.x0,x0) -->;
noun(Noun(chien),chien.x0,x0)-->;
noun(Noun(ville),ville.x0,x0) -->;
noun(Noun(hole),x0,x0)-->;
prep(pp(à),à.x0,x0) -->;
verb(tv(vont),vont.x0,x0) -->;
verb(tv(hole)) -->;
conjunction(et,et.x0,x0) -->;
```

Figure 3 : a simple grammar embodying the metagrammar

In figure 2 , there is not for instance the rule: "det(art(hole),x0,x0)---;" , because we do not allow the determiner to be missing. The parsing of a sentence S is done by the evaluation of:

CONJ(center(t,s,nil));

where t is the parse tree

4 CONCLUSION

The meta treatment we propose for coordination is elegant and linguistically relevant. A conjunction does not appear anywhere in a sentence; only some rules of the grammar can involve coordination. The solution we propose for embodying the meta-grammar , is to qualify the right hand side of non trivial rules with the predicate "CONJ". An extension of our work would be to set up rules of qualification; an interpreter will also be usefull for the qualification.

Because of the way string grammars have been defined , there are redundancies in the parsing. For the parsing of "John and Peter sleep" for instance ,two parse trees would be found: the first one will correspond to the coodination of two nouns in a nominal phrase , and the second one will correspond to the coordination of two nominal phrases with the empty string as left adjunct string to the noun. This is why a restriction component is included in the meta-grammar to eliminate the redundancies of the parsing.

The syntactic and semantic features can be used to obtain a good analysis; this can be done by adding a predicate for conjoining features in the rule "rest-conj". The grammar writer has to define himself how the features are to be conjoined.

The meta-grammar is efficient and simple to adapt ; moreover, the grammar embodying the meta grammar remains sensibly the same length as the original grammar.

AKNOWLEDGEMENTS

I would like here to thank A. COLMERAUER and M. SALKOFF for their advices during this work.

REFERENCES

[COLMERAUER,78]   COLMERAUER A. "Metamorphosis grammars", in natural language communication with computers, L. Bolc Ed, pp.133-189,

(Springer-Verlag, New York, 1978).

[DAHL & Mc CORD,83]   DAHL V., Mc CORD M. C. "Treating coordination in logic
                      grammars" Computer Sciences Departement University of
                      Kentucky.

[GAZDAR,81]   GAZDAR G. "Unbounded dependencies and coordinate structure"
              Linguistic Inquiry jrnl, vol 12, N[2.

[HUANG,83]   HUANG H. "Dealing with conjunctions in a machine translation
             environnement" ,in Proceedings of the first Meeting of the
             Association for Computational Linguistics, Europe, Pisa,(1983).

[PEREIRA,80] PEREIRA F., WARREN D. "Definite clause grammars for natural language
              analysis - a survey of the formalism and a comparison with augmanted
              transition networks", Artificial Intelligence jrnl. vol.13 PP. 231-278.

[ROSS,67]   ROSS J.R. "Constraints on variables in syntax" Indi'ana University lin-
            guistics Club, Bloomington, Indiana (1968).

[SAGER,81]   SAGER N. "Natural language information processing : a computer grammar
             of English and its applications",Addison-Wesley publishing company,
             inc. (1981).

[SALKOFF,73]   SALKOFF M. "Une grammaire en chaîne du français", Editions Dunod,
               Paris, (1973).

[SALKOFF,79]   SALKOFF M. "Analyse syntaxique du français :grammaire en chaine",
               John Benjamins B. V. (ed.), Amsterdam (1979).

[SEDOGBO,83]   SEDOGBO C. "About coordination treatment in metamorphosis grammars"
               Groupe BULL Research center (December 1983).

[SEDOGBO,84]   SEDOGBO C. "Tree Grammar: a PROLOG Implementation of the the string
               grammar of French", Groupe BULL Research center, (june 1984).

[VAN CANEGHEM,82]   VAN CANEGHEM M. "PROLOG II : Manuel d'utilisation",G.I.A,
                    Université de Marseille

[WOODS,73]   WOODS W. "An experimental parsing system for transition network
             grammars in Rustin R. (ed.) : Natural language processing,(algorithmic
             press, New York,1973).

APPENDIX

"THE META GRAMMAR"

```
CONJ(center(s3,x0,x2)) -→
   center(s1,x0,x1)
   rest-conj(center(s1,x0,x1),s3,x1,x2);
CONJ(object(s1,x0,x1)) -→
   encore-et(x0)
   object(s1,x0,x1)
   no-zero(s1.nil);
CONJ(p(s3,x0,x2)) -→
   autre(p(s3,x0,x2))
   p(s1,x0,x1)
   no-zero(s1.nil)
```

```
    rest-conj(p(s1,x0,x1),s3,x1,x2);

rest-conj(p(s1,x0,x1),s1,x1,x1) ->;
rest-conj(center(s1,t1,x0),conj(s1,cj(x),s3),x0,x3) ->
    conjunction(x,x0,x1)
    creature-bis
    center(s2,x1,x2)
    similar(s1,s2)
    creature'
    rest-conj(center(s2,x1,x2),s3,x2,x3);
rest-conj(p(s1,t1,x1),conj(s1,cj(x),s3),x0,x3) ->
    dif(p(s1,t1,x1),center(s1,t1,x1))
    conjunction(x,x0,x1)
    sans-vide(s1)
    p(s2,x1,x2)
    rest-conj(p(s2,x1,x2),s3,x2,x3);
```

"SIMILARITY OF TWO TREES"

```
similar(x,y) ->                          well-form'(e,x,e') ->
    same-node(x,y)                           sons(x,l1)
    sons(x,l1)                               well-form-respect(e,l1,e');
    sons(y,l2)
    asym(l1,l2)                          well-form-respect(e,nil,e) ->;
    well-form(x)                         well-form-respect(e0,x.l1,e2) ->
    well-form(y);                            well-form'(e0,x,e1)
                                             well-form-respect(e1,l1,e2);
asym(l,nil) ->;
asym(nil,l) -> dif(l,nil);               bascule(ind,hole,hole-enc) ->;
asym(x.l1,y.l2) ->                       bascule(hole-pos,hole,hole-enc) ->;
    same-node(x,y)                       bascule(hole-enc,hole,hole-enc) ->;
    asym(l1,l2);                         bascule(ind,x,hole-pos) -> dif(x,hole);
                                         bascule(hole-enc,x,hole-imp) ->
well-form(x) ->                              dif(x,hole);
    well-form'(ind,x,e);                 bascule(hole-pos,x,hole-pos) ->
well-form(x) ->                              dif(x,hole);
    dif(e,hole-enc)                      bascule(hole-imp,x,hole-imp) ->
    well-form'(ind,x,e);                     dif(x,hole);

well-form'(e,x,e') ->                    same-node(x,y) ->
    leaf(x)                                  arg(0,x,e)
    bascule(e,x,e');                         arg(0,y,e);

san-vide(x) ->
    leaves(x.nil,l)
    non-vide(l);

san-vide(x) ->
    leaves(x.nil,l)
    non-vide(l);

non-vide(x.y) -> dif(x,null);
non-vide(null.y) -> non-vide(y);

creature-bis -> affecter(lui,0) /;

creature' -> affecter(lui,1);
```

```
no-zero(x) -> val(lui,0) /  ;
no-zero(p(hole).nil) -> / impasse;
no-zero(p(q(hole)).nil) -> / impasse;
no-zero(x) ->;

encore-et(x0) ->
    val(lui,1)
    un-et(x)
    affecter(lui,0) /;
encore-et(x0) ->;

un-et(nil) -> / impasse;
un-et(t.x) -> conjunction(t) /;
un-et(t.x) -> un-et(x);

autre(center(s,x0,x1)) -> / impasse;
autre(object(s,x0,x1)) -> / impasse;
autre(t) ->;
```

Natural Language Understanding and Logic Programming
V. Dahl and P. Saint-Dizier (Editors)
© Elsevier Science Publishers B.V. (North-Holland), 1985

ABOUT THE ROLE OF CONTROL INFORMATION IN NATURAL LANGUAGE QUESTION ANSWERING SYSTEMS

Michael Hess
Seminar of General Linguistics
University of Zurich
Switzerland

ABSTRACT

Most existing Natural Language Question Answering systems written in a Logic Programming language such as Prolog make use of only one component of the information expressed in the questions, viz. the logic component. However, (many) Natural Language sentences also convey control information. If this type of information is ignored the interpreter must use an input-independent, in most cases fixed, control regime and can not always generate useful replies. We should like to draw attention to a few such cases in the context of Logic Programming: word oppositions like those between "what" and "which" determining whether a generalised solution or a fully evaluated solution is required; topic and comment in queries and DB entries and their use in guiding the search; restrictive and non-restrictive relative clauses and their use in interleaving data acquisition and query evaluation modes. We give a very short outline of a suitable query evaluator. The problem of actually parsing questions is not dealt with here.

ACKNOWLEDGEMENT

This work was supported under Grant No. 81.703.0.79 of the Swiss National Science Foundation.

Most Natural Language Question Answering systems written in the context of Logic Programming translate queries into a **logical form**, often cast in terms of straightforward Prolog terms, which are then evaluated direct by the system interpreter over a Data Base consisting of equally straightforward Prolog facts and rules.[1] It is very much in the spirit of Logic Programming to pay attention exclusively to the logical content of a query and to ignore questions of evaluation strategy, i.e. of control, at least in the first stage of designing a system. Moreover, the small and straightforward Data Bases used in those systems are kept very simple as they serve only as example material for the systems to work with. Under these conditions questions of control are fairly immaterial anyway and can be ignored even more safely. The success of many of these systems is ample proof that the concentration on the logical content of NL queries was good research strategy.

But NL as such is not pure logic; in the words of Kowalski:[2] "Natural Language = Logic + Control". Translating NL queries into a logical form very often means ignoring potentially valuable control information.[3] Sometimes this will only mean that the general-purpose evaluation procedure will be **less efficient** than one which makes use of the specific control information provided by the user. However, it often means that we will **not** get, in principle, **the type of answer** from a QA system which we intuitively expect. We will use examples from both categories but we will put more emphasis on the second, more serious, case. This will also be the topic of section 1.

1. FULL EVALUATION VS. GENERALISED SOLUTIONS

1.1 WHICH VS. WHAT

The two questions

1) **Which managers at IBM earn $ 100000 ?**
2) **What managers at IBM earn $ 100000 ?**

seem to call for two different types of answers,[4] namely

1a) **Hart, Miller, and Jones.**
2a) **Managers in charge of a branch office.**

In the first example the whole Data Base must be searched for entries of explicitly known managers, their salaries must be checked, and the names of all the managers meeting the criterion must be listed. The salary of a manager may be known explicitly, i.e. in the case of a Prolog DB be given as a fact (as in the case of Hart and Miller in Fig.1), or it may have to be

---

[1] This is the approach chosen, for example, in Pereira and Warren's system Chat-80, arguably the most powerful QA system written in Prolog so far (Pereira 1983).

[2] Kowalski 1975:129

[3] as emphasised by Klahr 1980:113 and Nilsson 1980:193-195

[4] as with most other problems of NL understanding we find a first solution of this problem in Winograd's SHRDLU (Winograd1972:164).

computed via a general inference rule (as in the case of Jones). In the second example it is this **general rule** itself which is the more appropriate reply rather than the list of individual instances.

Obviously we don't want a QA system to reply in full "All managers at IBM in charge of a branch office earn $ 100000"; it should return only those parts of the rule which were not given in the query.   But this is the result of filtering out information secondarily, on the basis of dialogue considerations. It doesn't change the fact that the rule had to be accessed as a whole, as a fact, rather than executed, as in example 1.   This kind of reply is sometimes called a "**generalised solution**" (Kowalski 1975:184).   The control decision whether a rule should be executed, or treated as a mere fact to be returned, is made by the user through the choice of the question word, i.e. "which" vs. "what".   It is a decision no interpreter, however intelligent it may be, can make on its own.[5]

```
manager(ibm,hart).
manager(ibm,miller).
manager(ibm,jones).

runs(branch_office,hart).
runs(branch_office,miller).
runs(branch_office,jones).

salary(hart,100000).
salary(miller,100000).

salary(X,100000)  :- manager(ibm,X),
                     runs(branch_office,X).
```

Figure 1: A sample Data Base

We can paraphrase 1 and 2 as 1b and 2b which intuitively have exactly the same meaning although they may be slightly less acceptable:

1b) Which are the managers at IBM that earn $ 100000 ?
2b) What are the managers at IBM that earn $ 100000 ?

Now we can see that we ask in both cases (of both versions of the two questions) for the **set of all objects** with certain properties, as expressed by the plural definite article.[6] However, we expect a different type of description for the set: In the first case ("which") we want an **enumerative,**

---

[5] which is basically what the variable-depth NL understanding system outlined in Kayser 1981 tries to do in a similar situation.

[6] We are not saying that the meaning of a plural definite article can be captured completely by a Prolog setof-predicate but it's a good approximation commonly used.

extensional description, in the second case ("what") a **constructive, intensional** one.

To further support our claim that "which" and "what" are two control versions of the same logical expression we look at two cases where only one of them can be used without difficulty.

In 3 and 3a we ask for a **unique object,** as expressed by the singular definite article, and reinforced by the superlative. 3 is quite normal as this constraint is compatible with the control information expressed by the interrogative pronoun, viz. with the demand that the result be an exhaustive enumeration of instances: It will simply be a list with exactly one member. Contrary to that 3a sounds odd because the interrogative pronoun asks for a general rule whereas article and superlative ask for a unique instance, and it is just a bit pointless to have a general rule generate a unique object. If we force ourselves to give 3a an interpretation we might come up with a description of the country which is general in character but at least consists of a sufficient number of constraints to make unique identification likely: "It is a constitutional monarchy, an island, and a reluctant member of the European Community".

3) Which is the European country with the longest coastline ?
3a) ? What is the European country with the longest coastline ?

The different control component in question words such as "which" and "what" also explains why 4 is perfectly normal

4) What is a country ?

where the reply is a general rule ("something is a country if it is a political, national, and geographic unit"), while 4a

4a) ? Which is a country ?

is quite odd and requires, in order to become acceptable, a reference to an exhaustively listed set from which the answer can be picked:

4b) Which (one, of the following, ...) is a country:
**   Lichtenberg, Liechtenstein, or Lichtenau ?**

When referring to people we can, in addition to the distiction between **indefinite reference** and **definite reference,** as expressed by "which" and "what", use the further category of **"individual reference",** through the use of "who". Now we ask for an individual, known by name if possible:

5) What's her husband? He is a film director.
5a) Which is her husband? He is the man smoking a pipe in the corner.
5b) Who is her husband? He is Paul Jones.

Note that 5 is precisely the kind of question mentioned as a bit pointless above. But 5 is an (almost idiomatic) special case: One's profession is, in our culture, considered the most important general criterion for social categorization, and "What's her X" asks specifically for X's profession. This becomes clear when we consider 5d

5d) ? What's her teacher?

which is definitely odd, and precisely because the (only conceivable type of) answer is given in the question itself.

One problem in this context has not been mentioned yet: What is a QA system supposed to do if we ask an indefinite question ("what") but there is no general rule in the DB, only individual instances? The easiest solution is to make the system treat an indefinite question as a definite question in a situation like that; if we removed the rule about salaries from the DB of Fig. 1 this would indeed be the only sensible behaviour. With a richer DB a more ambitious solution is conceivable: As before, the list of individual instances could be computed, but then the system could try to form equivalence classes from the list of instances, or even synthesize a rule which could generate this list.

Finally it is, of course, conceivable that the system finds several rules when looking for an answer to an indefinite question. Then it is reasonable to list them all as reply.

1.2   EVERY VS. ALL VS. EACH

Basically the same distinction of full evaluation vs. generalised solutions holds between "every" and "all" although the difference between them seems to be felt less clearly than in the case of "which" and "what".[7] "Each" finally seems to be a third control version of the same underlying universal quantifier.

**6)   Does every manager of an IBM branch
      office earn $ 100000 ?**
**6a) Do all managers of an IBM branch
      office earn $ 100000 ?**
**6b) Does each manager of an IBM branch
      office earn $ 100000 ?**

When asking question 6 we would expect a QA system to check every single instance of an entry about IBM managers, and then check the entry for his or her salary, **irrespective** of whether there is a universal rule about managerial salaries in the DB or not. The system should not fail if, for some managers, there is no entry at all about their salaries, provided there is a general rule it can execute; the system should then reply something like "nothing is known about Jones, but in general yes".

When asking question 6a we would be satisfied if the system found a general rule. A general rule says, of course, nothing about the existence of its antecedents (it does **not** say, in Fig. 1, that there are managers at IBM in the first place). However, this is clearly presupposed by the question, and the user therefore does not require the system to check the individual cases.

---

[7] However, the terminology frequently used to describe these words shows that there is a definite difference in their meaning: Leech/Svartvik 1979:50 call "each" and "every" (as opposed to "all") "distributive", Saint Dizier 1984:43 "universal distributive quantifiers" (as opposed to simple "universal quantifiers"). Jespersen 1974:599 describes "every" as "all, taken separately".

Only if no general rule can be found the system must test the individual cases and answer, if appropriate, "as it happens yes, but not necessarily so".

Questions with "each", such as 6b, seem to require an exact "matching" between the domain of the quantifier on the on hand, and the objects or events referred to in the restrictions on the other hand. If such a matching isn't obvious a sentence becomes odd, as the comparison between examples 7 and 7a shows; in our culture you have husbands one at a time, which makes it clear that there are separate events of admiration which can be matched with the husbands one to one. In 7a, however, the uncles aren't pre-ar- ranged in any discernible order, and so it isn't clear how the admiration is to be distributed among them. In order to make 7a unproblematical we must add information which explicitly creates different types of admiration, one for each uncle, as in 7b:[8]

7)   **Marge admired each of her husbands.**
7a) **? Marge admired each of her uncles.**
7b) **Marge admired each of her uncles in a different way.**

We can model these differences rather closely in terms of control informa- tion: A QA system, trying to find an answer to an "each"-question, should look only for **base facts** in the DB to be "matched" against each other (in our example: facts about managers and facts about salaries) but it should **not use** any **inference rules** to compute either domain or restriction terms (e.g. to infer that Jones must also earn $ 100000).

1.3   ANY VS. SOME

"Any" and "some" can also be seen as the two control versions of one and the same logical expression, viz. of the existential quantifier.[9] The conventional explanation is that the meaning of "some" and "any" is the same but that "some" is used in assertive positions and "any" in non-assertive positions (i.e. in questions, negations, conditionals, comparisons). However, "any" can be used in assertive positions ("Any colour will do"),[10] and "some" can be used in non-assertive positions, although in both cases this atypical use results in a particular connotation of the resulting sentence: In the case of the non-assertive "some" this connotation consists in a clear positive bias,

---

[8] McCawley 1981:98

[9] That "any" isn't a straightforward existential quantifier is shown by the following example where the intonation alone can turn it either into a uni- versal or into an existential quantifier: "I don't lend my books to any- body." With a rise-fall-rise tone on the "any" the sentence means "I don't lend my books to **just** anybody", with a high-falling tone "I don't lend my books to anybody **at all**". (Jespersen 1974:606)

[10] This is a simplification: They are not ordinary assertive positions. They always have some kind of "generalised", even "modal", connotation: "any colour **will** do", "you **can** take any colour", "you **may** come any day, but you must come some day" (Jepsersen 1974:604).

whereas "any", used in the same position, is neutral: 8 clearly is neutral, whereas in 8a the speaker knows for sure that there are female managers at IBM that make $ 100000, and the question is only whether the addressee knows them.

8)   Do you know any female managers at IBM that earn $ 100000?
8a) Do you know some female managers at IBM that earn $ 100000?

In 8a those female managers at IBM are treated as a group, and the addressee is expected to know them as a group: the famous four female top-managers at IBM, mentioned in all the newspapers, etc. He is not expected to know any individual instances. In 8, on the other hand, it is precisely individual instances he is asked about.

One more example to highlight the difference:

9)   Did you get any post cards last week?
9a) Did you get some post cards last week?

We could easily imagine a continuation of 9a "... which I sent you from Italy", which doesn't sound right for 9.[11]

The situation with "some" and "any" is an almost exact parallel to the relationship between "all" and "every". In both cases the first word, when used in a query, looks for a **whole group, or set** of objects, known (and assumed by the speaker to be represented in the receiver's mind) as **one single complex entry**, whereas the second word looks for **multiple simple entries** for multiple simple facts. And in both cases we have to use the same strategy if we can't find such a complex entry: we must then look for simple entries scattered in our mental DB, i.e. we have to treat all-questions and some-questions as every-questions and any-questions, respectively. And if, in this situation, the answer is in the affirmative it will usually be preceded by a phrase such as "as it happens" to indicate that the receiver couldn't simply "look up" the answer but had to compute it from scattered bits of information.

2.   ERROR HANDLING: VIOLATIONS OF EXISTENTIAL PRESUPPOSITIONS

It is well known that missing axioms are a source of trouble in Logic Programming and in common sense reasoning likewise. In some cases the absence of a piece of information may be a perfectly legitimate state of affairs (of which we make good use when we interpret negation as non-provability), but in other cases it is an "error" in our DB, i.e. we don't know something we ought to know.

------

[11] The same distinction is made, incidentally, between "already" and "yet":

10)   Has she gone to bed yet?
10a) Has she gone to bed already?

Particularly counter-intuitive is the situation where we try to prove a universally quantified statement using double negation, i.e. for 11 we have to prove 11a:

11)   Does every manager drive a Cadillac?
11a) not(manager(X), not(drives(X,cadillac))).

If there are no entries about managers in our DB the proof will succeed at once, but really "for the wrong reason".

In some implementations of Prolog we can tell the interpreter how to react when an axiom is found missing during a particular sub-proof: to either simply fail the sub-proof, to abort the whole proof with an error message, to fail but also issue an error message, etc.

Common sense, interpreting NL statements, shows a similar behaviour; we don't treat violations of existential presuppositions the same way we treat negations (given explicitly or as failure). English has special expressions for that: "There are no managers at IBM **to begin with**" or "**in the first place**", as opposed to "no, they don't".

Any useful QA system must make this distinction (as indeed most do).[12] If a system, during the evaluation of an **every- or each-question**, cannot find an entry for any one of the **domain terms** it should fail and **report the violation of an existential presupposition** instead of merely failing the proof. A missing **restriction term** should, of course, make the subproof simply fail. As an **all-question** asks for an explicit all-rule the system doesn't first have to care whether individual instances are also listed in the DB. However, if it cannot find any all-rule, and if it must resort to a search of the DB for individual instances, it must also report violations of presuppositions (i.e. it must treat the "all"-query **exactly** the same way as an "every"-query).

Analogous is the situation with "what"- and "which"-questions, and with "some"- and "any"-questions.

3.   ORDER OF EVALUATION: TOPIC AND COMMENT

There is yet another way of conveying control information in questions but it is almost too obvious to be noticeable: it is the distinction between topic and comment[13] by means of word order. Questions 12 and 12a

12)   Do any American female managers earn $ 100000 ?
12a) Do any female American managers earn $ 100000 ?

are, of course, logically equivalent, as are all the possible commutations of their translations into Horn-clause 12b

12b) ?- manager(X), female(X), american(X), salary(X,Y), 100000<Y.

---

[12] Berry-Rogghe   1980:192-195,   Berry-Rogghe   1979:293,   Bronnenberg 1980:253.   Cf. also Kaplan 1979.

[13] Both Berry-Rogghe 1980:165 and McKeown 1983 deal with the role of topic and comment in QA systems.

The order of words codes the order of evaluation which is considered most efficient by the speaker. However, the two orderings do not necessarily have the same direction: In English the order of adjectives and nouns in a NP is exactly the inverse of the most efficient order of evaluation, whereas post-modifiers already have the right ordering, as shown in 13 and 13a

13)   **Do any female American managers in their thirties with children above the age of four** ...

13a) manager(X), american(X), female(X), age(X,30$^+$),
     child(X,Y), age(Y,4$^+$), ...

If we represent the topic-comment distinction of **assertions** in an equally straightforward manner, viz. as the ordering of entries in the DB, the standard interpreter of Prolog will automatically use the most efficient strategy to evaluate the terms of a query, provided they are themselves arranged according to topic and comment.

A general query optimisation program could try to rearrange the terms of 12 on its own in such a way as to minimise the size of the search space, using estimates about the cardinality of the sets of entries in the Data Base.[14] However, even this rather sophisticated approach does not make use of the control information supplied by the user in the question, and this can be crucial if there are very general terms, such as "small" or "yellow", in a question - it will be next to impossible to give a reasonable estimate of the cardinality of the set of entries about yellow things in a DB.

4.   QUERY MODE VS. ASSERTION MODE: RESTRICTIVE VS. NON-RESTRICTIVE PHRASES

One more way to express control information in NL should be mentioned. QA systems don't normally deal with declarative sentences at all. If they do the system has, as a rule, two completely separate modes of operation: one for query answering, and one for data acquisition. However, in some cases NL mixes these two modes freely, for instance when using relative clauses:

14)   **Do managers who earn a lot pay a lot of taxes?**
14b) **Do managers, who earn a lot, pay a lot of taxes?**

While 14 is simply a query where the restrictive relative clause adds one more restriction, in 14b the **non-restrictive relative clause** functions as an embedded declarative sentence in a question. The speaker wants to make sure that the receiver knows certain relevant facts before he/she/it sets out to answer the question. While processing the query the receiver has to go from answering mode into data acquisition mode for a short while.

Quite complex combinations of processing mode information and mixed evaluation depth information are possible (although some of the examples sound awkward):

15) **What managers, some of whom pay taxes, are well-paid?**
16) **Which employees, whose bosses all earn a lot, are underpaid?**

---

[14] Warren 1981

17) Is a manager every employee of whom is underpaid unpopular?

or much better:

17a) Is a manager unpopular if every employee of his is underpaid?

Not only relative clauses can be restrictive or non-restrictive: appositions (18, 18a) and postmodifiers (18b,18c) can be used to make the same distinction:

18)   My friend Peter was here last night.
18a) My friend, Peter, was here last night.
18b) The substance discovered by accident which had the greatest impact on medicine is penicillin.
18c) The substance, discovered by accident, had an enormous impact on medicine.

5.   REPRESENTATION OF THE DATA AND OUTLINE OF AN INTERPRETER

If we want to have an input-dependent, flexible control regime which allows a system to access base facts one time, general rules another time, to issue different error messages in case axioms cannot be found during a proof, and to go from query mode to data acquisition mode and back again, we have to change the standard way of representing data, and we also have to modify the interpreter. In order to keep changes to the absolute minimum we simply sketch a small interpreter on top of the system interpreter.

The first requirement is that the interpreter should be able to access inference rules as facts.   Thus rule 19 becomes 19a[15]

19) salary(X,100000) :- manager(ibm,X), in_charge_of(X,branch_office).

19a) all(X, [manager(ibm,X),in_charge_of(X,branch_office)] ,
**   salary(X,100000)).**

As long as these all-expressions are nothing but Horn-clauses turned into Prolog facts, they should not have more than one term in the third argument position, and a conjunction of goals has to be written as follows
all(X, [manager(X,ibm)] , salary(X,100000)).
all(X, [manager(X,ibm)] , drives(X,cadillac)).

We can, of course, still use explicit inference rules as long as we do not require them to be available as generalised solutions. This may be the rigth thing to do for information about the type hierarchy, such as 20

20) animal(X) :- dog(X).

---

[15] This representation is now widely used for quantified formulas; it makes the restriction on the variable, its range, explicit in the second argument, as opposed to the classical quantifiers.   Cf. Moore 1981:9, and Pereira 1983:21.

20 is, to us humans, "obvious" in the same way as the grammar rules of our native tongue: In order to retrieve such a rule we must generate an example, and then abstract, from the proof tree of the specific example, what the underlying general rule must look like.

We already stressed the close parallel between all-statements and some-statements as far as their content of control information is concerned: Both have a positive bias, i.e. they presuppose the existence of whole contiguous "chunks" of data, of structured objects,[16] and both will look for individual DB entries corresponding to individual terms in a structured object only in case such a structured object cannot be found.   Accordingly we turn the Horn-clauses

> **kangaroo(sk1).**
> **in(sk1,africa).**
> **striped(sk1).**

for "some kangaroos in Africa are striped" into

21) some(sk1, [kangaroo(sk1), in(sk1,africa)], striped(sk1)).

The second argument carries the topical information, the third argument is used for the comment.

Information about individuals is represented the usual way:

> **manager(jim).**
> **american(jim).**
> **drives_a_cadillac(jim).**

An interpreter would accordingly have to prove an all- or some-query by first looking for a **matching** all- or some-entry in the DB and second, if that fails, **evaluate** the expression:

demo(Goal,Answer)   :- candidate(Goal,Candidate), match(Goal,Candidate),
**   difference(Goal,Candidate,Answer).**
demo(Goal,Answer)   :- evaluate(Goal,Answer).

candidate(all(X,Y,Z),all(U,V,Z))   :- all(U,V,Z).
candidate(some(X,Y,Z),some(W,V,Z))   :- some(U,V,Z).

evaluate(all(X,Y,Z),as_it_happens_yes) :- not(presup(Y),not(demo(Z,_))).
evaluate(some(X,Y,Z),as_it_happens_yes) :- presup(Y), demo(Z,_).

presup(G) is the same as demo(G,_) only it will report missing axioms as presupposition violations.

Matching all-expressions with each other is interesting. If we want to prove 22, given in Predicate Calculus notation,

22) ALL X(kangaroo(X) AND in(X,australia) AND female(X)) → brown(X).

---

[16] Nilsson 1980:361-415 uses the term for the representation of data in the form of semantic networks, but then semantic networks are only a convenient way to visualise logic anyway.

it becomes, in the notation used here,

22a) ?- all(sk1,[kangaroo(sk1),in(sk1,australia),female(sk1)],brown(sk1)).

(note that the matcher expects universally quantified variables in a query to be skolemized). This term will have to match (e.g.) with the DB entry

23) all(X, [kangaroo(X), in(X,australia)],brown(X)).

i.e the comments of the two terms ("brown(X)" and "brown(sk1)") have to be a direct match but it is sufficient that the **set of range constraints** of the DB entry be a unifiable **subset** of the constraints of the query. (By "unifiable subset" we understand a set which contains only members which are unifiable (not necessarily identical) with some members of a second set, i.e. the kind of subset we get automatically if we use the regular Prolog definition of "member".) We would, obviously, have to make sure that properties are inherited the usual way through the hierarchy of types, but this problem is of no interest in the present context.

Matching all-expressions through the computation of the subset relation between their topics can be seen as the **simulation on the meta-level of a direct object-level proof**. If we want to prove 22, we have to negate it and to transform it into clausal form, which will give 22b

22b) kangaroo(sk2), in(sk2,australia), female(sk2), :- brown(sk2).

22b can be used as a **direct proof for the existence of an inference rule** 22c

22c) brown(X)   :-   kangaroo(X), in(X,australia), female(X).

provided we interpret the unnegated terms in 22b as temporary additions to the DB, to be removed after the execution of the proof, and the negated expression (":-brown(sk2)"), of course, as goal to be proved. Given the uniqueness of the Skolem constant this proof can only succeed if rule 22c is in the DB. Additional unnegated terms in the query are harmless: They are additions to the DB which are never accessed. This is what the subset-operation of the matcher modelled on the meta-level.

If we want to match a some-query against a some-entry, everything is inverted. Obviously we will have the unbound variables in the query and the Skolem constants in the DB entry, and the set of range constraints of the DB entry has now to be a unifiable **superset** of those of the query. The query 24 must match the DB entry 25

24) ?- some(X,[manager(X),american(X)],drives(X,cadiallac)).
25) some(sk3,[manager(sk3),american(sk3),female(sk3)],
                                    drives(sk3,cadillac)).

In a direct proof, reordering DB entries and query terms is a simple way to improve efficiency, as mentioned above in the remarks on topic and comment. The ordering of the terms in the range constraints of both all- and some-expressions was made to preserve the ordering of the original query terms and DB entries. Thus we retain this gain in efficiency for direct proofs in their meta-level simulation: The computation of sub- and supersets proceeds from left to right, simulating the most efficient sequence for the direct proof sequence.

The distinction between every- and each-questions can be made as follows:

```
demo(every(X,Y,Z),yes)   :-  not(presup(Y), not(demo(Z,_))), !.
demo(each(X,Y,Z),yes)    :-  not(candidate(Y,U), match(Y,U),
                                 not(candidate(Z,V), match(Z,V))), !.
```

What-queries ask for (all) the rules (all-statements) matched by the query; the reply is the set of matched rules. If no rules can be found the query is treated as a which-query. A which-query evaluates to the set of instances found.

```
demo(what(X,Y,Z),Answer)   :-  ( setof(B, (candidate(all(X,Y,Z),C),
                                     match(all(X,Y,Z),C),
                                       difference(C,Y,B)),Answer) ;
                               demo(which(X,Y,Z),Answer) ).
demo(which(X,Y,Z),Answer) :-  setof(Y, (presup(Y), demo(Z,_)), Answer).
```

For data-acquisition mode we can, of course, use the system predicate "assert". We will have to make sure that existentially quantified variables are first skolemized. 14b ("Do managers, who earn a lot, pay a lot of taxes?") should accordingly translate into

```
11b) assert(all(X, [manager(X)] ,earns_a_lot(X))),
     demo(all(sk4,[manager(sk4)], pays_lotsa_taxes(sk4)),Answer).
```

whereas 15 and 16, repeated here for convenience, should translate into 15b and 16a, respectively:

15) **What managers, some of whom pay taxes, are well-paid?**
16) **Which employees, whose bosses all earn a lot, are underpaid?**
```
15b) assert(some(sk5,[manager(sk5)],pay_taxes(sk5)),
     demo(what(X, [manager(X)], well_paid(X)),Answer).
16a) assert(all(X, [manager(X),employee(X,Y)], earns_a_lot(X))),
     demo(which(X, [employee(W,U)], underpaid(U)), Answer).
```

Examples of declaratives embedded in other declaratives are simpler:
26) **Some car dealers, who are greedy, are crooks.**
as opposed to
27) **Some car dealers who are greedy are crooks.**
and
28) **Car dealers, some of whom are crooks, are greedy.**
as opposed to
29) **Every car dealer who is greedy is a crook.**

ought to translate into one or several "assert"-commands:

```
26a) assert(some(sk6, [car_dealer(sk6)] ,crook(sk6))),
     assert(all(Y, [car_dealer(Y)] ,greedy(Y))).
```

Note that the default interpretation of a plural as a universal quantifier is used for the relative clause: **all** car dealers are said to be greedy or else it would be said otherwise with an explicit quantifier, as in 28

```
27a) assert(some(sk7, [car_dealer(sk7), greedy(sk7)] , crook(sk7))).
```

```
28a) assert(all(X), [car_dealer(X)] , greedy(X))),
     assert(some(sk8), [car_dealer(sk8)] , crook(sk8))).
29a) not(demo(car_dealer(X),_), demo(greedy(X),_), not(assert(crook(X))))).
```

29a is interesting in that it will add, for each car-dealer found to be greedy, a separate elementary fact "crook(X)":

```
crook(jim).
crook(peter).
crook(bill)
etc.
```

There will, however, be no explicit "every"-entry, true to the definition of "every".

   Almost as a side-effect the data representation and the interpreter outlined here can cope with certain sentences which otherwise cause problems: Example 30 would be translated into Predicate Calculus as 30a

30) Managers whose employees are underpaid are unpopular.
30a) ALL X(manager(X) AND ALL Y(employee(X,Y) → underpaid(Y))
                                              → unpopular(X))

It translates, because of the implication in the antecedent, into the **non-**Horn-clauses

```
30b) unpopular(X) :-  manager(X), underpaid(sk1(X)).
     unpopular(X), employee(X,sk1(X)) :-  manager(X).
```

The second clause, with a disjunction in its head, cannot be processed by the Prolog interpreter. Also, the clausal form is highly un-intuitive. If we represent it by means of uninterpreted embedded all-statements we can use it direct as a DB entry

```
30c) all(X, [manager(X), all(Y, [employee(X,Y)] , underpaid(Y))] ,
                                              unpopular(X)).
```

which is also very close to the form of the original NL statement.   If our query is

"demo(unpopular(jim),A)"

the interpreter will access 30c) by means of the top "demo"-rule of the interpreter, and then work its way down through the embedded terms trying to find generalised solutions wherever possible, otherwise evaluating the terms. If it has to fully evaluate every subterm of 30c) this DB entry is interpreted the same way as the usual translation of 30) into Horn-clauses-cum-negation-as-failure

30d) unpopular(X) :- manager(X),   not(employee(X,Y), not(underpaid(Y))).

would have done it.

   If we want to prove the **general rule** that managers whose employees are underpaid are unpopular, we must turn 30) into the query 30e

30e) demo(all(sk6,[manager(sk6),
            all(sk7,[employee(sk6,sk7)],underpaid(sk7))],
                              unpopular(sk6)),A).

If the DB is as follows

    manager(jim).
    unpopular(jim).
    all(X, [employee(jim,X)] , underpaid(X)).

but 30c itself is not in the DB, we will get the reply "yes, as it happens", by partial evaluation of the subterms of the query. Finally, if the DB contains only base facts such as

    manager(jim).
    employee(jim,joan).
    underpaid(joan).

we will have to compute the answer as if the query had been given in the standard, fully reduced, form, i.e.

30f) ?- not(manager(X), not(employee(X,Y),
                not(underpaid(Y))),not(unpopular(X))).

Different is the case of question 31

31) Is a manager unpopular if every employee of his is underpaid?

which must be translated into 30f right from the beginning.

6. CONCLUSIONS

Many questions provide a QA system with valuable control information which either **must** be used to generate a pragmatically useful reply, as opposed to a merely logically correct reply, or it **can** be used to prevent the system from performing a search which is very unlikely to succeed. There must be many more types of control information conveyed by NL which might be put to good use in a similar way: Adverbs and adverbial constructions ("what are, generally speaking, the..."), "meta-nouns" ("the number of", "average value of"), adjectives (attributive adjectives for existential presuppositions).[17]

In this approach, some work is shifted from the parser to the query evaluator; all the quantifier and question terms mentioned, such as "every", "all" , "which", etc. are transferred unchanged from the text to either the DB entries or the query, and their embedding structure is also maintained (and taken care of by the query evaluator). Nevertheless the design of a parser dealing with the phenomena outlined will still not be a simple affair.[18]

---

[17] v.Hahn 1980:183 investigates this question in some detail.

[18] Porto 1984:228-232, made a beginning for a similar approach.

7. BIBLIOGRAPHY

Berry-Rogghe, G.L./Dilger,W., 1979. *Konzeption eines Terminterpreters.* in: Kolvenbach 1979, 289-304.

Berry-Rogghe, G.L, et al.,1980. *Interacting with PLIDIS a deductive question answering system for German* in: Bolc 1980, 138-220.

Bolc,L.,ed.,1980. *Natural Language Question Answering Systems.* Hanser: 1980.

Bolc, L., ed., 1980a. *Natural Language Based Computer Systems.* Hanser: 1980.

Bronnenberg, W.J.H., et al., 1980. *The Question Answering System PHILIQA1.* in: Bolc 1980, 217-305.

v.Hahn,W., et al., 1980a. *The Anatomy of the Natural Language Dialogue System HAM-RPM.* in: Bolc 1980a, 119-253.

ISLP 1984. International Symposium on Logic Programming, Feb 6-9 1984, Atlantic City. IEEE Computer Society Press: 1984.

Jespersen, O., 1974. *A Modern English Grammar* Part VII, Syntax. Allen and Unwin: 1974.

Kaplan, J. 1979. *Cooperative Responses from a Portable Natural Language Data Base Query System.* PhD Thesis, CS Dept., U. of Pennsylvania: 1979.

Kayser, D./ Coulon, D. 1981. *Variable-Depth Natural Language Understanding* in: Proceedings IJCAI-81: 64-66

McKeown, K.R., 1984. *Paraphrasing Questions using Given and New Information.* in: AJCL, vol.9, Nr.1, 1984, 1-10.

Klahr, Ph./ Travis, L./ Kellogg, Ch., 1980. *A Deductive System for Natural Language Question Answering.* in: Bolc 1980: 74-136.

Kolvenbach, M./ Lötscher, A./ Lutz, H.D., eds. *Künstliche Intelligenz und natürliche Sprache.* Narr: 1979

Leech, G./ Svartvik, J., 1975. *A Communicative Grammar of English.* Longman: 1975.

Kowalski, R., 1975. *Logic for Problem Solving.* North Holland: 1975.

McCawley, J.D., 1981. *Everything Linguists have Always wanted to Know About Logic* Blackwell: 1981.

Moore, R.C., 1981. *Problems in Logical Form.* SRI International, Technical Note 241.

Nilsson,N.J., 1980. *Principles of Artificial Intelligence.* Tioga: 1980.

Pereira, F.C.N., 1983. *Logic for Natural Language Analysis.* SRI International, Technical Note 275.

Porto, A., et al., 1984. *Natural Language Semantics: A Logic Programming Approach.* in: ISLP 1984: 228-232.

Quirk, R./ Greenbaum, S./ Leech, G./ Svartvik, J. *A Grammar of Contemporary English.* Longman: 1979

Saint Dizier, P., 1984. *Quantifier Hierarchy in a Semantic Representation of Natural Language sentences.* This volume.

Warren, D.H.D., 1981. *Efficient Processing of Interactive Relational Data Base Queries Expressed in Logic.* in: 7th International Conference on Very Large Data Bases, 1981.

Winograd, T. 1972. *Understanding Natural Language.* Edinburgh U.P.: 1972

Natural Language Understanding and Logic Programming
V. Dahl and P. Saint-Dizier (Editors)
© Elsevier Science Publishers B.V. (North-Holland), 1985

GENERATING SENTENCES FROM SEMANTIC NETWORKS

Michel BOYER, Guy LAPALME

Département d'I.R.O.
Université de Montréal
C.P. 6128, Montréal, Canada
Tel. (514) 343-6780

A working program generating all the sentences that can be
shown to have the "meaning" described by a given network,
using only a dictionary and tree transformation rules is
presented. Based on Mel'čuk's Meaning Text Theory (hen-
ceforth MTT), this dictionary driven program uses extensively two major PROLOG features, namely unification and
backtracking, the latter being essentially MTT's method of
producing synonymous sentences. Extension of the PROLOG
equality predicate is made to allow comparison and construction of trees with labeled arcs.

INTRODUCTION

Many linguistic models have led to working programs, either for the generation or
the analysis of sentences [2,7]. One of them however, the Meaning Text Theory
(MTT) which was put forward by K. Žolkovskij and A. Mel'čuk in 1965 [8] has been
neglected. Since it is based on backtracking and tree manipulation, it seemed natural to use it as the framework of a PROLOG generating program.

The aim of MTT is to establish correspondences between meanings, represented by
networks, and written (or even spoken) texts. MTT is made of several "components", each of which can be seen as an interface between two contiguous levels
of representation of a sentence. For instance, the semantic component describes
the relation between a Semantic Representation and a Deep Syntactic Representation; it can well be thought of as a PROLOG II [3] predicate, Sem-Comp, such that

        Sem-Comp(S-em-Rep, D-Synt-Rep)

holds if D-Synt-Rep is the deep syntactic representation of a sentence whose meaning can be described by the net S-em-Rep (Rem: <letter>-<identifier> is a PROLOG
II variable). The whole of MTT can be described by the procedure:

        MTT(S-em-Rep, T-ext) ->
            Sem-Comp (S-em-Rep,D-Synt-Rep)
            Deep-Synt-Comp (D-Synt-Rep, S-Synt-Rep)
            Surf-Synt-Comp (S-Synt-Rep, D-Morph-Rep)
            Deep-Morph-Comp(D-Morph-Rep, T-ext);

According to its authors, MTT should be fully reversible. However, since a PROLOG
program gives the same solution as many times as there are ways to prove it and
due to the combinatorial explosions that are unavoidable if no control is taken
(e.g. the use of cuts), this work will be concerned only by text generation (cuts
are reversibility killers).

This paper describes the implementation of a working system that, given a network,
produces actual sentences. The coding was done using the Marseille PROLOG II sys-

tem. After giving an overview of the problem to be solved, we will introduce a few tree manipulation techniques that were needed to deal with the various representations of sentences. Then will be presented the various components of the generating program, with examples and traces.

2. OVERVIEW OF THE SEMANTIC COMPONENT

The semantic component is made of two essentially distinct parts: the first one establishes relations between semantic representations and deep syntactic structures while the second applies transformations on a deep syntactic representation to give other deep representations. Together, these subcomponents use almost all the techniques that have been developed during this project; more emphasis will be put on them than on morphology.

What will be called a semantic representation is a network whose nodes are either predicates or names of objects. Its arcs are labeled by integers taken from the set $\{1,2,3,4\}$, the one labeled by i leading to the i-th argument of the predicate. Such a representation is not intended for deduction; it is simply an utterance in a pictorial language stripped of all the syntactic features of natural languages.

Here is a simplified example of SemR correcponding to the sentence: the sales increased by 20 units. To be complete, the net should have time indications.

(2.1)

$$\text{many} \xrightarrow{\ 1\ } \text{sale} \quad \begin{array}{c} \text{move} \\ {}^{1}\diagup {}^{2}\diagup {}^{3}\diagdown {}^{4}\diagdown \\ y \qquad z \qquad 20 \end{array}$$

It is understood here that move(x,y,z,w) means that x moved up w unit from y units to z units.

As for the deep syntactic structures, these are trees whose nodes are still predicates, the labels being chosen in $\{1,2,3,4, \text{ATTR,COORD,APPEND}\}$, where COORD accounts for coordinate constructions, ATTR for attributive relations and APPEND for parentheticals, interjections etc.

To get a DSyntR (Deep Syntactic Representation) from the SemR (Semantic Representation or Network), we have to (1) cut the network into connected pieces (2) find in a dictionary a tree corresponding to each of these pieces (3) glue these trees together.

Let us give ourselves a dictionary containing only three definitions; each of them gives a net, the associated tree and the list of conditions (possibly empty) to be satisfied before one can apply the definition. (The following nets are "degenerated" due to space limitations; the system handles real nets as well).

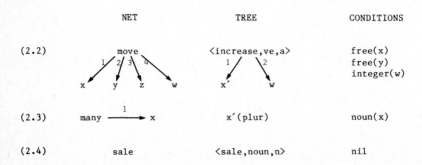

	NET	TREE	CONDITIONS
(2.2)	move x y z w	⟨increase,ve,a⟩ x′ w	free(x) free(y) integer(w)
(2.3)	many $\xrightarrow{\ 1\ }$ x	x′(plur)	noun(x)
(2.4)	sale	⟨sale,noun,n⟩	nil

The first rule means that if w is an integer, and if y and z are variables, then the tree corresponding to the given net has <increase,ve,a> as its root, where ve means verb and a is a variable to be instantiated to <t-ense, p-erson>; the node x′ whose value is unspecified should be instantiated to the correct value during the gluing operation. After applying these rules to the given net, taking into account the correspondence between the nodes of the net and those in the trees, we want to obtain the DSyntR:

(2.5)

$$
\begin{array}{c}
\text{<increase,ve,a>} \\
{}_{1}\diagup \qquad \diagdown{}_{2} \\
\text{<sale,noun,plur>} \qquad 20
\end{array}
$$

The following sections will show how this can be done.

3. TREE SURGERY TECHNIQUES

The trees we will be considering here have labeled arcs and non ordered leaves. Since we want to extract information from these structures and build new ones, it seems natural to extend the predicate eg (unification of PROLOG terms) so as to have tree unification. So doing, the programming remains natural and we take advantage of a major tool of PROLOG.

We define recursively tree templates as lists of the form

    root.<label-1,sub-tree-1>.<label-2,sub-tree-2>...<label-n,sub-tree-n>.W

satisfying the conditions:

- The sub-tree-s are either tree templates or free variables
- W is either free or nil
- the label-s are small integers or words (like ATTR, COND, predicative ...).
- The same integer cannot be used twice as a label in the same list of branches (we call branch a pair of the form <label-i,sub-tree-i>).
- If two branches have the same label (which is then a word) then their associated subtrees have distinct roots.

Equality of tree templates and branches (or lists of branches) is defined recursively as follows:

- Two branches <label-i,sub-tree-i> and <label-j,subtree-j> (in different trees) are equal if they have the same label and if sub-tree-i is either equal or identical to sub-tree-j.
- Two tree templates are equal if they have the same root, the same number of branches and if it is possible to reorder them so that the corresponding branches in both trees are equal.

Two basic procedures are provided to work with these structures: equal and equal-1st. They are defined as follows:

- If the goal equal(t1,t2) succeeds, the free variables appearing in t1 and t2 take the more general values that make t1 equal to t2 as a tree templates, the trailing variables W being instantiated to lists of branches ending with nil or a free variable.
- The goal equal-1st(l1,l2) is equivalent to the goal equal(rt.l1,rt.l2) where rt is any root.

For instance, the goal:

    equal(nd1.<1,nd2.W1>.W2, nd1.<1,nd3.W3>.W4)

miserably fails, since nd2 and nd3 are unequal atoms. Here are a few examples of
questions and answers (this is a trace; the X__ are the free variables generated
by the program):

```
>equal (nd1.<1,nd2.W1>.W2, nd1.<ATTR,nd3.W3>.W4);
W2=<ATTR,nd3.W3>.X28   W4=<1,nd2.W1>.X28

>equal(nd1.<1,nd2.W1>.W2, nd1.<ATTR,nd3.W3>.<1,x>.W5);
W2=<ATTR,nd3.W3>.W5   x=nd2.W1

>eg(t1,nd1.<ATTR,nd2.W1>.W2)
 eg(t2,nd1.<ATTR,nd3.W3>.W4)
 equal(t1,t2);
t1=nd1.<ATTR,nd2.W1>.<ATTR,nd3.W3>.X42   W2=<ATTR,nd3.W3>.X42
t2=nd1.<ATTR,nd3.W3>.<ATTR,nd2.W1>.X42   W4=<ATTR,nd2.W1>.X42
```

It is self evident that these procedures can be used to extract information from a
tree. The last example suggests that they can also be used as builders. Since the
pieces we want to glue together do not have the same root, we define a procedure
sub-tree(x,y) which checks if x can be found somewhere in y (the root of x can be
any node of y). The tree t that is obtained by gluing t1, t2 ... tn is such that
sub-tree(t1,t), sub-tree(t2,t) ... sub-tree(tn,t) is true. However, this goal will
fail if the t's are not in a good order (for instance, if t2 is not a subtree of
t1, the first goal gives t=t1 and the second fails). The procedure "merge" will do
the reordering job.

```
sub-tree(x,y) ->              merge-1(t1,t2,t2) ->
    equal(x,y);                  sub-tree(t1,t2);
sub-tree(x.y,x1.y1) ->        merge-1(t1,t2,t1) ->
    dif(x,x1)                    sub-tree(t2,t1);
    sub-of-br(x.y,y1);
                              merge(t1.nil,t1) ->;
sub-of-br(x,<a,y1>.y2) ->     merge(t1.t2.r,t) ->
    bound(y1)                    merge-1(t1,t2,m)
    sub-tree(x,y1);              /
sub-of-br(x,y1.y2) ->            merge(m.r,t);
    bound(y2)                 merge(t1.t2.r,t) ->
    sub-of-br(x,y2);             append(r,t2.nil,r2)
                                 merge(t1.r2,t);
```

The goal merge (t1.t2. ... .tn.nil, t) succeeds if one can glue the templates t1,
t2 ... tn to get the tree template t.

4. GETTING OUR FIRST DEEP SYNTACTIC REPRESENTATIONS

Since the same word (e.g. time, before ...) can appear twice at the position of a
node in the SemR, the nodes will be pairs <i,w> where the i's are distinct integers and w is the word that labels the given node. In the example above, we
would have the nodes <1,move>, <2,many>, <3,sale>, <4,x>, <5,y> and <6,20> (the
actual choice of the integers is irrelevant, as long as they are different). The
nodes themselves are to be viewed as predicates, whose i-th argument is at the end
of the arc labeled by the integer i. Let us call <u>branching</u> at a node nd of the
SemR the labeled subnet of SemR whose nodes are nd and its immediate sons. Each
branching will be represented by the pair

        <N-ode, S-ons>

where S-ons is the n-tuple <s-1, s-2, ... ,s-n> where s-i is the end of the arc
labeled by i. The nets will be represented by the set of branchings at all its

nodes. The network (2.1) is represented by the list:

```
< <1,move>, < <3,sale>,<4,x>,<5,y>,<6,20> >>.
< <2,many>, < <3,sale> >>.
< <3,sale>, < >>.
< <6,20>   , < >>.nil
```

This represention is redundant. However, in all the cases we have seen, the coverings of a net leading to a DSyntR are such that no two of its subnets have a common arc. Consequently, once a branching has been recognized to figure in such a subnet, it can be discarded since it cannot be in any other one; moreover, the information needed to cover the remainder of the net is all contained in the remaining list of branchings.

It would still be expensive to try all possible coverings of a given net, as their number grows exponentially with the size of the net. Instead, we start with an arbitrary node, say <1,move>, and look in the dictionary to find an entry for the word "move" (we assume a direct access to the packet of clauses headed by the predicate move); we will find the following:

```
<move, SemDef,
    <<n0,move>, <<n1,x>,<n2,y>,<n3,z>,<n4,w>>>
    .nil,

    <n0, <increase,ve,a>>.
       <1, <n1,x′>
          .W1>.
       <2, <n4,w>
          .W2>
       .W3,

       free(y).free(z).integer(w).nil   )->;
```

This is how definition (2.2) has been coded. Definition (2.4) is given by:

```
<sale, SemDef, <<n0,sale>,< >>.nil, <n0,<sale,noun,a>>.W, nil> ->;
```

Now, if we unify the net pattern

```
<<n0,move>, <<n1,x>,<n2,y>,<n3,z>,<n4,w>>.nil
```

found in definition (2.2) with a subnet of SemR, we get

$n0=1$ $n1=3$ $x=sale$ $n2=4$ $n3=5$ $n4=6$ $w=20$ y and z free

The conditions free(y) free(z) and integer(w) being met, the rule applies and gives us the template:

```
<1,<increase,ve,X45>>.
              <1, <3, X46>.
                 X47>.
              <2, <6, 20>.
                 X48>.
           X49
```

As for definitions (2.3) and (2.4), they give us the templates:

```
<3, <X237, noun, plur>>.X238
<3, <sale, noun, X290>>.X291
```

A last rule is needed to take care of the value 20; it will give the template

```
<6, 20>.X338
```

and exhaust the branchings. If we merge these templates, we get:

```
<1,<increase,ve,X45>>.
          <1,
              <3,<sale,noun,plur>>.
              X47>.
          <2,
              <6,20>.
              X48>.
          X49
```

where the labels are put on isolated lines. This is exactly what   we   expected   at
the   end   of   section 2 (2.5) . The deep syntactic representation is obtained from
this template by unifying the trailing variables (X47, X48 and X49) with nil.   The
program that builds the template goes as follows:

```
semant(r,a) ->            elem(a,a.x,x) ->;
   tree-set(r,s)          elem(a,b.x,b.y) ->
   merge(s,a);               elem(a,x,y);

tree-set(nil,nil) -> /;   subset(a.nil,x,y) ->
tree-set(r,al.a2) ->         elem(a,x,y);
   figures(m,r)           subset(a.x,b,y) ->
   /                         elem(a,b,yl)
   trad(m,rl,al,c)           subset(x,yl,y);
   subset(rl,r,r2)
   exec(c)                exec(nil) -> /;
   tree-set(r2,a2);       exec(a.b) ->
                              a
   figures(t,r) ->            exec(b);
      elem(<<N,t>,x>,r,rl);
```

where trad(m,rl,al,c) is <m,SemDef,rl,al,c> when m is an identifier.

5.   SYNTACTIC TRANSFORMATIONS

In the first part of the semantic component, we obtained as   many   different   deep
syntactic   structures as there were different coverings leading to a set of merge-
able tree templates.

Once a deep structure has been obtained, there is still a   number   of   transformations it can undergo that will give rise to other synonymous deep structures: they
are performed by the syntactic transformations, most of which come from the use of
lexical rules. These rules can be seen as a definition of the "algebra" of lexical
relations (aften called functions).

The simplest lexical relation is probably that of synonymy, Syn; for   instance   we
would have, in our dictionary, under the "entry" shoot, the clause:

```
<shoot, Syn, fire> ->;
```

All the lexical functions of a given word will appear in the procedure defined   by
it.   The   coding   of   the   dictionary   is easy to read, the usefull information is
clustered and fastly retrieved.

Associated to Syn is the lexical rule stipulating that any node x   in   the   DSyntR
can be replaced by y to give an equivalent DSyntR if <x, Syn, y> holds. This could

well be seen as a definition of synonymy. Another lexical function, namely SS0, stands for "the noun corresponding to ..."; if increasel is the verb "to increase" and increase2 the noun, then

   ⟨increasel, SS0, increase2⟩ ->;

is in the entry for increasel. To show a non trivial example of a lexical rule, let's look at one of the 48 remaining functions, Operl: ⟨c,Operl,y⟩ holds if y is a verb whose only function is to make of the first argument of c the grammatical subject of a clause whose direct object will be c. For instance:

   ⟨increase2, Operl, show⟩ ->;
   ⟨analysis, Operl, perform⟩ ->;

Here, it is to be noted that

$$x \overset{1}{\longleftarrow} increase2 \overset{2}{\longrightarrow} y$$

represents : "an increase in x of y (quantity)". This is required by the fact that

$$x \overset{1}{\longleftarrow} increasel \overset{2}{\longrightarrow} y$$

represents: x increases by y (e.g. sales increased by 20 000 tons), and that coherence has to be maintained. The new lexical rule will garantee that the DSyntR corresponding to the sentence

   Sales increased by 20 units
   Les ventes ont augmente de 20 unites

can be transformed to the one giving:

   Sales showed an increase of 20 units
   Les ventes ont subi une augmentation de 20 unites

It is given by:

```
SyntR( ⟨v,ve,a⟩.
             ⟨2, y⟩.
             W,
         ⟨o,ve,a⟩.
             ⟨2,⟨S0,noun,sing⟩.
                     ⟨ATTR, an⟩.
                     ⟨2, y⟩.
                     nil
             ⟩.W,
         ⟨v, SS0, S0⟩.⟨S0,Operl,o⟩.nil
     ) ->;
```

The pattern is: SyntR(t-emplatel,t-emplate2,c-onditions), where conditions is the list of conditions to be satisfied before t-emplatel can be replaced by t-emplate2. There are about 60 lexical rules valid for any language. The program that uses them is only 11 lines long.

6. THE DEEP SYNTACTIC COMPONENT

A surface syntactic representation is a tree where the arcs bear as labels the function of the phrase described by the branch they determine. The auxiliaries and prepositions, that were absent in the deep syntactic representation, are also introduced at this level. More generally, all the constructs that depend on individual words are expanded.

As it was noted earlier, the first completive of the noun increase2 is introduced by the preposition in; we talk of "increases in sales". This information must be coded in the dictionary, in the entry for increase2. It will look like:

        <increase2, 1, in, first-completive> ->;
        <increase2, 2, of, second-completive> ->;

What appears as:

        $<increase2,noun,sing> \xrightarrow{\quad 1 \quad} <sale,noun,plur>$

in the deep syntactic structure will then be transformed to

        $<increase2,noun,sing> \xrightarrow[\text{first-completive}]{\qquad\qquad} in \xrightarrow[\text{prepositional}]{\qquad\qquad} <sale,noun,plur>$

As for the auxiliaries, here is a clause for the future of a verb:

        Deep-Synt-Comp(t, <will, ve, pres>.
                          <predicative, X'>.
                          <auxil, <V, ve, inf>.
                                    W'
                          >.nil
) ->
                  equal(t, <V,ve,future>.<1,X>.W)
                  Deep-Synt-Comp(X, X')
                  Deep-Synt-Comp(<V,ve,pres>.W, <V,ve,pres>.W');

The standard PROLOG unification of arguments does not handle directly labeled trees; as we see here, a simple use of the predicate "equal" removes rapidly this limitation. In fact, "equal" figures in almost all the clauses for the procedure Deep-Synt-Comp.

7. THE SURFACE SYNTACTIC AND MORPHOLOGICAL COMPONENTS

Since this research was not primarily interested with morphology, the corresponding component was reduced to a minimum: a set of ad hoc procedures whose role is to write all words with the proper form and ending.

As for the surface syntactic component, its programming is fairly straightforward: it looks for the possible constituants of the sentence - subject, pronominal direct object and verb or verb or verb and non pronominal object, other complements - and expands them into a list. Here we use the fact that PROLOG executes from top to bottom and from left to right. We do not try to generate all the legal orderings of words in a sentence. The first linearization found is the only answer that is kept.

CONCLUSION

Despite the fact that we had to extend the unification procedure to make it more suited to the data structures used in the MTT, it seems that PROLOG was the best language to choose for an implementation: it provides the necessary mechanisms for a direct access to words in the dictionary; the backtracking facilities needed for paraphrasing sentences is given free and finaly, its global semantic was easily extendable to handle networks and labeled trees.

With this technique, we were able to generate french sentences [1] from given se-

semantic networks containing time indications. The implementation was realized   on a VAX 750 running Prolog II.   Our priority was to produce a working MTT system and, to our knowledge, we were the first to succeed in that direction. To do so, we   had to take liberties with MTT, our choices being dictated by efficiency, not orthodoxy. I wish to thank I. Mel'čuk who, nevertheles, spent much time   introduc- ing us to his theory and hope that, in return, he will be able to take advantage of our work.

BIBLIOGRAPHY

[1]   Boyer, M., Génération de phrases à partir de réseaux sémantiques, doc. de trav. no 152, Dept. d'IRO, Université de Montréal (Aug 1984, 117p).

[2]   Colmerauer A., Metamorphosis Grammars, in: Bolc L. (ed), Natural Language Communication with Computers (Springer-Verlag, NY, 1978).

[3]   Colmerauer A. Kanoui H. and Van Caneghem M.,. Prolog, bases théoriques et developpements actuels, TSI 2 no. 4 (1983) 271-311.   ʼ

[4]   Kittredge R.I. and Melčuk I., Towards a Computable Model of Meaning-Text Re- lations within a Sublanguage, IJCAI-1983, Karlsruhe, 1983.

[5]   Mel'čuk,I.A., Opyt Teorii Lingvističeskix Modelej "Smysl <=> Tekst" Semanti- ka, sintaksis (Nauka, Moskow, 1974, 314p).

[6]   Mel'čuk,I.A., Théorie de langage, théorie de traduction. META vol 23 no 4 (1978).

[7]   Simmons R.F., Chester D. Relating Sentences and Semantic Networks with Pro- çedureal Logic, Comm. of the ACM vol 25 no 8 (1982).

[8]   Žolkovskij,A.K. and Mel'čuk,I.A., O vozmožnom metode i instrumentax semanti- českogo sinteza, NTI 5 (1965) 23-28.

[9]   Žolkovskij,A.K. and Mel'čuk,I.A., O semantičeskom sinteze, Probl. kibern. 19 (1967) 177-238. English trans: systems Theory Research, vol. 19, New York.

Natural Language Understanding and Logic Programming
V. Dahl and P. Saint-Dizier (Editors)
© Elsevier Science Publishers B.V. (North-Holland), 1985

FORMAL REPRESENTATION OF TEXTUAL STRUCTURES
FOR AN INTELLIGENT TEXT-EDITING SYSTEM

Saïd Tazi
Jacques Virbel

Langages et Systèmes Informatiques
Université Paul Sabatier
118, route de Narbonne
F - 31062 Toulouse Cedex

In this paper, we try to point out the problem of the communication to an intelligent text-editing system of knowledge
that will make it able to simulate a human editor's behaviour. This knowledge is essentially of linguistic nature
and defined thanks to a new application of the speech-
act theory: the set of physical characteristics of the
text is seen as non-discursive traces of particular meta-
textual performatives. We will propose a general model
of such an intelligent editing system, and will illustrate
the representation of this knowledge trough the example
of the enumeration phenomenon. We will use a local Definite
Clause Grammar (DCG) to express it.

The set of the textual function representations linked
to edition constitutes a kind of an editing-expert-system.

I. PRESENTATION

The project presented here, aims at designing an intelligent text-editing system
in which the human expertise used in formatting and editing natural texts is represented. The conception of such a system is based on three hypothesis that can
be summed up so:

a. First, we think that the set of a text physical characteristics (nature and
style of the characters, disposition arrangement - layout - medium properties,
...) contributes, in a specific way and on different levels, not only to the
legibility, as is well-known, but also to the literacy, i.e.: the meaning of
this text, in a broad sens (Card 1980, Spiro 1980, Waller 1980). This aspect can
be underlined if we modify, experimentally, the text physical characteristics
and if we estimate the correlative modifications of meaning (Ballmer 1978, pp
82-95).

All existing text-editing systems, so far as we know, are available under the
constraint of an explicit and exhaustive definition by authors of their wishes
or intentions about the ultimate shape of one's text ; the definition is reali-
sed by introducing sequences of marks into the properly so called "message". On
the other hand, these text-editing systems indeed may differ about the part, or
level of syntactical integrity (if a priori models of document types are communi-
cated to the system) ; or about the procedural/declarative value of marks used,
and their more or less concrete or conceptual correspondence with actual marks
in a printed text. But in traditional modes of writing, (hand-writing and typing

---

(*) This project is supported in part by a grant provided by CNRS (ATP Intelligence Artificielle).
Authors are indebted to Mario Borillo for helpful discussions.

in particular) authors's intentions about editing are directly formed out by
"natural" marks, available according to the mode of writing used (upper and
lower case characters, indendation, underlining, line feed, and so on). It is
a matter of experience that these natural marks are in general well-identified
and understood by readers, or human editors with a view to printing. So we came
to the conclusion that automatic processing of a "natural layout", based on
linguistic and editorial knowledge is a realistic means for inferring authors's
intentions about the specific level of meaning denoted by the physical (visual)
aspects of any text ; and also that, conversely speaking, some aspects of the
text content can make it possible to control systematically the composition
and the edition operations on this text. In the meantime we assume that the
high polysemic and polyvalent rate of natural marks will presumably make it
necessary to have some semantic knowledge about fields of processed documents
which are referred to, and/or interactive dialogue between parser and user.

Then we tackle two questions:

. What kind of linguistic knowledge holds the understanding of a text within
the prospect of its edition ?

. By which formalism can we represent and use this knowledge in this prospect ?

b. Then we introduce a cognitive and linguistic hypothesis about the semantics
of the text's physical characteristics. We held the text physical aspects to
be non-discursive traces of particular performative speech-acts. For example:
to introduce, to develop, to conclude, to entitle, to subtitle, to enumerate,
to give an example, to demonstrate, to remark, to comment, to insist, to under-
line, to quote, etc... In austinian terms (Austin 1962, Searle 1980), we are led
to study the locutory empiric aspects of various markers (punctuation symbols,
diacritics, line feed, indentation, etc.) in terms of their illocutory (writers
intents) and perlocutory (effects induced on the legibility and the intelligibi-
lity) implication.

These performatives (about a hundred in the reader) correspond principally to
the "fifth" class of Austin's classification ("expositives") and to the "8T"
class of Ballmer's typology ("Theme Models"). They have a component of meta-tex-
tual meaning: they do not describe the primary content of a text segment but
give a characterization of it on a generic level.

c. Methodologically speaking, we follow two ways of representation. On one hand,
from a linguistic point of view, we draw an inspiration from Hjelmslev's analyses
(1961), about the double distinction form/content applied to two levels signi-
fié/signifiant (emic/etic) and from Harris's (1968) in order to define the editorial performatives as metalinguistic operators.

From an information-processing point of view, we think that it is possible,
as a hypothesis, to interpret these operators as editing plan generating trig-
gers in the light of the research about the speech-acts planification. (Allen
1980, Cohen 1979).

The representation of "graphical-linguistic" knowledge led us to define textual
entities - for a given natural language - on two levels: a micro-level and a
macro-level.

On the micro-level we defined the word and the sentence, and on the macro-level
we have the indented line, the enumeration, the paragraph, the title and all
the entities defined by the titles organization (for instance: chapters, parts,
sections...). Our aim is to study, in the same way, other phenomena such as
foot notes, bibliographical references, tables references...

The originality of our project is also linked to the way we studied these phenomena, since this analysis is not restricted to taking certain of them into account
- as it is already done with most of the existing systems - but it is also interested in the semantics and the link between these phenomena and the logical
organization of the text from an editing point of view. This means that we want
to study the interest lying in the fact that a text-editing and manipulating
system recognizes and represents these phenomena. The semantic definition of
the textual phenomena (see the example of the enumeration further on) enables
us to tell that we are in presence of new problems, but we are also confronted
with the usual difficulties that we meet with new methods such as the logical
grammars and the use of the programming language PROLOG (see   Clocksin 1981):
the definition of text grammars increases the complexity of the problem, since
the parsing is made in a much detailed way.

II. GENERAL STRUCTURE OF THE SYSTEM.

The most recent text-editing and manipulating systems, whi'ch can process structured texts, leave it entirely to the user to define this structure as well as
all the formatting commands. But, when an author writes his manuscript, he thinks,
somehow or other, of the structure that his text is going to have, he implici-
tely reveals his intentions of structuration in the way he uses a certain number
of graphical linguistic knowledge such as the use of capital letters, of lower
cases and of some diacritic signs, or the use of space indentation and the change
in line (see Verges, 1973, Reid, 1980, Goldfarb, 1981 and Allen,1981). In the
same way, a human editor uses a certain number of editing and typographic knowledge to format and produce the document.

Starting from these statements, we defined a model of a text editing and manipulating system based on the following ideas:

- We construct a linguistic knowledge base, by representing the necessary knowledge to structure a written text, and we define a parser able to recognize
this knowledge in a text in order to structure it.

- An editorial knowledge base, constructed with the model-markers', typograph'
and editors' skill, will enable the system to format the text from its structure
by mapping between the two knowledge bases via the text and its structure (see
the diagram of the system model).

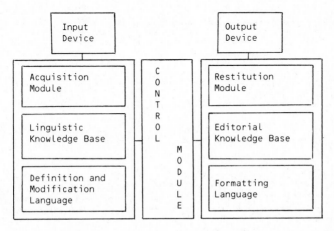

figure 1

The diagram (in figure 1) shows that the system is composed of three main modules:

a) The first one consists in the acquisition of the text, the definition of its structure and the modifications which may be made on a text during an editing session ; this module is made up of three parts:

     * an <u>acquisition module</u> makes it possible to store the text in a text-file from a computer terminal or from several other files in a secondary memory.

     * a <u>linguistic knowledge base</u> with a parser to recognize the text organization and to represent its hierarchical structure in a structure-file.

     * a <u>definition and modification language</u> enables the user to do all the editing operations on the text or on its logical structure, it also enables him to break in on parsing when there is an ambiguity.

b) The second one is concerned with the formatting and restitution of a document from the structured text and an editorial knowledge base on an output device, it is also composed of three components:

     * an <u>editorial knowledge base</u> on which the editors', typographs' and printers' expertise is represented, a mapping between the rules of this base and the structured text is made to produce a document.

     * a <u>formatting language</u> allows the user to modify the formatting parameters (taken in the editorial knowledge base) to have a final presentation of the document dependent on the output device.

     * a <u>restitution module</u> makes it possible to output the final document.

c) A <u>control module</u> satisfies the needs of the following aims:

- the system must be able to process written texts in several natural languages, then the <u>control module</u> allows to pass from one language to another without confusion.

- the knowledge initially put in the system is not exhaustive, and the knowledge bases must be able to change (adding of rules, modifications ...), the control module enables the knowledge bases to remain coherent after any modification.

Inside this kind of frame, we give a definition of a systematic structure of a text, from the highest level (principle title) to the lowest one (character). The principal part of these textual units is well-known in text-editing studies: titles, chapters, paragraphes, sentences, and the like ; but it is also necessary to define some units which are not, in general, identified in spite of their contribution to the structure of the message, and therefore in its visualization. We present now an example of this kind of unit, the enumeration.

III. AN EXEMPLE OF THE ANALYSIS AND PROCESS OF A TEXTUAL STRUCTURE:
    THE ENUMERATION

In order to communicate to the above mentioned system the required knowledge and expertise, we examined, in a very much detailed way, the behaviour of all the textual phenomena (see I) in relation with their expressive power of authors' intentions. The conceptualization of the representation of these phenomena enables us to define algorithms of parsing and generating of corresponding textual structures. To give an illustration, we develop hereafter some aspects of the enumeration.

1. Intuitive presentation

The enumerative way of writing is extremely frequent in texts of different style, and particularly in scientifical, technical, instructional or learning texts.

Moreover it is a complex phenomenon, as much in its significance as in its structural and visual implementation.

Let's first consider a simple example of enumeration that we can schematize intuitively in figure 2.

$$
\begin{array}{l}
* \ A_1 \\
* \ A_2 \\
\qquad \text{a) } A_3 \\
\qquad \text{b) } A_4 \\
* \ A_5 \\
\qquad - \ A_6 \\
\qquad - \ A_7
\end{array}
$$

figure 2.

(in which A_i called item, is any text segment).

We note that two elementary functions, corresponding to simple performatives, are attested and inter-composed: a function (herafter called LIST-ENUMERATION) consists in enumerating items A_i in a linear order with no other explanation of this order, the A_i are introduced by different marks (here [*] and [-] which do not possess any ordering relation generally admitted.

The relation of the items A_5, A_6 and A_7 show that this function can be applied recursively, and create a hierarchy. Moreover, indentation is used to visualize some items.

We can see another function (hereafter called NUMBER-ENUMERATION) which is concerned with A_3 and A_4, in so far as they are introduced by marks [a),b)] supplied with an ordering relation (that would also be the case with [1), 2)], or [α), β)], or [(i), (ii)], or [+, ++] and so on).

2. Conceptual definition

We consider that when an author wants to make an enumeration in his text, it is as though he has to apply a function which has two effects:

- the first one is to organize his text under the enumeration structure

- the second effect is to separate the different textual segments (items) to be enumerated by marking them visually.

Moreover, we noticed that the enumeration phenomenon in a text is composed of two basic functions ; the first being when the order of the occurence of the items is not important, the second being when the order is of some importance.

We called the first function <u>LIST-ENUMERATION</u>, and the second one <u>NUMBER-ENUMERATION</u>.

Each basic function uses a certain mark for the visualization effect. Thus, the marks of Number-Enumeration denote the order of the items [1), 2), 3)] or [(i), (ii), (iii)] or [*, **, ***] or again [α), β), γ) ...] and the marks of List-Enumeration do not denote any order [*)], [+], [(-)] ... (except the linear order of items). Then we noted that these basic functions can be composed in different ways.

Therefore we defined two compositions of the functions: the <u>concatenation composition</u> and <u>recursive composition</u> ; before explaining the composition, let's try a closer study of the basic functions.

2.1. Basic functions

2.1.1. The List-Enumeration Function

This basic function enables the writer to enumerate the text-items without arranging or counting them.

We will represent this function by the predicate <u>List-Enumeration (M,T)</u> which means that we have the text T, enumerated by the list-enumeration function M is the mark, it is taken within the set of marks:

$$= \{*, *), (*), +, +), -, -), (-), ., .), ...\}$$

This set is extensible.

Example

$$\begin{array}{l} * \ A_1 \\ * \ A_2 \\ * \ A_3 \end{array}$$

Figure 3.1.

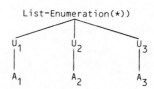

figure 3.2.

The figure 3.1. shows List-Enumeration function with the "*)" mark on the three items A_1, A_2 and A_3, the structural organization is represented by the figure 3.2. (U_i is the label of the A_i item).

2.1.2. The Number-Enumeration function

This is the basic function which enables the writer to enumerate the text items by arranging them in the natural order of occurences of these items, the order, denoted by the semantic of marks.

We represent this function by the predicate <u>Number-Enumeration (M,T)</u> in which M is the mark code representing one of the following situations:

- "numerical": when the marks are noted by cardinal Arabic 1 ; 2 ; 3; ...
- "numerical)": when the marks are the cardinal Arabic followed by a bracket
          1) ; 2) ; 3) ; ...
- "lower-case": when the marks are lower case a ; b ; c ; ...
- "upper-case": when the marks are upper-case A ; B ; C ; ...
- "upper-case)": when the marks are upper-case followed by a bracket
          A) ; B) ; C) ; ...
- "lower-case Roman": when the marks are i ; ii ; iii ; iv ; ...
- "upper-case Roman": when the marks are I ; II ; III ; ...
- "replicated tallies": when the marks are * ; ** ; *** ; ...
etc.

Example

a) A_1
b) A_2
c) A_3

figure 4.1.

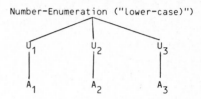

figure 4.2.

Figure 4.1. represents the Number-Enumeration function when mark M is "Lower-case)". The structure of this function is represented by the figure 4.2.

2.2. Composition of basic functions

2.2.1. Concatenation composition

We will say that we concatenate two enumeration functions f_1 and f_2, on a given text T, when we successively apply the function f_2, then f_1 on T. This composition is noted $f_1(f_2(T))$.

In order to see the effect of this composition, let's study an example :

Number-Enumeration ("numerical", List-Enumeration (*,T)) is the predicate that represents the enumeration phenomenon of the figure 5.1.

1* A_1
2* A_2
3* A_3

figure 5.1.

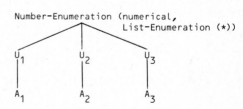

figure 5.2.

The organisation fo this composition is presented in figure 5.2.

2.2.2. Recursive composition.

This composition corresponds to the cases when an enumeration is made in an enumeration. This means that in the text definition which constitutes the item, the author makes another enumeration. This composition may be illustrated by the example of the figures 6.1. and 6.2.

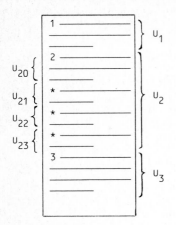

figure 6.1.

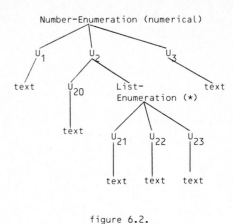

figure 6.2.

In the text that constitutes the 2nd item the author makes another enumeration, there is then a recursive composition of both List-Enumeration and Number-Enumeration.

The structure of the text that has been submitted to this composition is such that we can find a new enumeration structure on the level of the item. Thus we'll have for the preceeding example the structure showed in the figure 3.8.

We studied, in a more detailed way, all the combinations of composition, in order to find out the formal properties which will enable us to lay down constraints to define the algorithms of generating or parsing of these phenomena.

Here is a recapitulatory example:

```
  │ * A₁
  │ * A₂
  │    a) A₃
  │    b) A₄
  │ * A₅                          figure 7.1.
  │    - A₆
  │    - A₇
  │    A₈
  │ * A₉
```

Figure 7.1. shows a general enumeration phenomenon. If we decompose this phenomenon, we realize that there is, first, a List-Enumeration with the "*" mark. There are four items, the first one is a simple text A_1, the second item is an enumerated text, we first find the text A_2, then the Number-Enumeration with the "lower-case)"mark and two items A_3 and A_4. The 3rd item of the first List-Enumeration is also a text composed of a simple text A_5 followed by another List-Enumeration with the "-" mark, and two simple items A_6 and A_7, the end of this item is a simple text A_8. The last item of List-Enumeration is a simple text A_9. The structure of this phenomenon is represented in figure 7.2.

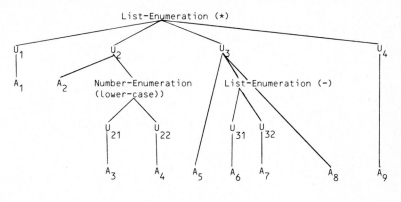

figure 7.2.

3. Logical grammar to represent textual phenomena

Since the birth of Metamorphosis Grammar one has witnessed a great development of the logical grammar formalisms, which intend to represent properties of natural language (Extraposition Grammar, Modifier Structure Grammar ...). These formalisms may have many application fields (natural language generation and understanding, programming languages compiling, etc.).

Both top-down and buttom-up parsing methods are available with logical grammars (Tazi, 1984a). Thus Definite Clause Grammars (DCGs), (Pereira, 1980) are logical grammars which constitute the parsing program (written in PROLOG) ; the parsing process (with DCG) is done through the inference technique of the PROLOG interpreter in a top-down way. Another formalism exists, in which parsing is done in a bottom-up way: a Bottom-Up Parser embedded in Prolog (BUP) (see "Facilities of the BUP Parsing System": Y. Matsumoto et al. in this volume and also (Matsumoto 1983)).

Both methods have their advantages ans weaknesses ; we choose the DCG formalism to represent grammar rules, because of its perspicuity. In DCG, each Prolog clause is built from a grammar rule by adding extra call procedures and arguments to check contextual information. Thus we wrote grammars in order to parse textual phenomena, then we translate these grammars into DCG ; the corresponding Prolog programs are translation of each rule into a clause which, besides contains calls to structuration and visual procedures.

We are interested in the DCG formalism for multiple reasons:

- First we evaluate the power of these new formalisms which were especially used until now to parse natural languages in a totally different level of structuration (sentencial syntax).

- then the DCG formalism enables us to add contextual information process to the parser, something that is well adapted to our problem.

- procedure calls to structure or to display, for example, while parsing are possible by the DCG formalism.

- lastly the PROLOG interpreter uses the inference mecanism necessary to parse.

3.1. List-Enumeration grammar

We do not develop here thoroughly the concept of DCG, but we merely explain how we used the syntax (Pereira, 1980).

Non-terminal symbols are translated into predicates, they are written in lower-case, variable names are capitalised and terminal symbols are in inverted commas.

As one can see, the grammar has two kinds of rules ; one of them is a set of rules having two sides left and right separated by "→", on the right side we can find "," to separate predicates and "." to terminate a rule.

The other kind of rules are under the same form: a simple fact, they constitue the "data base". This grammar is not listed completely here, it should be completed by visualisation and structuration call procedures.

The first rule can be read as "a list-enumeration with the M mark extands from T0 to T if there is a heading-enumeration from T0 to T1 and a set of list-items within the mark M form T1 to T".

The second rule can be read as "a set of list-item within the list mark M extands from T0 to T if there is a list-item marked with the list-mark M from T0 to T1, followed by a sequence of list-items made with the mark M from T1 to T".

$$list\text{-}enumeration\ (M, T0, T) \rightarrow heading\text{-}enumeration\ (T0, T1),$$
$$set\text{-}of\text{-}list\text{-}item\ (M, T1, T).$$

$$set\text{-}of\text{-}list\text{-}item\ (M, T0, T) \rightarrow list\text{-}item\text{-}marked\ (M, T0, T1),$$
$$set\text{-}of\ list\text{-}item\text{-}marked\ (M, T1, T).$$

$$set\text{-}of\text{-}list\text{-}item\text{-}marked\ (M, T0, T) \rightarrow list\text{-}item\text{-}marked\ (M, T0, T1),$$
$$set\text{-}of\text{-}list\text{-}item\text{-}marked\ (M, T1, T).$$

$$set\text{-}of\text{-}list\text{-}item\text{-}marked\ (M, T0, T) \rightarrow list\text{-}item\text{-}marked\ (M, T0, T).$$

$$list\text{-}item\text{-}marked\ (M, T0, T) \rightarrow list\text{-}mark\ (M, T0, T1),$$
$$body\text{-}of\text{-}list\text{-}item\ (M, T1, T2),$$
$$end\text{-}of\text{-}list\text{-}item\ (T2, T).$$

$$body\text{-}of\text{-}list\text{-}item\ (M, T0, T) \rightarrow text\text{-}not\text{-}enumerated\ (T0, T).$$

$$body\text{-}of\text{-}list\text{-}item\ (M, T0, T) \rightarrow text\text{-}not\ enumerated\ (T0, T1),$$
$$rest\text{-}body\text{-}of\text{-}list\text{-}item\ (M, T1, T).$$

$$rest\text{-}body\text{-}of\text{-}list\text{-}item\ (M, T0, T) \rightarrow nested\text{-}enumeration\ (M, M1, T0, T1),$$
$$body\text{-}of\text{-}list\text{-}item\ (M, T1, T).$$

$$rest\text{-}body\text{-}of\text{-}list\text{-}item\ (M, T0, T) \rightarrow nested\text{-}enumeration\ (M, M1, T0, T).$$

$$text\text{-}not\text{-}enumerated\ (T0, T) \rightarrow connects\ (T0, W, T1),\ words\ (W),$$
$$text\text{-}not\text{-}enumerated\ (T1, T).$$

$$nested\text{-}enumeration\ (M, M1, T0, T) \rightarrow list\text{-}enumeration\ (M1, T0, T),\ M1 \neq M.$$

$$nested\text{-}enumeration\ (M, M1, T0, T) \rightarrow number\text{-}enumeration\ (M1, T0, T).$$

$$list\text{-}mark\ (M, T0, T) \rightarrow connects\ (T0, M, T),\ is\text{-}list\text{-}mark\ (M).$$

heading-enumeration (TO,T) → connects (TO,C,T), is-heading-enum (C).

is-list-mark ("").*

is-list-mark (")").*

is-list-mark ("-").

is-list-mark ("-.").

is-heading-enum ("CR").

is-heading-enum (":CR").


```
/* we consider the ASCII code of strings between " " */
```

words (W) means that W is a string of characters different from those used to mark the list-enumeration and number-enumeration, and different from those used in the heading-enumeration and end-of-list-item.

We used the same connects-predicate as the one used by Pereira, connects (T1,W, T2) means: "Terminal symbol w lies between T1 and T2 in the text to be parsed.

In order to achieve the recognition of the text structure from the level above mentionned, the parser must analyse the lower level, i.e.: sentences, words, abbreviations, characters and other graphic symbols. This stage of the analysis is not presented here, but, method and procedure are by some way of the same kind.

In order to exemplify the range of textual data that this grammar takes into account, we may give an analysis of some passages of our text. For instance, one can observe that Section II ("General structure of the system", - above) contains two enumerations (which are spontaneous written products, and are not any ad-hoc compositions).

The first one lies on § 3, and it is composed of two units (items) introduced with a hyphen (without indentation) followed up by a space and the first letter of the first word is capital. It is a List-Enumeration, in our terms. It must be noticed that the enumeration itself (as the second one) begins with a sequence of marks generally bound up: a colon, a blank space, a line feed, and particular lead (in comparison with the current lead in the body of the text), which is also the same between items.

The parsing process on this example will be done so: the computer program takes in input the text as it is presented in § 3, section II ; in this example the processing will start at the beginning of the enumeration, and we assume that there has not been any problems in the parsing process up to now. The parser will find a colon followed by a carriage return, which will be interpreted as a heading enumeration thanks to the "is-heading-enum (":CR")" predicate ; there is a set of list-items which will be recognized by the "set-of-list-item" predi-cate, the mark will be recognized thanks to "is-list-mark ("-")" predicate. Thus two list-items are found, and the structuration procedure will produce the tree of figure 8 as their representation:

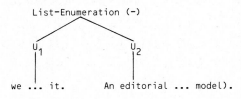

figure 8.

The second enumeration is more complex. It consists in a discursive commentary
of figure 1 and it contains three upper-level items introduced with alphabetic
marks "a", "b", "c", combined with a close parenthesis separator ("lower-case)").
On a lower-level, each one of these items is composed again of respectively
three, three and two items introduced by an asterisk associated with a particular
indentation in the first two cases, and by hyphen mark without indentation in
the third case. This second enumeration is made of a Number-Enumeration with
a recursive composition of List-enumeration inside of each first level item.
We give here the representation of this enumeration.

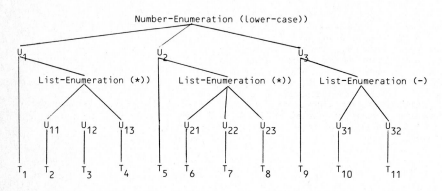

figure 9.

T_1 is the text "the first one ... parts"

T_2 is the text "an acquisition module ... memory."

T_3 is the text " a linguistic ... file."

T_4 is the text " a definition ... ambiguity."

T_5 is the text "the second one ... compenents"

T_6 is the text "an editorial ... document."

T_7 is the text " a formatting ... device."

T_8 is the text "a restitution ... document."

T_9 is the text "A control ... aims"

T_{10} is the text "the system ... confusion."

T_{11} is the text "the knowledge ... modification."

We can point out a remark about these examples. It appears that the above so-
called "non-discursive equivalence" between physical aspects of text and meta-
textual content associated with the performative value of marks, is a gradual
relation ; for instance in the second enumeration, the first and the second
items marked by a) and b) begin with a discursive enumerative phrase, very closed
to a conjunction or an adverb ("The first one", "the second one"). This "dual-
like" relation, to say it in a rather analogical way, makes it possible to study
the semantics of marks into the natural language itself.

IV. CONCLUSION

In this paper we presented a rather general pattern of intelligent text-editing system, as well as a method to analyse the conception of such a system, and also a detailed example of the textual structures that we want to recognize and characterize. It is sometimes required (Meyrowitz,1982, Furuta, 1982) that the classical formatting and editing system have to be augmented by new and more powerful conceptualizations. We agree with this requirement and we wish that our research contributes to it.

The project is still in its conception phasis, and we design its implementation within the Prolog language. The use of such a language will increase the system prover but it could bring some drawbacks. Indeed, we conceived the text-editing system round knowledge bases (linguistic and editorial) and the implementation of knowledge bases is quite adequate in Prolog. The parsing tools offered by the Prolog environnement (i.e. DCG) will enable us to analyse, to represent and to manipulate easily the text logical structures. The command language will be parsed within the same methodology. On the other hand, the character manipulation is not efficient within Prolog and a compromise could be found in the use of a machine language to implement the character manipulation primitives (Konagaya 1984). Nevertheless, our first care is to analyse and formalize the textual structures.

REFERENCES

Allen, A.V. and Ullman J.D., The theory of parsing, translating and compiling, (vol.1), Prentice-Hall, Series in Automatic Computation, S.D.

Allen, T., Nix, R. and Perlis, A., PEN A hierarchical document editor, in: Proc. ACM SIGPLAN SIGOA SYMP. Text Manipulation, Sigplan Notices (ACM) 16,6 (1981), 74-81.

Allen, J.F. and Perrault, C.R., Analysis Intention in Utterances, Artificial Intelligence, 15 (1980), 143-178.

Austin, J., How to do Things with Words (Oxford University Press, 1962).

Ballmer, Th. and Brennenstuhl, W., Speech Act Classification. A study in the Lexical Analysis of English Speech Activity Verbs (Springer Verlag, 1981).

Ballmer, Th., Logical Grammar (North-Holland, 1978).

Beaugrand (de), R., Text Production. Toward a Science of Composition (Ablex 1984).

Borillo, M. (ed.), Representation des connaissances et raisonnement dans les sciences de l'homme, Colloque INRIA, Saint-Maximin, 1979 (Ed. INRIA 1979).

Carbonnel, J.G., Meta-Language Utterances in Purposive Discourse, Dept. Of Comp. Sc., Carnegie-Mellon University (1982).

Card, S.K. and all., Computer Text-Editing: An Information Processing Analysis of a Routine Cognitive Skill, Cognitive Psychology, 12 (1980), 32-74.

Clocksin, W.F. and Mellish, C.S., Programming in Prolog, (Springer-Verlag, Berlin, Heidelberg, New-York, 1981).

Cohen, P.R. and Perrault, C.R., Elements of a Plan-bases Theory of Speech Acts, Cognitive Science, 3 (1979), 177-212.

Davis, R. and Lenat, D.B., Knowledge-Based Systems in Artificial Intelligence (Mc Graw-Hill, 1982) Advanced Computer Science Series.

Document Composition Facility Generalized Markup Language: Concepts and Design Guide. Program Product (IBM Ed., april 1980).

Fredericksen, C.H. and Dominic, J.F. (eds), Writing: the Nature, Development, and Teaching of Written Communication, Volume 2: Writing: process, development and communication (Lawrence Erlbaum, 1981).

Furuta, R., Scolfied, J. and Shaw, A., Document Formatting Survey, Concepts and issues, ACM Computing Surveys, 14, 3 (1982), 417-472.

Goldfarb, C.F., A generalized approach to Document Markup, in: Proc. ACM SIGPLAN SIGOA SYMP. Text Manipulation, Sigplan Notices ACM, 16,6 (1981), 68-73.

Gregg, L.W. and Steinberg, E.R. (eds), Cognitive Processes in Writing (Lawrence Erlbaum, 1980).

Grimes, J.E., The Thread of Discourse (Mouton, 1975).

Harris, Z.S., Mathematical Structures of Language (John Willey and Sons, 1968).

Hjelmslev, L., Prolegomena to a Theory of Language (Univ. of Wisconsin Press, Madison, 1961).

Kolers, P.A., Wrolstad, M.E. and Bouma, H. (eds), Processing of Visible Language. NATO Conference Series (Plenum Press, 1980).

Konagaya, A. and Umemura M., Knowledge Information Processing Language: Shape Up, New Generation Computing, 2, 2 (1984).

Kowarski, I., Les bases de données textuelles : Etude du concept de document et application à deux réalisations, Thèse, Grenoble (1983).

Matsumoto, Y., Tanaka, HA., Miyoshi, H. and Yasukama, H., A bottom-up Parsed Embedded in PROLOG, New Generation Computing, 1, 2 (1983), 145-158.

Melese, B., MENTOR-RAPPORT, Manipulation de textes structurés sous MENTOR ; les éditeurs dirigés par la syntaxe, tome 2, in: Proc. INRIA-Aussois (1983).

Mellish, C.S., Towards Top-down Generation of Multi-Paragraph Text, in: Proc. of the Sixth European Conference on Artificial Intelligence, Pisa, Italie, (1984).

Meyrowitz, N. and Van Dam, A., Interactive Editing Systems, Part I and II, ACM Computing Survey, 14, 3 (1982) 321-416.

Pereira, F, and Warren, D., Definite Clause Grammar for Language Analysis. A survey of the Formalism and a Comparison with Augmented Transition Networks, Artificial Intelligence, 13 (1980), 231-278.

Reid,K.B., Scribe: a document specification language and its compiler, PhD Carnegie-Mellon University, (October 1980).

Searle, J., Speech Act Theory and Pragmatics (Reidel, 1980).

Small, S., Viewing Word Expert Parsing as Linguistic Theory, in: Proc. IJCAI 7th (1981), 70-76.

Soulhi, S., Un modèle logique de certains actes de communication, Rapport Interne, LSI-CRN, Toulouse (1984).

Spiro, R.J. and all (eds), Theoretical Issues in Reading Comprehension. Perspective form Cognitive Psychology, Linguistics, Artifical Intelligence and Education (Lawrence Erlbaum, 1980).

Stromfors, O., and Jonesjo, L., The implementation and experiences of a structure-oriented tex editor, Research Report, Datalogi Linkoping (March 1981).

Tazi, S., Elimination of left-recursion, bottom-up and top-down parsing in Prolog, Rapport Interne LSI-CRN, Toulouse (1984a).

Tazi, S., Recherche sur la représentation de connaissances textuelles en vue d'édition "intelligente", Rapport Interne LSI-CRN, Toulouse (1984b).

Verges-Escuin, J.C., and Verjus, J.P., Reconnaissance automatique des structures des textes en vue de l'édition, RAIRO,B-3 (octobre 1973), 85-120.

Virbel, J., La composante matérielle des structures textuelles, in: Borillo, A., Borillo, M., Farinas del Cerro, L. and Virbel, J. (eds), Approches formelles de la sémantique naturelle, (LSI, Toulouse, 1982).

Virbel, J., Quelques nouveaux contours de l'informatique linguistique et de l'ingénieurie du langage naturel dans l'analyse et le traitement des données textuelles, Rapport Interne LSI-CRN, Toulouse (1984).

Virbel, J., Représentation des connaissances et édition de textes, Bulletin de la Recherche en Informatique et Automatique, 90 (1984), 27-33.

Warren, H.D., Perpetual Processes. An Unexploited Prolog Technique, in: Proc. of the Workshop on Prolog Programming Environments, Linköping (1982).

Werlish, E., A text Grammar of English (Quell & Meyer, 1976).

Whiteman, M.F. (ed.), Writing: the Nature, Development and Teaching of Written Communication, Volume I: Variation in Writing: functional and linguitic-cultural differences (Lawrence Erlbaum, 1981).

Natural Language Understanding and Logic Programming
V. Dahl and P. Saint-Dizier (Editors)
© Elsevier Science Publishers B.V. (North-Holland), 1985

LOGIC BASED NATURAL LANGUAGE PROCESSING

Camilla B. SCHWIND

Centre National de la Recherche Scientifique
Groupe Représentation et Traitement des Connaissances
31, Chemin Joseph Aiguier
13402 Marseille Cédex 9
France

We describe the theory and the implementation of a natural
language processing system which is designed as an interface for knowledge base access. Our system is characterized
on each of these two levels by a uniform representation language : LOGIC on the theoretical level and PROLOG on the
implementation level. The knowledge base contains in addition to the proper "database knowledge" all natural language processing components ; i.e. lexical and parsing laws,
semantic laws, frame and possibility laws. All these laws
are logical formulae resp. PROLOG clauses. Natural language
queries and assertions are transformed into intermediate
tree structures and are interpreted with respect to the
knowledge base frames which are related by deduction laws
to the proper database knowledge. A dialogue is accompanied
by metalaws which state what is the context, the focus, and
the meaning of previous sentences. These metalaws are used
for the resolution of ellipses and pronouns.

1. INTRODUCTION.

This paper describes the theoretical as well as the applicational aspect of our
research on natural language understanding and processing. On the theoretical level
the system is presented in logic and on the implementation level it is programmed
in PROLOG. Our system is conceived as a knowledge base access module. Hence the
natural language processing is viewed as the understanding of assertions and
queries on the background of a specific domain. Moreover we do not interpret single
isolated sentences but sentences within a dialogue. For that reason we are concerned with the central problems of ellipses and pronoun resolution.

Our whole system is described in logic. Therefore, at different moments, we will
introduce non-logical predicates which are needed for the description of the
different parts of our system (lexical and parsing predicates, frames and semantic
predicates, meta predicates for dialogue and context description). In this paper,
we limit ourselves to classical predicate logic for the representation of the
natural language itself. Sometimes, it does not look like that, because we have
second order predicates for frames and semantic relations. But these "second-
order" predicates together with their axioms turn out to be representable in first
order logic ; i.e. we can define them in first order in such a way that their
axioms are deducable from that definition. Therefore, our logical language is a
conservative extension of classical first order predicate logic. We insist a little
bit on this remark, because we have observed that people are often not very careful
when they pretend to need some extension of classical logic. This seems to be the
case on a superficial level but is not always profoundly true. Claims for the need
of extensions are frequently based on some arbitrary examples which seem not to be
representable in first order logic. But the only way to know if some phenomenon is

or is not describable in first order, is to show that <u>any</u> of its representations
is not-first-order. In order to say something on "any representation" one has to
define what is a representation at all (and what isn't). We think that there are
hard philosophical problems involved here which are by non way resolved or even
grasped in a formal way.

The whole understanding process focus on the adaptation of the natural language
sentences to predefined frames. These are inspired by semantic case structures
and are formulated around verbs. Clearly, it is not possible to find general frames and we did not try that. We formulated completely domain specific frames
around domain specific verbs. It was possible and necessary to proceed in this way
because our understanding of verbs is largely based on the assumption that a verb
represents an action on the knowledge base and we have observed that those actions
are never the same for two different domains. The frames we defined are <u>minimal</u> in
two aspects : on the one hand, we always tried to find the most general <u>semantic</u>
attributes for the noun phrase complements and to deduce more specific frames by
frame deduction laws. On the other hand, we tried to find a minimal set of noun
and prepositional phrase complements for every verb. The adaptation device of sentences to frames allows then more complements within sentences under certain conditions. We proceeded in this way because we think that we have a better chance
to find so <u>the good frames</u> for a domain.

PROLOG is our implementation language but we used it in the spirit of a descriptive
language, not as a procedural programming language (which it is too !). Therefore -
we have in almost all parts of our system an equivalence logic (HORN-clauses) -
PROLOG Program.

We think, that the greatest benefit of PROLOG is, that it allows (and conducts you)
to a big extent, to formulate your problems and your ideas in a very direct and
descriptive way without bothering you with too much problems related to execution,
briefely procedural problems. On the other hand, the powerful feature of PROLOG to
conduct one to a clear programming style most near to the conceptual level, is at
the same time a considerable disavantage with respect to efficiency. Unfortunately,
pretty programs are very often very unefficient and any trial (last not least the
slash !) to render them more efficient (or simply executable) distroys the beautiful descriptive program. In some cases however the necessary changements are so
mechanical and formal that we could think of an automatic transformation of a
PROLOG program description to an executable PROLOG program.

2. THE DEDUCTIVE KNOWLEDGE BASE.

On the theoretical level, the knowledge base is a conjunction of formulas, i.e. a
set of formulas. Conceptually, we distinguish the following parts :

- Natural language processing laws

- Semantic predicate laws

- Frame laws

- Possibility laws

We will present the lexical and parsing laws in the next paragraph about natural
language processing.

Semantic predicates as well as frames and possibility laws are defined on sets of
concepts and constants. The constants are the primitive objets of the base itself
(e.g. in a database about musical work the composer names, the names of the elements
of the attribute sets) and the verbs. Concepts are represented as one place predicates (e.g. composer, piano concert,...). We think, that the semantic predicates
and their properties, which are formulated by axioms, are general. We have found
and used a common set of predicates for different domains . As pointed out above,

our semantic predicates are second order but are representable within first-order logic, i.e. are only a conservative extension.

Definition.

Let P be a set of predicates of higher order and let A be a set of axioms about the elements of P. Then P is conservative iff their is a definition of the predicates of P within first order logic such that the axioms in A are true under that definition.

Let us illustrate this definition by two of our semantic predicates :

isa (X,Y) where X is a concept and Y a constant (not a verb), means that Y is an X, e.g. isa(opera,fidelio).

sup (X,Y) where X and Y are concepts means that X is superordinated to Y ; e.g. sup(concert,piano concert).

The axioms belonging to these two predicates are :

(i)   isa $(X,Y) \wedge$ sup $(Z,X) \rightarrow$ isa (Z,Y)

(ii) sup $(X,Y) \wedge$ sup $(Y,Z) \rightarrow$ sup (X,Z)

The first order representations of sup and isa are defined as follows :

$$\text{sup } (a,b) \Longleftrightarrow_{df} \forall \: x \: b \: (x) \rightarrow a \: (X)$$
$$\text{isa } (a,b) \Longleftrightarrow_{df} \quad a(b)$$

It is easy to see that (i) and (ii) are deducable from these definitions.

Possibility laws define prepositional restrictions, i.e. they are used to verify if two nouns may be related to a propositional phrase. Possibility laws are partly defined by use of the semantic predicates.

Example :

can-mod $(X,Y) \rightarrow$ possible $([of,X,Y])$

mod $(X,Y) \rightarrow$ can-mod (X,Y)

fit $(X_1,X) \wedge$ fit $(Y_1,Y) \wedge$ mod $(X_1,Y_1) \rightarrow$ can-mod (X,Y)

isa $(X,Y) \rightarrow$ fit (X,Y)

sup $(X,Y) \rightarrow$ fit (X,Y)

star $(Y,Y_1) \wedge$ fit $(X,Y_1) \rightarrow$ fit (X,Y)

It is possible to relate two concepts X and Y by "of" to a prepositional phrase whenever X can modify Y. "modify" is given explicitely as a semantic relation and it can be derived via isa and sup-relations. The application of the star-operation takes into account that the noun phrases under question are eventually complex, i.e. have prepositional or adjective complements.star (X,Y) is true whenever X is the "main" concept of a noun phrase Y.E.g. :

star([with,[the,ref(little,boy)],[the,ref(big,ref(sharp,knife))]],boy)

Our language frames are completely domain specific. Frames are verb concentrated, i.e. for every (domain specific) verb, there is a frame which specifies the semantic properties of the verb complements. Formally, a frame $F \subset \bigcup_{j>3} (V \times \bigtimes_{i=1}^{3} B)$, where V is the set of verb constants and B the set of concepts.

Example :

frame ([create, human world])

frame ([V,X,Y]) ∧ sup (X,Z) → frame ([V,Z,Y])

frame ([V,X,Y]) ∧ sup (Y,Z) → frame ([V,X,Z])

By these laws, new frames can be generated. The frames are the proper interface between the natural language sentences and the database.

The database itself consists of sets of tuples together with deductive laws (in the spirit of the relational model).

Example : Chamber music pieces

piece (N,K,O,C,D,T,L,I) means that :

N is the name of the piece

K is the category

O is the opus (or KV or BWV) number

C is the composer's name

D is the date of creation

T is the duration

L is the key

I is the list of the instruments

e.g. piece (-,sonata, op-69, Beethoven,1805,29 min,A-dur,[violoncello,piano])

Composer (N,D1,D2) means that :

N is the name of a composer

D1 is his/her birth date

D2 is his/her death date

e.g. composer (Beethoven,1770, 1827)

Sample integrity laws :

piece (-, string quartet,-,-,-,-,-,[1.violin,2.violin, viola, violoncello])

The instruments of a string quarter are 1.violon, etc.

piece (-,-,KV-NR, Mozart,-,-,-,-)

Mozart's compositions have KV-numbers.

Sample deduction law :

piece (-,X quartet,-,-,-,-,-,[X,violin,viola,violoncello])

In order to deduce answers to questions we have to relate on the one hand the questions to language frames and on the other the language frames to database entries respectively to facts deducable from the database. The former process will be described in the next paragraph. The derivation of facts from the database is carried out by the application of deduction laws. Since both, the language frames as well as the database structure are predefined, this derivation rules do not depend on specific questions and they can be defined once for any given database structure. We think that the language frames are not liable to change once they have been well chosen. But the database structure may change, producing then a derivation rule change. In this paper however, we are not concerned with that problem. We assume that the derivation rules are invariant. Clearly, they are completely domain specific, since they depend entirely on the domain specific parts of the knowledge base. The database entries are generally not organized around the verbs.

In order to describe the deductions, we use the one place predicate "fact". Facts are more or less structured as frames, i.e. a fact is a tuple $[V,C_1...C_n]$, where V is a verb constant and the C_i are complements. On the contrary to frames, facts contain rather constants or their descriptions than concepts. And facts can have more complements for a given verb than the frames for the same verb. Facts are generally derived from database entries.

Some of the typical database deduction laws for our sample base are :

piece $(X,Y,Z,C,D,T,K,I) \rightarrow$ fact $([\text{compose},C,X])$

piece $(X,Y,Z,C,D,T,K,I) \rightarrow$ fact $([\text{compose},C,X,[\text{in},D]])$

Note that a fact can be "longer" than a frame. We will see in the next paragraph that sentences too may be adapted to frames which are shorter than they are.

On the other hand some semantic relations may be deduced from the database frames, e.g.

piece $(X,Y,Z,C,D,T,K,I) \rightarrow$ mod (K,X)

piece $(X,Y,Z,C,D,T,K,I) \rightarrow$ mod (I,Y)

piece $(X,Y,Z,C,D,T,K,I) \rightarrow$ isa (Y,X)

Fig. 1 shows a schematic representation of the semantic relation assertions deducable from our sample database.

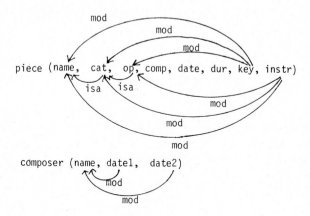

Fig. 1

Frames are minimal and do not contain information about possible embedded prepositional phrases of their concept complements. Given a frame and semantic relations on its complements, and a fact "belonging" to that frame, we can derive other more specific facts from it :

frame $(V,C,D) \wedge$ fact $(V,X,Y) \wedge$ fit $(C,X) \wedge$ fit $(D,Y) \wedge$
   mod $(U,X) \rightarrow$ fact $(V,[prep, X,U], Y)$

Analogous laws exist for other frame schemas and the other complements of the frame schemes. prep is a constant and should indicate that there is some preposition for this pair of concepts (e.g. "for" for the pair (instrument, category), i.e. "concert for piano").

3. NATURAL LANGUAGE PROCESSING.

The parsing laws are formulated as described in (1). PROLOG can be used as a meta-compiler for such type of grammars (2). We will briefly recall the mechanism of logical parsing. Every syntactic category k (e.g. S, NP, V,...) is associated with a predicate which has most times three places. (The number of places depends on the different informations which have eventually to be sent around within a parsing tree). k (X, XR, S) means that the beginning of the list X is a k ("belongs to the category k), the tail is XR and the meaning is S.

Example :

np ((all children play in the garden),(play in the garden),($\forall$x children (x))).

To every parsing rule (context-free grammar rule) of the form

$A \rightarrow B_1 B_2...B_k$ is associated a clause

$B_1(X,X_1,S_1) \wedge B_2(X_1,X_2,S_2) \wedge ... \wedge B_k(X_{k-1},XR,S_k) \rightarrow A(X,XR,S)$

where $S=f(S_1,...S_k)$ is the result of building the semantic representation expression belonging to A out of the expressions belonging to the B_i.

Example :

$np(X,X_1,N_1) \wedge v(X_1,X_2,V) \wedge np(X_2,XR,N_2) \rightarrow s(X,XR,[V,N_1,N_2])$

This rule describes and analyses a sentence X with one np-complement X_2 and produces the list structure $[V,N_1,N_2]$ where V is the structure generated by the verb group and N_1 (resp. N_2) the one generated by the subject (resp. object).

The german grammar presented here is based on (4) and on our previous work on the translation of natural language sentences into temporal logic formulae. In (15) this translation function has been described by an attributed feature grammar, run by a meta-compiler. One of the problems with german grammar is the "free" word order, i.e. the subject of a sentence can occur after the verb and any verb complement, i.e. any noun phrase or prepositional phrase can occur before the verb. For an example, the sentence

Der Vater gibt dem Kind die Milch in der Küche.

(The father gives the milk to the child in the kitchen)

can have the following permutations :

Dem Kind gibt die Mutter die Milch in der Küche.
Die Milch gibt die Mutter dem Kind in der Küche.
In der Küche gibt die Mutter dem Kind die Milch.

Our grammar includes all of the following sentence patterns together with all possible permutations :

np v (ap)   (elements within parentheses are optional)

np v np (ap)

np v (ap) pp

np v np np (ap)

np v np (ap) pp

np stands for noun phrase.

v stands for verb.

ap stands for adverbial phrase.

pp stands for prep np.

Noun phrases admet all types of prepositional as well as relative clause embeddings.

The syntactic analysis laws generate an intermediate "semantic-syntactic" structure for every sentence. These S-expressions are defined as follows :

(1) [V,N1,...Nk] is an S-expression where V is a verb-expression, Ni are N-expressions.

(2) Every verb predicate name is a verb expression.

(3) If A is an adverbial expression, and V a verb then [V,A] is a verb expression.

(4) Every proper name is an atomic N-expression.

(5) Every pronoun is an atomic N-expression.

(6) Every noun predicate or every list of noun predicates is an atomic N-expression.

(7) ref(A,N) is an N-expression where A is an adjective predicate and N is an atomic N-expression or an N-expression formed by (7).

(8) [ART,N] is an N-expression where ART is d, u, all, or w and N is an N-expression by (7) or atomic.

(9) [P,N1,N2] is an N-expression where P is a prepositional predicate and N1, N2 are N-expressions and N1 is not formed by (10).

(10) Every S-expression, containing an expression rp(N) with N an N-expression not formed by (10) at some Ni-position, is an N-expression whenever the position of rp(N) within the N-expression is the same as the position of the N-expression within is S-expression.

One can see that S-structures are lists where the head is a verb structure and the other elements are the structures belonging to the noun phrase and prepositional phrase complements of the sentence. These semantic trees (13) appear also in (15) as an intermediate state when sentences are translated to logical formulae. From this it is easy to see that S-structures are transducable to the logical formulae which represent the meaning of the original sentence.

As we have mentioned in the last paragraph, natural language sentences have to be adopted (or matched) to language frames, in order to be interpreted correctly with respect to an underlying database entry or fact. Informally, we proceed in the following way. First, the verb-expression of the S-expression is matched against the verb concept of a frame expression. Either an identical verb constant is found or the verb of the sentence is subordinated to the verb constant within the frame. We see that the appropriate frame is accessed by the verb and its semantical relations (i.e. subordinated verbs). By a second step the np and pp complements of the sentence are matched against the cases whereby the pattern is eventually permuted, fulfilled or extended. Permuation can become necessary because of the free word order. Sometimes, an np at the top of a sentence can be identified to be the object of the sentence because of the morphological manifestation of its case. This is however not always possible since nominative and accusative have often the same form. For that reason, we check semantically if an np can be the subject or object or indirect object of the verb. We take the first element of the language frame and look for a noun phrase in the S-structure which can fit it, by use of the fit-axioms defined above. If one such np is found it will get the place within the S-structure which corresponds to the place of the corresponding concept within the frame. If no np can be found which could belong to the frame concept, we fulfil that place within the S-structure by that concept. By continuing in the same way through the whole language frame, we produce a transformed sentence structure which has its np permuted and its lacking complements fulfilled by the semantic descriptions which are required by the underlying frame. If the S-structure contains additional complements, then these are kept at the end of it provided that those additional elements meet some restrictions. In German, we allow only prepositional phrases occurring unforeseen. In French there would be moreover a small list of concepts which could occur additionally (e.g. la nuit = in the night). Fullfilling is necessary, because all kinds of complements may be absent in sentences whenever they do not play any role in some context. Often, sentences do not specify certain cases, which however have to underly semantically, because they are just not important in some situations. The following is the more formal definition of this adaptation process.

Definition

Let $S = [V, N_1, \ldots N_K]$ be a S-structure. Then S is adaptable to the language frame $[P, C_1, \ldots C_n]$ if V is adaptable to P and there are subsets $\{M_1, \ldots M_m\} \subset \{N_1, \ldots N_k\}$ and $\{B_1, \ldots B_m\} \subset \{C_1, \ldots C_n\}$ such that M_i fits B_i and $\{N_1, \ldots N_k\} \subset \{M_1, \ldots M_m\}$ contains only pp-structures. A verb expression V is adaptable to a verb concept P iff $star(V,P)$ or $sup(V,P)$ or there is W such that $star(V,W)$ and $sup(W,P)$.

A noun phrase (resp. prepositional phrase) expression M is adaptable to a noun concept C iff $star(M,C)$ or there is N such that $star(M,N)$ and ($sup(C,N)$ or $isa(C,N)$).

If a sentence cannot be adapted to a frame in this way, this may be the case for two reasons : either the verb cannot be found as frame verb or the complements cannot be adapted. In this case the system asks the user a counter question by giving him the parts of the sentence it has understood. Such counter questions are already asked during the lexical analysis whenever a word cannot be found in the lexicon.

4. DISAMBIGUATION.

There are typical syntactic ambiguities in natural language grammars. E.g. one can never decide if a prepositional phrase occurring after a noun phrase is embedded into that np or belongs to the verb. We only accept embedded noun phrases if they are possible for semantic reasons i.e. we look in the knowledge base for a possibility law involving the two respective noun concepts. Our logical parsing grammar allows the incorporation of such semantic control axioms in a very elegant and flexible way. The corresponding parsing law is :

$$np(X,X_1,N_1) \wedge prep(X_1,X_2,P) \wedge np(X_2,XR,N_2) \wedge possible\ ([P,N_1,N_2]) \rightarrow np(X,XR,[P,N_1,N_2])$$

5. BACKTRACKING DIMINUTION HEURISTICS.

The parsing process may be considerably ameliorated when backtracking is minimized, i.e. when the algorithm is formulated as deterministic as possible. For that purpose, we have incorporated some heuristic laws in the grammar which eventually prevent the call of some type of clauses :

An expression is only sentence-parsed, if it contains a verb. If not we proceed immediately to ellipses analysis. If it contains only a verb we proceed to ellipses analysis too.

The relative clause law is only called if the rest of the sentence being parsed contains a verb or auxiliary.

Whenever a subexpression begins with an article, it is invariably a noun phrase and no other law will be tried.

Although generally we do not analyse morphological properties of German, i.e. we do not verify that the adjectives, verbs, nouns, etc. have the proper number, case, person, genus, we exploit these morphological properties in order to prevent backtracking.

The law describing genetive embeddings after nouns (e.g. die Tasche des Vaters = the father's pocket) is only called when the embedded noun phrase begins with an article in genetive form.

The case of relative pronouns is used in order to find more quickly the correct order of the other complements and their correct case role.

6. ELLIPSES PROCESSING.

Noun phrase ellipses are resolved by inserting the ellipses parts into the S-expression belonging to the last sentence, whereby each part is inserted at the place of that part of the last sentence which is most similar to it. Again, "similar" is a logical predicate involved in general semantic knowledge base laws, and the similarity is uniquely decided on that semantic background. The elliptic sentences are processed in the following way. The S-structure of the last sentence is kept and accessed as term of the dialogue control predicate "old", which is typically one of the predicates which changes at every dialogue state. Then we look for that element in the S-structure which fits the best the ellipses structure.

A verb fits only a verb and a np or pp fits another one if they are fitted by a common element. When a fitting element is found within the S-structure it is replaced by the ellipses structure. "Fitting" is checked by the same clauses as described above. The following is the ellipses processing law. Note that PROLOG calls a clause by calling the consequence of the formula (testell (N,T)).

$$ellipsis(N) \wedge old(S) \wedge replace\text{-}similar(N,S,T) \rightarrow testell(N,T)$$

$$fit(Z,X) \wedge fit(Z,Y) \rightarrow similar(X,Y)$$

replace-similar replaces the element of S similar to N by N and renders T.

We can proceed the following types of ellipses :

How many symphonies did compose Beethoven ?

And Mahler ?

And Bruckner ?

And piano concerts ?

The second and third sentence have the same S-structure as the first with Beethoven replaced by Mahler and Bruckner resp. and the fourth one has again the same with "symphonies" replaced by "piano concerts" :

[compose, Bruckner, ref ([?, many], symphonies)]

We can also process ellipses which lack of one part inside a noun phrase structure :

Who is the composer of Fidelio ?

and the text book writer of Figaro ?

We cannot yet process ellipses of the following type but we think this presents not a very difficult problem :

Did the father give the book to Mary ?

And the mother the bag to John ?

This approach to ellipses resolution is exclusively semantics based. Implementations as described in (5) are only syntax based. But it is clear, that we can only resolve very few kinds of ellipses, and we cannot resolve many of the problems described in (6, 18). In (17), we developed a dialogue theory based on an action logic (12, 14) which permits anaphora resolution on a theoretically well-founded background.

7. PRONOUN RESOLUTION.

Our approach to pronoun resolution is based on our previous work on the representation of natural language analysis by logic (16).

Pronouns are processed after the syntactic analysis when the whole S-structure is built up. When a pronoun referent is found the pronoun is replaced by it. Pronoun referents are processed by three approaches. First, we try to find a referent with the same gender ; if no unique referent is found we recur to semantic based preference laws ; if semantically there is still more than one possible referent, we choose the one who is "nearer" within the context. Before undertaking the search in this three directions we check if there are referents at all and we only proceed to the next step when there are too much referents (more than one). In order to access to the elements with the same gender or belonging to the same concept we use meta predicates which describe the actual context of a situation :

context (X) is true when X is the S-structure of a sentence which occurred "some" instances before.("some" is actually 10).

beforeo (X,Y) is true when X has been mentioned for the first time one instance before Y has been mentioned for the first time.

before (X,Y) is   the transitive closure of beforeo.

focus (X) is true when there have been asked questions about X at few preceding states.

onlyg (X,Y) is true when X is the only constant occurring in elements of the context which belongs to a concept of gender Y.

onlyc (X,Y) is true when X is the only constant out of the context which belongs to a concept Y.

All these meta predicates are constatly "updated", i.e. during sentence analysis we add or retract clauses about them to the knowledge base. For an example, whenever a "new" sentence X has been parsed, after the call of s(X,XR,S), rendering the S-structure S we have calls assert(kontext (S)), old (T), assert (beforeo (T,S)) which add the positive clauses kontext(S) and beforeo(T,S) to the knowledge base.

The referent of a pronoun P within an S-structure S is then found (hopefully !) by the following refer-clauses :

onlyg $(X,Y) \land$ genderp $(P,Y) \rightarrow$ refer (P,X)

genderc $(C,X) \land$ genderc $(B,X) \land$ genderp $(P,X) \land C \neq B \land$ prefer $(S_C^P, S_B^P) \rightarrow$ refer (P,C)

possf $(A) \land \neg$possf $(B) \rightarrow$ prefer (A,B)

possf $(S_C^P) \land$ possf $(S_B^P) \land$ before $(C,B) \rightarrow$ prefer (P,C)

S_Y^X is the result of replacing X by Y in S. genderp and genderc are the gender of a pronoun resp. of the noun which is the name of the concept c. possf is a predicate which works along the same lines as the frame adopting laws in the third paragraph. It checks if A can be adapted to some frame.

We think that our approach to manipulate context descriptions by assertions is not just a way to describe such problems in LOGIC and to implement them in PROLOG but reflects the philosophy of our approach. We do not feel that people in a dialogue situation search for a pronoun referent in some list, but we think that they access pretty directly to the "good" referent. Hence this referent has to be present for an immediate access and we feel that our description is very near to this situation.

8. CONCLUSION.

The most important properties of our logic based natural language system are :

(1) The whole system, i.e. parsing, meaning, inference and translation is represented in a uniform language on the theoretical as well as on the implementation level : our representation language for the theory is LOGIC and for the implementation it is PROLOG.

(2) The uniformity of the description language allows a smooth and rich interaction between syntactic, semantic, and pragmatic axioms and inference rules.

(3) Syntactical laws bear a logical relationship between syntactic categories.

(4) Syntactical laws can refer to the meanings of the sentences being analysed.

(5) Meanings may interact with general world knowledge during the analysing process.

(6) The system is general enough to be adapted to different domains. We have applied it to a database on musical works and on a knowledge base on the grammar of natural language (actually grammatical laws of German).

(7) The treatment of ellipses and pronouns in logic grammars is a rather new
approach. Most of the papers about natural language and logic programming do
not treat with anaphora (3, 9, 10, 11). There are only very few and very recent
papers including ellipses and pronoun processing (7, 8). Our resolution of anaphora is not as complete as discussed e.g. in (6) or (18). Our objective in
treating this problem has rather been to incorporate the representation of anaphoric expressions into a more general formal system, as described in (17).
Clearly, we did not aspire to procedurally oriented approaches (e.g. 5)
although we did aspire to comparable results.

The organization of dialogues has also been described in (8) ; but it seems to me
that this approach does not have a logical theory as background but is rather a
procedurally oriented solution programmed in PROLOG.

Verb templates have also been used by McCord and Lopes (7, 9).

REFERENCES.

(1) BROWN F.M., SCHWIND C.B. - Outline of a Integrated Theory of Natural Language
         Under-Standing,in : Representation and Processing of Natural Language.
         Natural-Language Communication with Computers, (L. Bolc, ed.), Hanser
         Verlag, München 1980.

(2) COLMERAUER A. - Metamorphosis grammars, in : Natural Language Communication
         with Computers (L. Bolc, ed.), Lectures Notes in Computer Science 63,
         Springer Verlag, 133-189, 1978.

(3) DAHL V. - On Database Systems Development through Logic. In : ACM Transactions
         on Database Systems, vol. 7, n° 1, March 1982.

(4) DUDEN. - Grammatik der deutschen Sprache.

(5) HAHN von W., HOEPPNER W., JAMESON A., WAHLSTER W. - The anatomy of the Natural
         Language dialogue system HAM-RPM. In :(Bolc, L. ed.) : Natural Lan-
         guage based computer systems. München, London, Hanser, 1980.

(6) HIRST G. - Anaphora in Natural Language Understanding : A Survey. Lecture
         Notes in Computer Science 119, Springer-Verlag, Berlin Heidelberg,
         New York, 1981.

(7) LOPES G.P. - Implementing Dialogues in a Knowledge Information System. This
         Volume.

(8) LUBONSKI P. - Natural Language Interface for a Polish Railway Expert System.
         This Volume.

(9) McCord M.C. - Using Slots and Modifiers in Logic Grammars for Natural Lan-
         guage. In : Artificial Intelligence 18, 1982, pp. 327-367.

(10) PEREIRA F., WARREN D. - An Efficient Easily Adaptable System for Interpreting
         Natural Language Queries. In : AJCL 8, 1982, pp. 110-122.

(11) PIQUE J.F. , SABATIER P. - An informative adaptable and efficient natural
         language consultable database system. European Conference on
         Artificial Intelligence, Orsay, France 1982.

(12) SCHWIND C.B. - Representing Actions by State Logic. Proceedings of the AISB/
         GI Conference on Artificial Intelligence, Hamburg, 18-20 July, 1978.

(13) SCHWIND C.B. - Semantic Trees for Natural Language Representation. In : Infor-
      mation Processing and Management. Vol. 19, n° 4, 1983.

(14) SCHWIND C.B. - Action logic. LISH, August 1982, Marseille 1982.

(15) SCHWIND C.B. - A Formalism for the description of Question Answering Systems.
      In : L. Bolc : Natural Language Communication with Computers. Lecture
      Notes in Computer Science 63, Springer Verlag, 1978.

(16) SCHWIND C.B. - Natural Language Analysis by Theorem Proving Methods : Disam-
      biguiting Pronouns in Natural Language Texts. In : "Knowledge Represen-
      tation and Reasoning in the Humanities and Social Sciences". Colloque
      Saint Maximin 1979, publication IRIA.

(17) SCHWIND C.B. - Un modèle logique de dialogue. In : Les modes de raisonnement.
      Colloque ARC 1984.

(18) WEBBER B. - A Formal Approach to Discourse Anaphora. Thesis Harvard 1979.

Natural Language Understanding and Logic Programming
V. Dahl and P. Saint-Dizier (Editors)
© Elsevier Science Publishers B.V. (North-Holland), 1985

PROGRAMMING IN A NATURAL LANGUAGE ? AT WHAT COST ?

Anne Daladier

C.N.R.S. L.A.D.L.
Université Paris 7
Tour Centrale 9e
2,Place Jussieu 75005 Paris

How far the semantics of a programming language could lend itself to the expression of the formulation of informations in natural languages? We locate the
role of Logic Programming in that objective and in connection raise some questions
about tools used in applicative language semantics. We believe that some of the
existing treatments could be significantly enlarged if we split the notion of
text comprehension into (at least) two levels of interpretation: (a) what we call
literal information and (b) denotational or other aspects of information vehiculed by NL. We concentrate on (a) and describe the features of a syntactic modulus which should yield at once syntactical analysis and automatic reconstruction
of implicit information in terms of actual simple sentences.

1. COMPARISON BETWEEN OUR APPROACH AND OTHER RELATED ONES.

    Generally speaking, the interest of syntactic analysis is to make the systems
transportable. The proposal of a syntactic component is not new in itself. We
depart from current opinions on its importance and on the role to be devoted to
syntax and semantics in the design of NL interfaces.
    Surprising as it may seem at first, well-formedness in NL is still an open
question. There does not exist a set of strings characterizing all and only well-
formed sentences for a whole language. A notion of reduction is needed in order to
characterize assertability in NL and the question of determining such a notion
which would always yield finite derivations is clearly not trivial as we shall
show. One of the main issues underlying all our approach is the proposal of a
linguistic reduction rule which should account for both well formedness of a
sentence and for the reconstruction of its implicit informational structure.
In addition, we give it the form of a deduction rule in order to automatize the
derivations. This attitude goes together with a formulation of all available
grammatical and lexical constraints inside our applicative representation of
word insertion and word reduction. In particular, our treatment of anaphora reconstruction does not involve metatheoretical co-indexing of coreferent words, nor
semantic primitives, which have the drawback of being relative to pecular and
specified in advance universes of discourses. The semantic interpretation of coreference is produced here as being induced by an underlying co-assertion operator
which allow identifying two identical or partially identical instanciations in
its arguments.

PS grammars, as other grammar formalisms used in the lexicalist framework, do not
provide a way of producing all the word sequences interpretable as well formed
sentences and only those. One of the main differences between the way information
is formulated in NL as compared to programming languages or predicate calculi,
is the property of not expliciting all the information, something sometimes
refered to as elimination of redundancies. Aside sequences (1), (3), (5), (7)
which are not assertable, sequences (2), (4), (6), (8) which only differ by
replacement of terms belonging to the same grammatical categories, are perfectly
good sentences:

(1) ≯ Le Luc de Jean a déteint.
(2)   Le Lewis de Jean a déteint.

(3) ≯ Les murs de Jean sont herbe.
(4)   Les murs de Jean sont prune.

(5) ≯ Jean voyage Luc.
(6)   Jean voyage Pan Am.

(7) ≯ Le clocher et vitraux de Notre-Dame dure deux heures.
(8)   Le son et lumières de Notre-Dame dure deux heures.

The inassertability of sequences (1), (3), (5), (7) comes from the fact that we
are not able when trying to interpret them, to reconstruct subjacent predicates
which would enable us to combine the existent arguments and predicates of the
sentence in a conventional way. We can consider as an extra-linguistic accident
the fact that in French the single word <u>prune</u> represent a kind of colour which is
like the colour of a plum and that in opposition, the word <u>herbe</u> does not mean a
pecular green like colour. The use of these words may be pecular to French but
the use of such reductions is not. It is also very common inside a given language.
From a linguistic point of view, what is involved here seems to be a quite general
process of reduction of classifier predicates like: <u>colour of</u> , <u>action of</u>, <u>content
of</u>, <u>thing of the name of</u> etc. We consider metonymy as an aspect of this process.
Seeking for a sound notion of assertability in NL, we give up grammar formalisms
making use of auxiliary categories and immediate constituent rules. PS grammars
are not sufficient nor necessary. Instead, we assign directly an applicative status
to lexical entities and we recognize correct assertions by mean of a domain of
types (see section 2. below).Moreover, we briefly review in section 2. a few empirical constraints such as lexical dependencies involving more than two terms or
non immediate dependencies. These constraints cannot be accounted for by mean of
context-free rules and we see only advantages to take the dependency structures
which seem to be adequate for determining the interpretation structures as the
adequate ones for determining the syntactic   structures.

This is not to say that traditional grammatical categories such as noun, verb,
preposition etc. used in PS grammars are not useful but we locate their role at
the level of lexical informations, in labels of boolean features. There,they have
a role in the making of applicative dependencies which define literal interpretation structures of sentences.

The question of a characterisation of assertability in NL is related to the price
we are ready to afford for it. Producing and recognizing all assertable sequences
and only those, would require a tremendous list of adhoc reductions. On another
hand, we can propose a semi-decidable solution, that is a way of recognising
assertable sentences, by mean of a domain of constructed types. This solution
also enable us to produce reconstruction structures where zero morphemes of appropriate types indicate word combinations under which a sequence might be understood.
If in addition, we use classifiers in our labels of lexxical features, we can
reconstruct approximations of the subjacent lexical content of reduced sentences:
the more features, the best the approximations. At worst, zero morphems can be
replaced by indefinite lexical items. For example, corresponding to the reduced
sentences (8) and (2) above we could reconstruct:
     La chose son et lumière de Notre-Dame dure deux heures.
     La chose Lewis de Jean a déteint.
From the production point of view, we can obtain a good many reduced forms by mean
of the linguistic rules we propose here, for example those involving anaphora, and
the unreduced ones. We do not believe that it is useful for an interface to produce
all the possible reduced forms of sentences having the same informational content.

Our syntactical modulus provides a representation for checking the well-formedness of a sentence by mean of a type which has to belong to a certain order relation. Before applying type reductions, this type also provide the implicit structure of information of the sentence. The reconstruction of the informational structure is what we call literal information processing in opposition to denotational properties that those informations can have in various applications. Literal information structures are independent from applications for which NL formulation is used. Obviously, this is not the case for denotational properties.

Supposing we can explicit the way NL formulation of informations is compositional, there is no reason to consider this compositionality as the one involved in denotational properties. Any well-formed word sequence in a language is interpretable but well-formedness in predicate calculi does not account for well-formedness in sentences.

In fact, it is not even proved that the relevant criterion of well-formedness for some languages is the relevant one for all natural languages.

The compositional character of interpretations in predicate calculi cannot be confused with the compositionnal character of literal interpretations even after the explicitation of sujacent informations. This is why we believe that approaches making use of a direct translation of sentences into predicate formula can be interesting in pecular applications but not for dealing with natural language as a whole.

What we have in mind can be represented by the following schema:

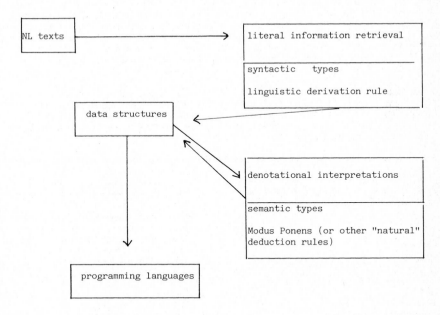

We recall that our goal is to use programming languages semantics to represent NL formulation of informations. It seems realistic, if we use on the one hand linguistic work on lexical and syntactical properties in NL formulation, and on the other hand, works on programming language design and semantics, to construct text representations as data structures allowing a modular implementation. It seems quite promising to keep in mind the two points of views. First, we can use

all the expressivity and flexibility of tools involved in the design of programming
languages when we conceive the NL decompositions. In our opinion, these tools are
not fully exploited in many AI works. Second, we should have in mind empirical
constraints of the formulation in NL when we conceive the data structures. In
opposition to a current opinion, we believe that empirical constraints on natural
language formulation can be used to restrict the expressive power of a NL grammar
provided they are properly restated as internal restrictions on the formal syntax
of this grammar. We use these constraints to eliminate undesirable ambiguities
that is to replace variables by constant terms.

We present in next section how we intend to represent the literal information
vehiculed by a text as data structures . In our syntactic   modulus, we use an
applicative language and the applicative formulation of a linguistic reduction
rule which can be used as the deduction rule of this modulus. Texts and their
decomposition can be expressed in the same applicative language. These applicative
expressions can be restated as sentences using appropriate linearization rules
(see |3|). The output of the syntactical modulus is the data structure modulus
which in turn can be used as an input for one or several semantic modulus,
according to what goals are to be achieved involving use of informational content
of texts. These modulus would use logical deduction rules and have the same data
structures as output. The semantic behaviour of all necessary intermediary
programs could be controled at once at this level.

The main purposes of the syntactical modulus are the following:
1) Intoduction of a type caculus providing a notion of assertability in NL
   and automatic checking in NL recognition.
2) Use of those types for recovering implicit information (anaphora, ellipsis,
   scope properties)
3) Use of the labels of boolean lexical features and binding properties of
   linguistic reductions under identification to replace constraints on variable
   dependencies by a hierarchy of constant terms in a context of assertion.
   Before insertion of expressions in contexts, higher order constraints are
   involved in very broad NL interpretation mechanisms such as:
   a) recursive modification of word meaning
   b) pronominalisation of complex noun phrases or anaphora depending
      on lexical dependencies involving two or more terms
   c) variable scope properties
4) Semantic free access to literal information in question-answering systems
   and its automatic reformulation in terms of simple sentences.

2. OUTLINES OF AN APPLICATIVE REPRESENTATION OF LITERAL INFORMATION PROCESSING

The notion of linguistic reduction plays a central role in the treatment proposed
here. It is borrowed to a large extent to the recent theory proposed by Z.S. Harris.
In particular, we take up the idea of a direct representation of the well-formedness
of a sentence by the structure of its informational reconstruction. This idea
goes together with a direct representation of lexical entities by operators. The
literal structure of a sentence is taken into account the operator order insertion.
These operators are either explicit or reconstructed words. The applicative order
of words is not the occurence order of words in sentences contrary to phrases
order in PS grammars. We also take up from the last theory of Harris the idea of
giving up the classical transformation rules, that is operations from sentence
structure to sentence structure . It is then equivallent for sentences to belong
to the same derivation and to have the same informational structure. In other
words, it is equivalent for a sentence to be derived from another one and to have
the same informational structure although showing in its surface form less explicit
information. No kind of restructuration on applicative structures is allowed.

Linguistic reduction can be identified here with lexical reduction. It takes two forms:

first,the so-called appropriate reduction. Usually, reduced operators take a zero shape but sometimes they have conventional morphemic contractions. These reductions are recoverable in a sentence when this sentence shows apparent discrepancies in the syntactical requierements of its explicit words.

Second, the reduction of an elementary argument or of an operator together with its descendents involved in a linguistic rule of identification. The goal of this identification is to account for anaphora. Reduced elements can be zeroed or pronounded. In Harris conception, reductions only take place in immediate applicative dependencies. Non elementary arguments such as completive are directly inserted under the main verb. Types are not introduced as operators can only be constant terms either 0-order, 1-order, or 2-order.

One of the most important hypothesis which is behind the proposals briefly summarized here, is that the metalanguage of a language could be described inside this language. In particular, the steps of a derivation which reconstructs the structure of a sentence in terms of successive reductions are themselves sentences. We shall stay as closed as possible to that attitude even if some modifications invoving technical primitives seem unavoidable.

The modifications that we propose here have two goals. First, to account for empirical constraints which could not else be adequatly described and generalize some of the existing solutions. Second, to give a deductive form to the reductions such that the treatment could be automatized. A consequence of our solution is to generalize the use of a syntactic   identification to the decomposition of all lexical insertions of non elementary operators and of determiners either determinate or undeterminate. The introduction of a pecular restriction of functional completness plays a central role in our proposals. We use a Lamda-calculus with non finite types and weak extensionality.

Our modifications involve an enlargment of the notion of operator used to represent lexical entities insertion in the interpretation structures. The notion of operator constant used by Harris is not sufficient. His operators can be 0-order, that is elementary arguments, such as John, apple or 1-order such as eat for instance: eats (John , apple)   or else 2-order, such as think for instance : think (Mary , eat (John , apple)). It seems inescapable to introduce a notion of operator variable to take into account non immediate dependencies relations such as variable scope properties or anaphora depending on complex lexical dependencies or on other anaphoric reconstructions (see |4|). But this introduction will not make our derivations uncontrolable, nor does it imply higher-order extensions at the level of programming languages. Another important modification is the introduction of continuity, in the sense of Scott, for our operators. We also need to introduce a representation of lexical constraints put to work in reductions or in scope determination inside the applicative dependencies which account for syntactical restrictions of selection (i.e. number and elementary or not elementary status of arguments.).

Previous to text analysis proper, we propose to associate to each lexical entity an initial type scheme and a label of boolean features corresponding to lexical properties. In particular, properties of "normal" lexical selection may be necessary to determine the scope of a word in a sentence and eliminate undesirable ambiguities in the reconstruction of an informational structure. For example, sentence (9) is ambiguous because contre can be interpreted as an operator on attaque or on a mentionné , which have the compatible type of non elementary arguments with contre and both belong to its normal lexical selection. In contrast, 10) is not ambiguous because a oublié does not belong to the normal lexical selection of contre :

    (9) Jean a mentionné cette attaque contre Luc.

        Jean a mentionné (cette attaque contre Luc).

        (Jean a mentionné cette attaque) contre Luc.

(10) Jean a oublié cette attaque contre Luc.
     Jean a oublié (cette attaque contre Luc).

Immediate constituant structures would not account for those differences, they would either generate two syntactic   structures and predict ambiguity for both examples or inadequatly generate only one structure in both cases. Of course it would be possible to redefine the correct interpretation structures at a semantic level, but it is unnecessary to do so.

Initial type schema are used to recover implicit information. For example in sentence (11), the missing elementary argument of partir has to be identified with Paul , the elementary argument of a permis. In addition with the fact that an operator like partir has an elementary argument, we must attach lexical features to operators like promettre and jurer to account for the difference in the rank of the antecedent of the missing argument of partir in (11) and (12):

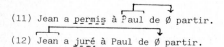

(11) Jean a permis à Paul de Ø partir.

(12) Jean a juré à Paul de Ø partir.

Initial type schema are also used to account for the difference in lenth of the respective antecedents of chose in examples (13), (14):

(13) Marc a préparé un gâteau, chose que nous allons manger maintenant.

(14) Marc a préparé un gâteau, chose qui a duré longtemps.

The operator a duré requiers a non elementary argument as opposed to manger .

An operator like espoir requiers a non elementary argument because it can construct with a completive, as in (15):

(15) Jean a l'espoir que Luc viendra.

espoir still requiers a non elementary argument even if it is not explicitly instanciated as in (16) where it has to be reconstructed as being the same as the non elementary argument of a dit :

(16) Jean leur a dit qu'il viendra et ils ont bon espoir Ø pour Luc.

→ Jean leur a dit qu'il viendra et ils ont bon espoir pour Luc qu'il viendra.

Sentencial arguments may be combined into complex non elementary arguments, that is the length of non elementary arguments may vary. Depending on further lexical constraints and/or other reconstructions under the identification rule in the same context, the missing non elementary argument of an operator may refer non ambiguously to a whole combination of operators or to a subcombination. For example in (17), cette action has to be interpreted as l'action de Jean d'avoir escaladé la tour montparnasse , in (18) as l'action de Jean d'avoir fait semblant de commencer à escalader la Tour Montparnasse. In (19), l'action de Luc is l'action de Luc d'avoir révélé que Jean avait escaladé la Tour Montparnasse and in (20), l'action de Jean is l'action de Jean d'avoir escaladé la Tour Montparnasse . We present the operation of reduction under identification in a co-assertion below, it sufice here to say that the repetition of Jean or Luc in (19) or (20) plays a central role in the reconstruction.

(17) Jean a escaladé la Tour Montparnasse. Cette action nous a étonnés.

(18) Jean a fait semblant de commencer à escalader la Tour Montparnasse. Cette action nous a étonnés.

(19) Luc a révélé que Jean avait escaladé la Tour Montparnasse.L'action de Luc nous a étonnés.

(20) Luc a révélé que Jean a escaladé la Tour Montparnasse.L'action de Jean nous a étonnés.

Linguistic reduction is made out of two reduction operations:

1) Local reduction of either indefinite operators or appropriate classifiers
2) Non local reduction under the co-assertion operator ";" allowing identification of instanciations which can be uncomplete.

We introduce two distincts operators corresponding to the same word chose (or thing in English),contrary to what we do for most lexical entities: the elementary one, as in (13), (22),   and the non elementary one, as in (14), (23), (25). They both can be zeroed as in (21), (24). penser requires a non elementary argument as (26) can be asserted:

    (21) Jean a trop mangé Ø.
    (22) Jean a trop mangé de choses.
    (23) Que Marc ait préparé un gâteau est une chose étrange.
    (24) Jean ne pense pas Ø, il agit.
    (25) Jean ne pense pas de choses, il agit.
    (26) Jean pense que Luc viendra.

The non elementary operator chose is itself an operator requiring a non elementary argument as (23) shows. So chose in an example like (25) has itself a non explicit argument and we have to specify its syntactic   form. Unbounded recursive insertion of non elementary arguments is allowed, so the indefinite operator takes value in the whole domain of assertable sentences. It is not possible to approximate the missing argument by the elementary indefinite operator because that would make the system contradictory.

    Assuming that a non explicit argument is either reconstructible in the context or indefinite, it is possible to avoid an infinite syntactical form, that is an infinite list of indefinite operators as the argument of the initial one in examples like (24), (25). Such infinite syntactic   forms can be avoided using the property of continuity of functional expressions, that is the fact that all lexical operators requiring non elementary arguments have fixpoints. We consider that the least informative value of an operator is produced when it is applied to a lexically indefinite operator itself operating on its least fixpoint. We don't loose any relevant information when we approximate the interpretation of thing or chose taking its value in the domain of sentences by the interpretation of thing or chose on its least fixpoint. Its intuitive linguistic signification could be the autoreferential interpretation of thing or chose.

We use lexically indefinite operators on their fixpoint to close the domain of interpretation of an operator requiring a non elementary argument when its argument is zeroed and that it cannot be reconstructed in the context. This form of continuity also enable us to account for situations where the evaluation of the interpretation structure of a sub-expression must be postponed untill the evaluation of another sub-expression belonging to the same assertion context and which is not necessarilly contiguous. Using this mechanism of postponed evaluation, completive insertion come down to relative clause insertion.

It should be noted that the indefinite operator on its fixpoint can be inserted under higher operators without altering the monotonous increase of informations. We consider then that the possibility of asserting a sentence whose informational content is partially undefined is a property of the formulation in natural languages.

Non local reductions, that is reductions involving non immediate dependencies, come down to zeroing of identified instanstiations under the co-assertion operator ";".

In our approach, the semantic notion of coreference is acconted for as being induced by the repetition (eventually partial repetition) of two instanciations having equal or ordered types under the co-assertion operator ";". We propose an applicative formulation of identifications in subjacent lambda-expressions, where the localisation of the syntactical position of the words to identify is produced internally. In the case of the analysis of relative clauses, Harris describes the

syntactic. localisation of the words to be identified using some pecular lineari-
sation properties in English. Unfortunatly, his solution cannot be generalized to
other languages nor to many other anaphora reconstruction in English. It also
raises some internal problems of formalization and could not be computerized
because the pecular linearized sentence that he uses has an applicative structure
which does not account for the interpretation structure of the reduced sentence.
The identification must be accounted for at the applicative level.

We identify instanciations of variables and not the variables themselves. The
variables are then bund. The location of the variable to be reinstanciated
by a pronoun or a zero morphem is produced using successive projections in embedded
conditional expressions. These operations have a trivial functional expression in
lambda-calculus.

Examples (27), (28), (29) all have the same applicative structure represented in
short by (30), they have the same informational content. Word order in these
sentences corresponds to various linearizations of their applicative structure
and not to permutations on that applicative structure.

(27) Jean est arrivé. Luc connaît Jean.
(28) Jean est arrivé, Luc le connaît.
(29) Jean, que Luc connaît est arrivé.

(30)

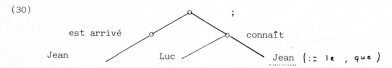

This identification process apply to non elementary operators like decision,
and in particular, uncompletly instanciated ones as in (32). Identification
of partially incomplete instanciations is allowed because they can be closed.
decision requiers a non elementary argument as shown by the existence of the
noun phrase (31). (32) would be reduced from (33), represented in short by (34):

(31) La decision de Jean de partir
(32) Une decision de Jean Ø que Paul approuve est importante.
(33) Une decision de Jean est importante; Paul approuve une decision de Jean.

(34)

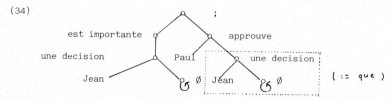

We want to stress on the fact that here the interpretation of coreference is
produced by the grammar as a property of co-assertion. From a recognition point of
view, anaphoric bindings are reconstructed by mean of apparent types discrepancies, elements having no type scheme (such as pronouns), pattern matchings on
boolean lexical features.

In order to recognize the interpretation of example (17) above, it is not necessary
that the analyser knows that to climb something is an action, it suffices to use
in a proper way the formulation itself. More precisely, it is the fact that action
requiers a non elementary argument which makes it possible to suppose that if this
argument is not explicit, it might have been zeroed under identification with a
non elementary argument of the same assertion context. The demonstrative pronoun
cette confirms that hypothesis and we are then able to reconstruct the complete
noun phrase as there is only one possible candidate. This kind of approach is

interesting as there are many operators which could be inserted in place of action in same examples, like ce fait, la détermination de Jean etc. . A framework which would use semantic primitives would requier a quite impressive list of adhoc analytical relationships. Moreover, such a list could hardly be exhaustive as other operators can combine with action.

We introduce a universal type μ for indefinite operators on their fixpoint and an order relation on types of assertion. As more than one incomplete subexpression can be inserted in a sentence, we introduce a complete semi-lattice structure on the types of well-formed linguistic expressions. The identification rule apply under type control of instanciations which are either equal or ordered one toward the other. For example, it is not possible to identify an elementary indefinite word with a non elementary occurrence of the same word.

Compatibility of boolean features can be tested in conditional expressions which have an immediate applicative expression. Our use of normal lexical selection is not contradictory with the fact, often stressed by Harris, that these normal selectional restrictions can be violated in assertable word combinations, because in such unusual combinations, no local reduction apply. For example, it is possible to assert to dream with an argument not having the lexical feature animate and this argument may be non explicit under anaphoric interpretation, as in (35), but an argument like teapot will not be implicit in (36) if it is asserted without a context:

 (35) In this fairy-tale, teapots enjoy ∅ dreaming.
 (36) It is pleasant to ∅ dream.

Unlike the connective in predicate calculi, negation in NL has variable scope properties depending on the context where it is inserted. In the examples below, negation bears on arguments which are not already bound by an identification taking place in the assertion context. An example like (37) is many times ambigüous if it is asserted without a context. Sentences (38) to (41) are not ambiguous:

 (37) John did'nt eat the apple pie.

 (38) John did'nt eat the apple pie, it is Mary who ate it.

 (39) John did'nt eat the apple pie, it is a pear that he ate.

 (40) John did'nt eat the apple pie, he is going to eat it.

 (41) John did'nt eat the apple pie, he was out all day long.

As it can bear selectively on an operator, negation in NL can even be interpreted as a mere modality on the assertion. If (42) was to be interpreted as a proposition (43) would certainly not be interpreted as its negation:

 (42) John did'nt say that Bob was coming, he shouted it.
 (43) John said that Bob was coming, he even shouted it.

To sum up this section, we start with an applicative higher order language and restrict it with internal representation of all available lexico-syntactic constraints on NL formulation.

Assigning a type to a linguistic expression provides a proof of its assertability as well as a reconstruction of its informational structure. Before their insertion in a pecular sentence structure, lexical entities, which are not elementary, are operator variables whose domain of interpretation is constrained by a type scheme. After their insertion in a sentence, they become constant terms whose entry order in the applicative structure of the sentence are given by actual types. These informational structures can be rephrased as co-assertions of simple sentences using additional linearization rules.

The reconstruction of informational structures result from:
a) generation of linguistic hypothesis of reductions
b) elimination of variables
Linguistic reduction hypothesis are generated when are recognized:
 - type schema discrepancies on explicit words
 - anaphoric words
 - lexical features discrepancies
Elimination of variables result from different processes of reduction:
 - classical β-reduction and μ-reduction (substitution of approximated normal
   form$_s$ to incomplete instanciations).
 - pattern matching on boolean lexical features of labels which are initially
   attached to lexical entities.
 - type introduction and elimination rules.
 - binding of variables in the environment of higher assertion under application
   of the linguistic reduction rule.

3. LOGIC PROGRAMMING AND LITERAL INFORMATION PROCESSING

We have been using an applicative formalism so far to express our derivations.
But, as formalisms underlying programming languages are interconvertible, the
question of what programming language should be used is still open. In particular,
D.H. Warren has made propositions about translating some properties of applicative
languages in Prolog. We review some of these questions here, transposing them to
our perspective.

Replacement of variables by constants is obtained in Prolog using unification.
In Lamda-calculus it is obtained by β -reduction. For example, the β -reduction
in (1) can be translated by unification of schema (a) and (b) below. The result
of unifying (a) and (b) is represented by (c), which also represent the normal
form of the lambda-expression, that is the second member ofthe equality in (1):
    (1) λxy. eats(x,y) (John) (an apple) $\underset{\beta}{=}$ eats(John,an apple)

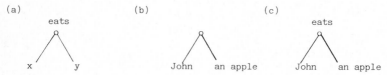

We would have to represent in Prolog NL interpretation mechanisms for which we
used Scott's notion of continuity, such as using a fixpoint to postpone an evaluation or to close the syntactical expression of operators. We dont know if Frozen
procedures would fit all situations.

Initial type schema assigned to lexical entities correspond to a static binding
of variables. It is a touch of stone of our treatment for recovering implicit
informations. It can be expressed in Prolog using a pair of pointors. One points
on the code of the operator and the other points on the "environment" which
contains the non local instanciations of the variables of this operator, that is
variables which are bound because of application of identification under our
co-assertion operator ";".

We do not want to introduce quantifiers to express the binding of variables because
they have duality and scope properties which are not adequate £or literal information
processing. We have already said that one of the main difference between NL and
artificial languages was the NL property of reducing the form of assertions
without reducing their informational content. Another important difference is
the variable scope properties that many operator words can have and the ways the

context disambiguïse them. Again, we want to stress on the interest of dissociating pecular scope properties, proper to NL formulation of informations and symbolic manipulations of these informations in order to fullfil some applications. Careful and detailed examination of the linguistic properties of the formulation appear to allow eliminating some higher -order constraints and enables us to replace them by linear dependancies on constant terms. It seems promising to see how far we can go.

Before ending this section, we shall emphasize the interest of using environments to reconstruct and decompose the interpretation of a word combination, even when this combination represents an apparently simple sentence. We use a definition of elementary sentence in terms of our typed operators. The analysis of a sentence involve its environment in a very general way. Programming languages have in common a tree representation of the programs. We can also represent as a tree the deduction of the literal interpretation of a sentence as advocated here. But some current confusions about tree representation for sentences should be exposed.

The question of being for or against tree representation appear to me to be a wrong debate because to adopt a tree representation does not imply to adopt a grammar of immediate constituants. It seem to me that the question of the choice of the relevant categories to describe word insertion in underlying structures clearly deserves further attention. This question should be raised together with that of what the representation structures should account for. Do we want to account at once for the surface order of word occurrences and complexify the representation of the sentences or should we define informational structures which account at once for well-formedness and literal interpretation and then use some simple additional linearization rules to account for surface word order? These linearization rules can be defined using the type of operators and some of the lexical features which are needed anyway. As to the descriptive power of trees, it depends on the kind of categories involved. We recall that the well-formed expressions of the Lambda-calculus have a tree representation, when if we don't restrict to the classical type calculus, its descriptive power is not even limited to recursive languages.

CONCLUSION

The price to pay to achieve an implementation of the treatment proposed here is two fold. On the one hand, the reformulation of NL constraints in our representation is still a work in progress. On the other hand, we will have to enter a large amount of lexical data. A part of it is already available at the L.A.D.L..

Of course, our propositions do not imply that we could computerize or even approximate the expressive power of natural languages. In particular, we don't think that one could ever account for the property of creating new sublanguages related to new universes of discourse that natural languages have. But we think that we can stimulate text comprehension at the level of literal interpretations, without previous knowledge on their domain of discourse. This kind of comprehension can be used to enlarge some of the existing logical treatments.

Acknowledgements
We wish to thank André Lentin, Zellig Harris and Paul Sabatier for lengthy and very stimulating discussions concerning the issues discussed in this paper.

REFERENCES:

|1| Colmerauer A., Metamorphosis Grammars, in: Natural Language Communication
    with Computers Lecture Notes in Computer Science Springer Verlag I975

|2| Daladier A., Problèmes de représentation d'une langue naturelle en lambda-
    calcul in Approches formelles de la Sémantique Naturelle C.N.R.S. U.P.S.
    Toulouse 1982

|3| Daladier A., Informational Linearizations: an Example from French, in:
    Form of Information in a Science - a Text Case in Immunology, Z.S. Harris eds.
    to appear

|4| Daladier A., Traitement de coréférences dans une représentation applicative
    des textes,in: Proceedings du Colloque Intelligence Artificielle et Reconnai-
    ssance des Formes INRIA AFCET Paris 1984

|5| Gross M., Méthodes en Syntaxe Herman Paris 1975

|6| Harris Z.S., A Grammar of English on Mathematical Principles Wyley New-York
    1982

|7| Huet G., In Defense of Programming Language Design,in: Proceedings ECAI Orsay
    1982

|8| Scott D;, Data Types as Lattices SIAM Jnrl. of computing Vol. 5, No 3 1976

|9| Warren D.H.D., Higher Order Extensions to Prolog: Are they Needed? Mitchie
    and Pao eds. Machine Intelligenge 10 1982

Natural Language Understanding and Logic Programming
V. Dahl and P. Saint-Dizier (Editors)
© Elsevier Science Publishers B.V. (North-Holland), 1985

UNIFICATION IN GRAMMAR

by
Martin Kay

*Xerox Palo Alto Research Center
and The Center for the Study of Language and Information,
Stanford University*

A number of grammatical formalisms that are currently gaining popularity
are based on a notion of unification that differs slightly from the one used
in logic programming. The differences are such as to make logic programming, at least as commonly practiced, relatively unsuitable for grammatical
description. However, the minor modification on which these formalisms appear to converging has a great many desirable properties. Most important
among these is that the notion of a completely specified formula is missing.

INTRODUCTION

Language is an abstraction from observed processes of communication and ratinociation.
A particular language is abstracted from a subset of such processes and a grammar is a
characterization of such a subset. One of the major goals of linguistics in recent times has
been to design ways of writing grammars that do justice to their essentially procedural
nature while not ascribing more to linguistic processes than the evidence supports.

Transformational grammar is based on a carefully articulated process of sentence generation which is, however, explicitly dissociated from the processes that occur when language
is used. By ignoring these processes it closes itself off from an important potential source
of evidence about the nature of language. At the other extreme, augmented transition
network grammars contain a detailed specification of the sequence of events that must
be followed to analyze each individual sentence. Much of the detail that they contain is
therefore without empirical motivation. Context-free grammar occupy a middle ground
in that they are associated with a simple and effective class of well behaved procedures
which leaves open most of the underdetermined questions, such as the specific order of
low-level events. However, context-free grammar was long thought not to have the expressive power necessary to capture natural linguistic processes, and it is still generally
agreed that the formalism requires supplementing in various ways if it is to be capable of
capturing important generalizations and stating the facts in an irredundant manner.

Such considerations as these have lead to the development over the last few years of
several new linguistic formalisms with associated interpretive procedures that can be
specified without laying out specific sequences of events. These include generalized
phrase-structure grammar (GPSG), Lexical Functional Grammar (LFG), and Functional
Unification Grammar (FUG). All of them are phrase-structure grammars in the sense that
they assign constituent-structure trees to sentences and determine the kinds of constituents
that a phrase can have solely on the basis of that phrase's grammatical description. They
are also all *monotonic* in that the processes involved in their interpretation can add
information to existing structures but never require an existing structure to be modified.
Monotonicity is a property of context-free grammars and also of definite-clause grammars
and, in the latter, much of what makes this property important is clearly exhibited.
Definite-clause grammars are nonprocedural in the usual sense of not determining a

unique sequence of events.[1] However, when offered almost unmodified to a standard Prolog interpreter, sequences of events are generated that result in sentences being generated and analyzed.

These facts about definite-clause grammars come as no surprise to habitual Prolog users who are the constant beneficiaries of a monotonic formal system. Typically, these people resist allowing their activities to lead them into Prolog's embarassing periphery where monotonicity no longer holds. Monotonicity is a feature of Prolog because it is a feature of the principal operation on which Prolog is based, namely unification. This is an operation that compares a pair of expressions and determines whether they could be descriptions of the same object or state of affairs. If they could not, it declares as much and this is its only result. If they could, it constructs a new expression, in general more specific than either of the originals, because it contains all the details from both of them. The unification operation is also at the heart of the new grammatical formalisms just mentioned. However, the grammatical version of the operation differs in some important details from the logical version. In this paper, I propose to explore why unification has come to fill so central a role and also why the linguists prefer to work with their own version. To this end, I shall construct examples using a "pedagogical" formalism, which I will call *Simple Unification Grammar (SUG)*, which is none of the above, but which shares the relevant properties of all of them.

SIMPLE UNIFICATION GRAMMAR

Like all the formalisms under discussion, SUG associates a *functional description (FD)* with every word and phrase. This is a complex object that takes the place of the simple grammatical label or category of phrase-structure grammar. A FD is a list of names called *attributes* each of which has a value associated with it. Several kinds of value are possible but, for the moment, we will restrict our attention to two, namely unanalyzable *atoms* and FD's. I will write attributes to the left of an "=" sign and the corresponding value to the right. The FD in Fig. 1 describes the sentence *All dogs chase cats* according to the grammar in Fig. 2.

Each rule has a left and a right-hand side separated by an arrow. The left-hand side is a functional description, possibly preceded by the negation sign "~", and the right-hand side is a Boolean expression over three types of primitive, namely

1. FDs,

2. A constituency expression consisting of the word *Constituent:* followed by a sequence of one or more *paths*.

3. An ordering expression consisting of the word *Order:* followed by a sequence made up of paths and zero or more occurrences of "$\cdots$".

A path is a sequence of words enclosed in angle brackets. It is simply a means of identifying a value within the FD; if $[a_1 = [a_2 = \cdots [a_n = v]\cdots]]$, then the path written $< a_1 a_2 \cdots a_n >$ has the value v in that FD. Paths in FUG fill much the same role as variables do in logic programming, namely to link sets of unified values. When a location in a FD is occupied by a path that identifies some other location, the two values are

---

[1]A sequence of events is, of course, implicit, if one supposes that the grammars will be interpreted by a Prolog program in the usual way. However, this is clearly not the only procedure, or even the one obviously to be preferred.

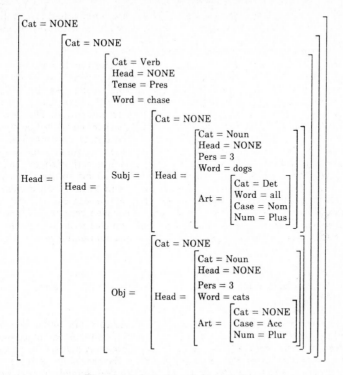

Fig. 1—A functional description

unified. Usually, we write the value itself in one place and paths identifying that place in all others where the value is unified with that one. The advantage of this scheme is that it makes it possible to stipulate identity between parts of a FD without allowing for special expressions to establish equality between variables and values.

If the label of a word or phrase is unifiable with the left hand side of a rule, then that rule must be applied to it. Where an alternation appears on the right of the rule, at least one of its clauses must apply; where a conjunct appears, all its clauses must apply. The notion of unification involved is straightforward. A pair of FDs is unifiable just in case there is no attribute with a value in one of them that cannot be unified with its value in the other. Atoms, of course, unify only with themselves. The result of the operation is a FD with the union of the attributes of the contributors. The value of each attribute has its original value if it comes from only one of the contributors, and otherwise the result of unifying the corresponding input values. Thus, FDs differ from more familar expressions in two ways: first, corresponding subexpressions are identified by name rather than position, and second, each FD behaves as though it had indefinitely many subexpressions, all but a finite subset having empty values.

One virtue of the attribute-value scheme is that of convenience. It is possible to work with linguistic descriptions in this formalism without having to remember the exact layout of every possible expression. More importantly, it is necessary to include in an expression only those parts that will appropriately restrict its possibilities of unification with other

1. $[\ ] \longrightarrow$ ([Head = NONE] **and** ([Cat = noun] [Cat = verb])) **or**
   (~[Head = NONE] **and** [Cat = NONE])

2. [Head = [Cat = Verb]] $\longrightarrow$ *Order:* <Head> ...

3. ~[Head = [Cat = Verb]] $\longrightarrow$ *Order:* ... <Head>

4. [Head = [Head = [Cat = Verb]]] $\longrightarrow$ [Head = [Head = [Subj = [Head = [Art = [Case = Nom]]]]]] **and**
   Constituent: <Head Head Subj>

5. $\left[\text{Head} = \begin{bmatrix} \text{Cat} = \text{Verb} \\ \text{Obj} = [\text{Cat} = \text{NP}] \end{bmatrix} \right] \longrightarrow$ [Head = [Obj = [Head = [Art = [Case = Acc]]]]] **and**
   Constituent: <Head Obj>

6. [Head = [Art = [Cat = Det]]] $\longrightarrow$ *Constituent:* <Det>

Fig. 2—A Simple Unification grammar

expressions. There is in FUG that there is no notion of a completely specified FD just as, in everyday life, there is no notion of a complete description of a object—it is always possible to add more detail. This means, for example, that it is possible to suplement the supposedly complete FD constructed by unification by the syntactic component of a grammar with semantic or other information, also by unification.

Rather than give an explanation of the formalism, I will summarize what the rules in Fig. 2 say. This will provide enough detail for present purposes.

1. An item either has NONE as the value of its Head attribute, indicating that it is a word, or it has some other value for that attribute indicating that it is a phrase. A word must have a Cat attribute with the value det, noun, or verb and a phrase must have NONE for that attribute. Since the FD on the left of the rule is empty it will unify with anything and the rule therefore applies to all words and phrases: It has the status of a redundancy rule.

2. If the Head of a phrase is a verb, then the phrase is a verb phrase and its Head is its first member. If there are other members, they take the position of the dots.

3. The Head of a phrase that is not a verb phrase comes last. For the present grammar, this covers sentences and noun phrases.

4. A phrase whose Head is a verb phrase is a sentence so that it has a verb as the Head of its Head. The subject of this verb is a constituent of the sentence and its article, described by the value of its Head's Art attribute, has the property [Case = Nom].

5. If a verb phrase has an object, then the article of that object has the property [Case = Acc], and the object itself is a constituent of the verb phrase.

6. If a noun phrase has a Head whose article has the property [Cat = Det], then that article is a constituent of of the noun phrase.

Rule one implements a principle known in linguistics as X-bar theory. I do not intend to

$$\begin{bmatrix} \text{Cat} = \text{Noun} \\ \text{Word} = \text{dog} \\ \text{Art} = \begin{bmatrix} \text{Cat} = \text{Det} \\ \text{Num} = \text{Sing} \end{bmatrix} \end{bmatrix} \quad \begin{bmatrix} \text{Cat} = \text{Noun} \\ \text{Word} = \text{dogs} \\ \text{Art} = \begin{bmatrix} \text{Cat} = \text{Det} \\ \text{Num} = \text{Plur} \end{bmatrix} \end{bmatrix}$$

$$\begin{bmatrix} \text{Cat} = \text{Noun} \\ \text{Word} = \text{Fido} \\ \text{Art} = [\text{Cat} = \text{NONE}] \end{bmatrix} \quad \begin{bmatrix} \text{Cat} = \text{Noun} \\ \text{Word} = \text{sheep} \end{bmatrix}$$

$$\begin{bmatrix} \text{Cat} = \text{Verb} \\ \text{Word} = \text{chases} \\ \text{Obj} = [\text{Cat} = \text{NP}] \\ \text{Subj} = [\text{Head} = [\text{Art} = [\text{Num} = \text{Sing}]]]] \end{bmatrix} \quad \begin{bmatrix} \text{Cat} = \text{Verb} \\ \text{Word} = \text{Chase} \\ \text{Obj} = [\text{Cat} = \text{NP}] \\ \text{Subj} = [\text{Head} = [\text{Art} = [\text{Num} = \text{Plur}]]] \end{bmatrix}$$

$$\begin{bmatrix} \text{Cat} = \text{Verb} \\ \text{Word} = \text{slept} \\ \text{Obj} = \text{NONE} \end{bmatrix} \quad \begin{bmatrix} \text{Cat} = \text{Verb} \\ \text{Word} = \text{ate} \end{bmatrix}$$

Fig. 3—Lexical entries

argue for this theory but only to used it to illustrate the flexibility of the formalism. What the theory says is that every phrase has a distinguished constituent called its *head*. If a phrase has something with the grammatical category X as its head, then it is an X-phrase. Since a sentence has a verb phrase as its head, it might more strictly be referred to as a *verb-phrase phrase*. The theory is implemented here by representing categories explicitly only in the descriptions of lexical items. Thus, a sentence is a phrase whose head's head is a verb.

The lexical entry for a word is an FD, or several FDs if it is grammatically ambiguous. Fig. 3 gives some lexical entries to go with the preceding examples. Notice that the grammar embeds the description of a determiner within that of the noun it determines and ascribes properties in respect of which a determiner and a noun agree to the more deeply embedded of the two. It follows that *dog* can be used only with a singular determiner and *dogs* only with a plural. A determiner like *the* has no "Num" attribute in its lexical entry and can therefore be used with either singular or plural nouns. *Fido* is a proper noun and has a lexical entry that prevents a determiner from occurring with it. An analogous strategy is used for encoding the frames and agreement information of verbs. The description of a verb within the description of a sentence contains the description of the subject of the sentence, and the object if there is one. These must therefore be unifiable with the appropriate parts of the lexical description of the particular verb. *Chases* and *chase* require singular and plural subjects respectively, whereas the past-tense forms *slept* and *ate* agree with subjects of either number. Both forms of chase exclude the possibility of a null object (incorrectly, as it happens); *slept* excludes the possibility of an object, and *ate* can be used transitively or intransitively.

It is not difficult to show that the week generative capacity of SUGs, like the others in the class we are considering, excedes that of context-free grammars—it is, for example, possible to write a grammar that generates the language $a^n b^n c^n$. Very probably, these grammars have the same week generative power as Definite-Clause grammars. But their value does not come from this. One of their principle advantages is that, as well as the traditional constituent structure that they obviousy assign to sentences, they also assign a label each node in these trees that typically contains the labels of all the nodes that it dominates. As the example just explored illustrates, this structure is far from isomorphic with that of the constituent tree. This *functional structure* plays a role reminiscent of the deep structures of transformational grammar, and its value is argued for extensively and persuasively in Bresnan (1982). I have attempted to show how agreement, and various other phenomena that are lexically bound can be treated naturally within a formalism of this class.

The rules of SUG function strictly as constraints on the kinds of structures that a language allows. I have already pointed out that there is no notion of a completely specified FD, a fact that I shall exploit in the next section where we shall see that an existing grammar can be made to play host to important additional information. The grammar in Fig. 2, while too small to reveal important generalizations in a convincing way, gives clear indications of some of the ways in which this might be done. Rules 2 and 3, for example specify the ordering relations for the language by restricting the position of the head of a phrase. If these rules were removed, the grammar would be that of a free word order language. Rules 2 and 3 also state the generalization that the value of a head attribute always describes a constituent. Rules 4 and 5 specify that subjects and objects are constituents without saying anything about how they are ordered relative to others.

Semantics

I now hope to show that the benefits of unification go well beyond those just outlined. Let us augment the lexical entries for "all" and "dogs" so that they become as shown in Fig 4. Lower-case italic letters are used as variables. Thjey are used here in an inessential way simply to indicate when to values are unified. Unbound variables are never used. Observe what will happen now when, following rule 4, these two words are incorporated in a noun phrase. The determiner's description is unified with the value of the *Art* property of the noun, causing the variable p to take on the value of the *Meaning* property of the determiner unified with the value of the meaning property of the noun. This unification gives the following result:

$$\begin{bmatrix} \text{Type} = \text{all} \\ \text{Var} = \quad q \\ \\ \text{Prop} = \quad \begin{bmatrix} \text{Type} = \text{and} \\ \text{P1} = \begin{bmatrix} \text{Pred} = \text{dog} \\ \text{Arg} = \quad q \end{bmatrix} \\ \text{P2} = [\text{Arg} = \quad q \quad] \end{bmatrix} \end{bmatrix}$$

Without going into elaborate detail, this can be seen as description of the logical expression

$$\forall q.dog(q) \land P(q)$$

The predicate P remains to be specified. It would come to be specified if the noun phrase "all dogs" became the subject of the verb "ate", and the lexical entry of "ate" were provided with a *Meaning* as follows:

$$\begin{bmatrix} \text{Cat} = \text{Verb} \\ \text{Word} = \text{sleep} \\ \text{Meaning} = r \\ \text{Subj} = [\text{Meaning} = r = [\text{Prop} = [\text{P2} = [\text{Pred} = \text{eat}]]] \end{bmatrix}$$

The meaning of the verb is unified with that of the subject, and P2 of the Prop of that meaning is unified with [Pred = eat]. It is not difficult to see that the result of this is effectively

$$\forall q.dog(q) \wedge eat(q)$$

$$
\begin{bmatrix}
\text{Cat} = \text{Det} \\
\text{Word} = \text{all} \\
\text{Num} = \text{plur} \\
\\
\text{Meaning} =
\begin{bmatrix}
\text{Type} = \text{all} \\
\text{Var} = q \\
\\
\text{Prop} =
\begin{bmatrix}
\text{Type} = \text{Implies} \\
\text{P1} = [\text{Arg} = q] \\
\text{P2} = [\text{Arg} = q]
\end{bmatrix}
\end{bmatrix}
\end{bmatrix}
$$

$$
\begin{bmatrix}
\text{Cat} = \text{Noun} \\
\text{Word} = \text{dogs} \\
\text{Art} =
\begin{bmatrix}
\text{Num} = \text{plur} \\
\text{Meaning} = p
\end{bmatrix} \\
\\
\text{Meaning} = p \quad =
\begin{bmatrix}
\text{Prop} =
\begin{bmatrix}
\text{P1} =
\begin{bmatrix}
\text{Type} = \text{Pred} \\
\text{Pred} = \text{dog}
\end{bmatrix}
\end{bmatrix}
\end{bmatrix}
\end{bmatrix}
$$

Fig. 4—Semantic lexical entries

CONTROL-STRUCTURE

I have tried to make a strong argument for monotonic processes in grammatical analysis. Before an audience of logic programmers, the argument probably does not need to be urged particularly strongly. What doubtless requires more justification here is building special programs to carry out these monotonic processes when Prolog lies readily at hand. The argument the is most frequently made for not using Prolog is based on the claim that the most straigthforward implementations—those using recursive decent in the spirit of standard definite-clause processors—generally require an amount of time that is exponentially related to the length of the sentence analyzed, whereas a chart parser such as I in fact use requires only polynomial time. As the linguistic coverage of the grammar and the length of the sentences analyzed get large, this may become an issue. But they are not an issue for me, nor are they likely to become important in the near future. Prolog programmers usually claim that the time taken by their parsing programs on actually occurring sentences are acceptable for all practical purposes, and I see no reason to take issue with this.

It is also argued that, if a case can be made for something other than straightforward recursive-descent analysis, this does not also constitute an argument against Prolog as the implementation system of preference because Prolog readily accomodates other strategies. I find this less persuasive, especially in a context where a model is being constructed is intended to serve as a psychological model of human language processing. Monotonicity makes for grammars with sufficient power to describe natural languages without building into them commitments about how they are to be processed which do not blong there. But this is not to say that they do not belong somewhere and that they are not a proper object of linguistic investigation. Indeed, one of the benefits of removing all such issues from the grammars of particular languages to the linguistic faculty that is presumably common to the speakers of all languages should make it more readily available to be studied in the manner it deserves. If this is one of the aims of computational linguistics, then one of the strengths of Prolog, namely that it frees the programmer form many of the usual concerns about controls structure, becomes a weakness.

CONCLUSION

I have tried to display some of the advantages of grammatical formalisms that construct functional structures for sentences by means of a strictly monotonic process based on unification. To an audience of logic programmers, it should not be necessary to urge this case particularly strongly. However, the principal argument for the formalisms in this class do not flow automatically from simply embedding a grammar in a logic programming system. There are two important reasons for this: First, logic programming systems do impose strong constraints on the order of the events that make up the linguistic process. But, for the linguist, this order is an empirical matter. Even if the only aim were to analyze or generate sentences efficiently, without regard to psychological reality, it is possible to show that the strategies usually embodied in programming systems are extremely costly when faced with certain kinds of ambiguity. Second, standard mathematical notion, which distinguishes the parts of an expression and, in particular, the arguments to a function, by their serial order relative to one another does not serve linguistic ends nearly as well as the attribute-value notation. One reason for this is simple if shallow, namely that large numbers of arguments are easier to keep track of if they are named and if irrelevant ones are not mentioned at all. But more important is the fact that naming arguments gives rise to the situation in which expressions are never completely specified so that more detail can always be added to an existing grammar without affecting what is already there.

REFERENCES

1. Bresnan, Joan (1982). *The Mental Representation of Grammatical Representations*, MIT Press.

INDEX